THE JOY OF MAKING YOUR OWN

by the Editors of Consumer Guide Magazine

A basic book for do-it-yourself cooks, THE JOY OF MAKING YOUR OWN provides you with all the step-by-step instructions you need to stuff a savory sausage, knead a loaf of Cheddar bread, make spicy pickles, plus much more. THE JOY OF MAKING YOUR OWN brings together the best of old-fashioned taste treats and simplified modern cooking techniques with easy-to-follow tips that will save you money. Now you can experience the exciting transformation of fruit into wine, hops into beer and milk into cheese or yogurt. You will not want to miss the fun of making your own delicious eatables and drinkables when you read how easy it is. Sausage, bread, pickles, beer, and wine are just a few of the hundreds of recipes for fresh, pure, lively tasting homemade foods and beverages contained in THE JOY OF MAKING YOUR OWN. Created by the Editors of CONSUMER GUIDE Magazine, this fascinating cookbook presents step-by-step, easy-to-follow illustrated recipes including:

- Braunschweiger sausage
- Smoked turkey
- Dried apricots—no sulphur
- Raisins
- Soft pretzels
- Sourdough bread
- Champagne
- Dandelion wine
- Cold duck
- Rhubarb wine
- Drambui type liqueur
- Sauerkraut
- Cottage cheese
- Pickled eggs
- Almond butter
- Port wine cheese spread

THE JOY OF MAKING YOUR OWN makes it possible for the modern homemaker to join the movement away from over-processed and over-packaged foods. Each chapter carefully lists and describes the basic equipment and basic ingredients you need to make delicious food and beverages right in your own kitchen. Complete with simple-to-follow illustrated instructions that take you through the basic steps, THE JOY OF MAKING YOUR OWN is a treasure chest of delicious recipes that will make each meal a delightful experience.

You will be surprised at how much fun and how easy it is to make your own Super-Rich Vanilla ice cream (or diet ice cream), peanut butter, granola, soda pop, graham crackers, bagels, pizza bread and fruit leathers. These are just a few more of the special recipes you can bring directly from your kitchen to your table—no middleman, no chemical additives.

You will also be amazed at the money that can be saved when you make your own yogurt, smoked oysters, smoked shrimp, cordials, and fancy cheese balls. You probably have never enjoyed an old-fashioned Bounce—a quaint name for cordials made by steeping fresh fruit in spirits. Bounces are among the many tantalizing recipes you will discover in THE JOY OF MAKING YOUR OWN.

Watching bread rise, witnessing the startling cheese making process, fermenting beer—all of the fascinating processes are first-rate fun and family entertainment. Now you can continue the joyful tradition of making your own—for your family, for guests and for gift-giving.

The Joy of Making Your Own

Copyright© 1976 by Publications International, Ltd.
All rights reserved.
This book may not be reproduced
or quoted in whole or in part by
mimeograph or any other means or
for presentation on radio or television
without written permission from
Louis Weber, President
Publications International, Ltd.
3323 West Main Street
Skokie, Illinois 60076
Manufactured in the United States of America

1   2   3   4   5   6   7   8   9   10

Library of Congress Cataloging in Publication Data

Main entry under title:
The Joy of making your own.

  Includes index.
  1. Cookery.   2.   Food I. Consumer guide
TX652.J68   614.5   75-22478
ISBN 671-22197-3 pbk.

The Joy of Making Your Own

INTRODUCTION

Wave a magic wand over a large empty table and wish for the most delicious array of food and drink possible. What appears? To begin, there is a huge bowl of lusciously sun-ripened fruit and vegetables. After that come mouth-watering cold cuts, smoked shrimp and oysters, followed by wreathes of spicy grilled sausages, a whole smoked turkey, platters of fragrant smoked ribs and smoked beef, rounds of cheese, nut-crusted cheese balls and dips for raw vegetables. What is that heavenly smell? The hot, freshly baked breads, of course! Golden round loaves, braided cheese breads, a pyramid of pita bread and warm thick-crusted slices of sourdough. Here is a chilled bowl of creamy yogurt and tiers of dried fruits and nuts. Small dishes of pickled tomatoes, cucumbers and mushrooms punctuate the length of the the table. A silver bowl of rich strawberry ice cream balances on a mountain of ice. And, standing like sentinels beside every dish, you can see bottles of wine — vibrantly red wine, crystal clear sparkling wine. There are also homey brown bottles of beer. At the far end of this table, a row of red, yellow, green and purple cordials glitter like a stained glass window, promising a gracious end to this banquet. Your goblet of champagne stands ready. Please accept our invitation to this royal feast.

Our magical table groans with delectable foods you make in your own kitchen. An evil sorcerer's wand would have conjured up packaged wieners, cold cuts saturated with five kinds of chemical preservatives, outrageously

high prices dangling from wine bottles and pasted on smoked foods, plus sponge-like breads and boxes of junk snack foods. In other words, a nightmare of modern food processing and packaging.

Perhaps you have never seriously considered making your own sausages, smoking your own meat, drying fruit, making bread, wine or beer. Be prepared for three happy surprises: making these foods is fun and easy; they taste much better than their store-bought counterparts; they are inexpensive. Even wine, beer and cordials are simple to make. The cost of making these drinks is considerably lower than buying them at a liquor store.

All you need to start turning that imaginary feast into a real edible banquet is to follow the basic instructions in this book. Every chapter lists and describes the basic equipment and basic ingredients you will need. Then simple-to-follow instructions with step-by-step illustrations take you through the basic steps. Each chapter includes a wide selection of delicious recipes that follow the basic steps. What could be easier? CONSUMER GUIDE Magazine eliminates the confusion of elaborate instructions and clearly numbers each step in each recipe.

Sausages, smoked meats, dried fruit, cheese, bread, wine, beer, yogurt, pickled foods — these are mankind's most ancient foods. Civilization trundled onward busily developing these foods and glorifying them in religious rituals, myths, legends and festivals. But, today they are merely things to eat — packaging is their most interesting feature. Modern food processing and packaging has taken over some of the tastiest foods the world has known and found ways to mass-produce them. The easier they are to mass-produce, the less flavor they seem to have.

You do not have to be intimidated by advertising, you can make it yourself. Kneading dough is one of the most satisfying activities known. Watching bread rise, witnessing the startling cheese-making process, smoking fish and meat, fermenting wine and beer — all of these processes are fascinating and seem miraculous when you first try them. You are part of a heritage hundreds, even

thousands of years old when you follow the recipes in this book. Of course, you take advantage of modern methods and new ingredients, but the basic process is ancient. For instance, smoked fish found in burial mounds 10,000 years old was prepared by soaking fish in brine and hanging it over a smoking fire. You will use a more sophisticated smoker and check the temperature with a thermometer, but basically the cooking process is the same. The ancient Egyptians brewed beer and baked sourdough bread. The Greeks and Romans made sausages, cheese and bread and drank their wines with gusto. Medieval folk, from serf to master, loved festive revelry on every possible occasion. Renaissance men and women invented dishes with their newly found spices. Now you can continue the joyful tradition of creating the foods you eat and proudly serve your guests.

MAKING IT YOURSELF — SAFELY

An important part of making it yourself is knowing how to handle food properly and safely. It does not do much good, or save you much money, or make you feel better, if the result is a sick family.

Mild cases of food poisoning often resemble a 24-hour "virus." Food poisoning is a common result of poor food-handling practices. No one likes to think that his or her kitchen, or, even worse, his or her hands, could be the culprit, but unfortunately it could be true.

The cleaner your kitchen and your equipment are when you start to cook, and the cleaner you are when you start to cook, the safer your cooking will be. Clean clothes and hands are just as important as clean knives, pot and pans or countertops. If you have a cold or any other contagious disease, do not cook. Easier said than done, we know. If you have a cut or sore on your hand, wear rubber gloves when cooking, until the sore is completely healed. Always wash your hands after you touch any non-food item, whether you hug a kid, pat a dog, or blow your nose.

It is also important to handle each type of food sepa-

rately as you prepare it. If you are chopping meat, vegetables and salad greens for dinner, always wash your hands, the knife and the cutting board between each type of food. Use hot suds and rinse well. Bacteria from the raw meat, if not washed away, could be transferred to the vegetables and salad greens and you, or someone in your family, could become sick.

Temperatures are critical in food preparation, too. Always keep hot foods hot and cold foods cold, and get them to these temperatures as quickly as possible. The bacteria that can spoil food and make people ill grow best between 40°F and 140°F. Room temperature falls right in the middle of that danger zone, so do not let foods stand around on the kitchen counter. Heat them or cool them right away.

Mold thrives on bread, cheese and fruit. Some molds can make you sick, other molds are harmless. Cutting away moldy sections of food does not always eliminate the risk. Mold has deep roots. You are safer to throw out moldy bread, cheese or fruit.

SAUSAGES

Say "sausage" and most people think of breakfast sausage — well-browned pork links or patties that spark appetites with their spicy aroma. But sausages come in hundreds of varieties, including cold cuts and luncheon meats. Some sausages are perfect for snacks, others make elegant main dishes. Making sausages at home is nearly a lost art, yet the process is not complicated and much of the basic equipment can be adapted from ordinary kitchen ware. Homemade sausages have a rich savor that simply cannot be preserved and packaged commercially.

Imagine simmering your own marjoram-flavored sausages in red wine and serving the juicy morsels with boiled potatoes and asparagus. You have a dish fit for a Roman emperor. As a matter of fact, Roman emperors enjoyed just such dishes at their elaborate feasts. And, sausages grilled in the street were the most popular snack in the ancient Mediterranian world. Later, sausage making was raised to a proud art when European cities gave their names to their special sausages: Bologna, Frankfurt, Genoa, Wiener (Vienna). Germany still boasts its bockwurst, liverwurst, knockwurst and bratwurst. And, the Italians take pride in their dried sausages: Milano, Romano, Pepperoni, Salami, Coppicola.

Any spiced mixture of ground meat stuffed into a casing is a sausage. Beef and pork are commonly used, but veal and turkey make interesting sausages, too. Cold cuts, bologna and luncheon meat are all classified as sausages. Here in this chapter you will find recipes for sausages using finely chopped meats, ground meats and coarse cut meats. All of the recipes are for cooked sausages.

The loaves or rounds of cold cuts made from these recipes will remind you of very finely textured meat loaves. These cold cuts will not look like cold cuts from the supermarket. They will not slice like supermarket cold cuts. They will not taste like supermarket cold cuts. They will have no chemical additives or preservatives. They will, however, have a unique, subtle flavor. Indeed, all of these sausages made fresh in your kitchen will be surprisingly better than commercial products. They will cost less, too.

BASIC EQUIPMENT

1. **Blender.** Several of the following recipes require a blender to process the meat. A regular blender will do the job, if you work with small amounts of meat and allow the blender's motor to cool for ten minutes after each four or five minutes that it runs. (A heavy-duty blender, especially designed for nuts and grains, does a good and fast job, too.)
2. **Mixing bowls.** 5- to 6-quart mixing bowls are best.
3. **Spoons.** Large, smooth wooden spoons for easy stirring.
4. **Potato masher** for blending bulky ingredients.

5. **Spatula.** One or two wooden handled rubber spatulas — the bigger the better — makes handling the heavy meat mixture easier.
6. **Measuring cups.** You will need a set of dry measuring cups (metal) as well as a 1- or 2-cup glass liquid measuring cup.
7. **A set of accurate measuring spoons.**
8. **Loaf pans.** Two (9x5x3-inch) loaf pans. Loaf pans 8½x4½x 2 will also work.
9. **Meat thermometer**
10. **Sharp knives**

OPTIONAL EQUIPMENT

1. **Sausage stuffer.** Manual sausage stuffers will help you do a professional job of filling the larger casings. An electric meat grinder with a sausage stuffing attachment simplifies the stuffing procedure even further.

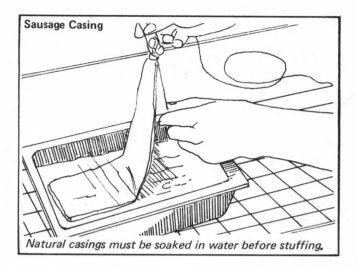

Sausage Casing

Natural casings must be soaked in water before stuffing.

Basic Ingredients

1. **Meat.** Sausage has always been the wise farmer's way to use up every bit of nutritious meat on an animal — "everything but the squeal," as the old saying goes. If you buy a whole animal, or even a half or a quarter, ask for the trimmings to take home to make your own sausage. Beef should be one-quarter fat, pork should be one-third fat. Or use the tougher cuts, or cuts that are not popular with your family, to grind for sausage.

   If the meat counter at the supermarket is as close as you get to animals, look for less tender and less popular cuts. You will recognize them by their prices — low. When buying ground beef, look for twenty-five percent fat content. Many markets now label ground meats with fat percentages. Ground beef that has been ground in federally inspected packing plants must be seventy percent lean. Ask the meat man. Tell him what you are doing and ask for his help. He can guide you to specials, or let you know about future specials. He will also help you spot the cuts that are best for sausage-making.
2. **Casings.** Casings are the packaging material for sausage. Natural casings are usually sheep or hog intestines and are most often used for link or country-style sausage. Natural casings must be refrigerated and must be soaked in warm water and thoroughly flushed out just before stuffing them. Synthetic casings are preferred because they are clean, easy to store and cannot spoil. Several types are available. The commonest size is about six inches in diameter and twenty-four inches long. This is the size used in the following recipes.
3. **Seasonings.** The amounts of seasonings given in the following recipes are for your guidance. You can change them to suit your taste. Just remember that a little spice can make a lot of flavor, so add or subtract from the given amounts of spices with a fraction of a teaspoon rather than generous handfuls. You can quickly test the flavor of your sausage by thoroughly frying a tablespoon of it before stuffing the casings.
4. **Extenders.** Nonfat dry milk or soy flour are ingredients that add protein, calcium and vitamins. They are not empty calories. Ground dry soybeans can replace soy flour as an extender. You can grind whole dry beans in your blender and store them in tightly covered jars until ready to use.
5. **Crushed ice.** Several of the recipes call for crushed ice to keep the meat cold while it is being processed in the blender. If you are weak of arm, an electric ice crusher or manual ice crusher is handy. Otherwise, dump a tray of ice cubes into a heavy duty plastic bag, or wrap the ice cubes in a clean dish towel and pound them with a hammer. Try to make almond-sized ice pieces because bigger chunks will not mix well.

STORAGE

All of the sausages in the following recipes including the cold cuts, are cooked meat. They should be stored and handled just as you would leftover roast beef or meat loaf — very carefully. Do not let the sausages or coldcuts stand around at room temperature. Store them in the refrigerator; re-wrap and return them to the refrigerator as soon as possible after cutting. Experts say that well-wrapped cold meats can be kept in the refrigerator for a week and in the freezer for up to six months. Many of the following recipes make about five pounds of sausage. So, you may want to keep one loaf or sausage-round in the refrigerator and wrap the other for the freezer. When ready to start on your second loaf, let it thaw in the refrigerator, not standing out on the counter.

Inexpensive and versatile, you will want to try your homemade sausage in place of ground beef in casseroles or in hearty soups. You can broil or grill chunks of sausage brushed with barbecue sauce. With these sausages you can build towering sandwiches and arrange artistic buffets — they are perfect for serve-yourself supper parties. You can try some on pizza, tucked in buns, crumbled over salads and in stuffings. And, of course there is that marvelously satisfying portable feast — bread, cheese and sausage.

Basic Steps

FINE-CUT SAUSAGE

These are the steps for fine-cut sausage. You mix the meat in the blender until it is almost like cake batter or peanut butter. The result is a finely textured loaf.

Basic Ingredients	**Basic Equipment**
See recipes for specific ingredients	*Blender*
Ground meat	*Measuring spoons*
Crushed ice	*Rubber spatula*
Extenders	*Large mixing bowl*
Seasonings	*Dry measuring cups*
	Large wooden spoon or very clean hands
	Meat thermometer

1. Drop 2 to 3 rounded measuring tablespoons of meat into your blender's container. (Use 4 tablespoons if you have a heavy-duty blender.)
2. Add a tablespoonful of crushed ice. Put on the cover and set the blender at "Liquefy" or "High" for about 5 seconds.
3. Turn the blender off, remove the cover and push the meat to the blades with a rubber spatula. Turn on and blend for 5 seconds longer.
4. Stop the blender and push the meat to the blades if necessary. Add a few more pieces of ice and blend about 5 seconds longer or until the mixture is the consistency of peanut butter.
5. Using a rubber spatula, remove all the mixture from the blender container to a large mixing bowl.
6. Repeat steps 1 through 5, blending the meat and ice until smooth, until you have processed about half the meat.
7. Let the blender cool while you measure the remaining ingredients in the recipe and add them to the meat in the mixing bowl.
8. Then finish processing the remaining meat in the blender.
9. Combine all the ingredients in the mixing bowl very thoroughly with a spoon, a potato masher or your hands. Seasonings must be evenly distributed or you will have hot spots of flavor.
10. Pack the meat mixture into a loaf pan, if recipe directs, or . . .
11. Tie one end of the casing with string. If using a sausage stuffer, follow manufacturer's directions.
12. If you do not have a sausage stuffer, pack meat mixture firmly into casing using a spoon, rubber spatula or your hands. Press out all the air that you can.
13. Tie the top of the casing, squeezing out the air at top and tying it close to the meat. Cut off the casing and tie the top.
14. Cook as the recipe directs.

FINE-CUT SAUSAGE

Basic Step 2

Basic Step 3

Basic Step 9

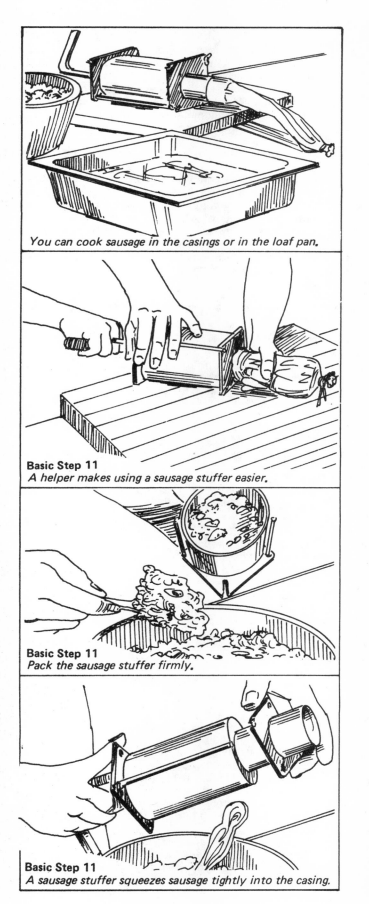

You can cook sausage in the casings or in the loaf pan.

Basic Step 11
A helper makes using a sausage stuffer easier.

Basic Step 11
Pack the sausage stuffer firmly.

Basic Step 11
A sausage stuffer squeezes sausage tightly into the casing.

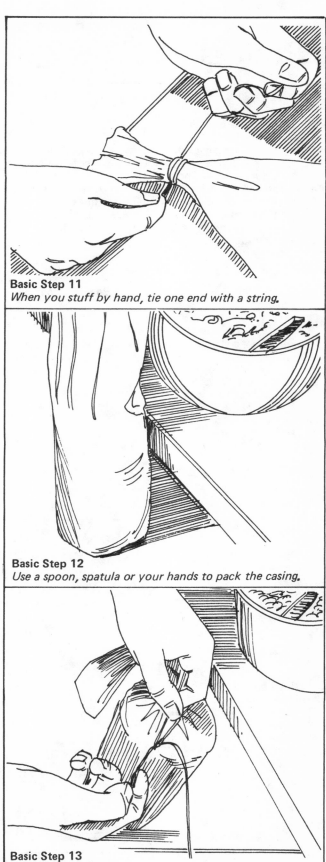

Basic Step 11
When you stuff by hand, tie one end with a string.

Basic Step 12
Use a spoon, spatula or your hands to pack the casing.

Basic Step 13
Tie the top of the casing close to the meat.

Recipes

PICKLE AND PIMIENTO LOAF

Have your meat man grind the beef and pork together once or twice. If you grind your own meats, put them through your meat grinder's fine cutter. This recipe makes about 5 pounds, 2 (9 x 5-inch) loaves. The meat will shrink some as it cooks, but you should get about 70 (⅛-inch thick) slices per loaf. Unless you have a huge family, or are planning a big party, you can freeze one loaf to enjoy later on.

Ingredients	Equipment
3 pounds 75% lean ground beef	See Basic Equipment
2 pounds ground pork	
1 tray ice cubes, crushed	
1 cup instant nonfat dry milk	
1 cup soy flour	
½ cup drained pickle relish	
1 jar (4 ounces) pimiento, drained and diced	
2 tablespoons salt	
½ to 1 tablespoon white pepper	
1 tablespoon sugar	
¾ teaspoon ground ginger	

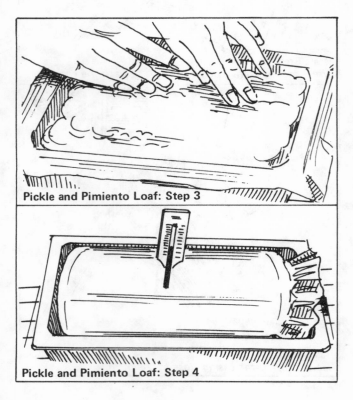

Pickle and Pimiento Loaf: Step 3

Pickle and Pimiento Loaf: Step 4

1. Preheat the oven to 275°F.
2. Follow Basic Steps 1 through 9.
3. Divide mixture between the two loaf pans. Put a piece of plastic wrap or waxed paper on top of the meat in each pan and press evenly but firmly, packing the meat into the pan. Remove the paper.
4. Stick a meat thermometer in the meat in one pan so that the tip of the thermometer is in the center of the meat mixture.
5. Put the pans on a rack in the center of the preheated oven.
6. Bake until the meat thermometer reaches 160°F, about 2 hours.
7. Remove the loaves from the oven and set in another large pan or sink of ice to cool quickly. After about 15 minutes put them in the refrigerator. Remove them from the pan to slice and serve.
8. Wrap the loaves in plastic wrap or foil, or seal them in a plastic bag to store in the refrigerator.

◆◆◆◆◆◆◆◆◆◆◆◆◆◆◆◆◆◆◆◆◆◆

LEONA BOLOGNA

Chunks of Leona Bologna stirred in sauerkraut, heated with caraway seeds and a splash of white wine or apple juice, make a quick and tasty main dish. This recipe makes about 5 pounds of bologna.

Ingredients	Equipment
3 pounds 75% lean ground beef	See Basic Equipment
2 pounds ground pork	String
1 tray ice cubes, crushed	Scissors
1 cup instant nonfat dry milk	Sausage stuffer (optional)
3 tablespoons salt	
1 tablespoon white pepper	
1½ teaspoons sugar	
1½ teaspoons ground coriander	
1½ teaspoons ground cardamom	
¼ to ½ teaspoon liquid smoke (optional)	
1 teaspoon dried sage	
¾ teaspoon ground allspice	
¾ teaspoon ground mace	
Few drops red food coloring (optional)	
1 casing, 6 x 24 inches	

1. Preheat the oven to 275°F.
2. Follow Basic Steps 1 through 13; stuff half the meat mixture into the casing and tie. Cut off the casing and tie the bottom of the remaining piece. Then continue stuffing with the second half of the meat mixture, tying the top.
3. Fit each filled casing into a loaf pan and press down firmly into the pan.
4. If the filled casing does not completely fill the pan from end to end, fill any space left over with a small metal measuring cup, crushed aluminum foil or any other heat-proof utensil that will hold the bologna tightly in place.

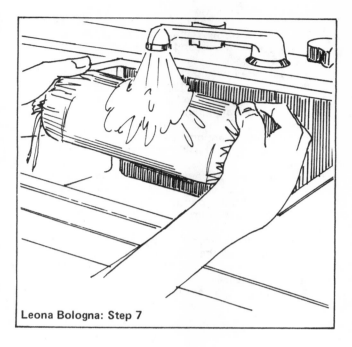

Leona Bologna: Step 7

BRAUNSCHWEIGER

Braunschweiger is so rich and flavorful that you can serve it simply. Slice it to eat with rounds of crusty French bread or Melba toast. Or sandwich it between thin-sliced Bermuda onions and tomatoes on very dark pumpernickel.

If you grind your own meat, use your meat grinder's fine cutter. Grind the onion along with the meat, if you like. Or have your meat man grind all meats together twice. The recipe makes about 1½ pounds of Braunschweiger.

Ingredients	Equipment
½ pound ground pork liver	See Basic Equipment
½ pound ground pork	1 (9 x 5 x 3-inch) loaf pan
½ pound ground beef	1 9x13-inch or larger baking pan
1 medium onion, finely chopped	
2 tablespoons instant nonfat dry milk	
1 teaspoon salt	
½ teaspoon sugar	
½ teaspoon pepper	
¼ teaspoon ground cardamom	
¼ teaspoon ground mace	
¼ teaspoon butter or margarine	

1. Preheat the oven to 275°F.
2. Follow Basic Steps 1 through 9.
3. Pack the meat mixture into the loaf pan. Put a piece of plastic wrap or waxed paper on top of the meat and press evenly but firmly to pack the meat down into the pan. Remove the paper.
4. Stick a meat thermometer in the meat with the tip of the thermometer in center of meat mixture.
5. Put the loaf pan in the larger baking pan and set

5. Stick a meat thermometer into one of the bologna rolls so that tip of thermometer is in center of roll.
6. Put the pans on a rack in the center of the preheated oven. Bake about 2 hours, or until the meat thermometer reaches 160°F.
7. Remove from the oven. Remove the meat thermometer. Hold the bologna under cold running water for a few minutes to cool, then refrigerate until ready to serve.
8. Slice to serve. Cover the cut portion of bologna with plastic wrap or foil and store in the refrigerator.

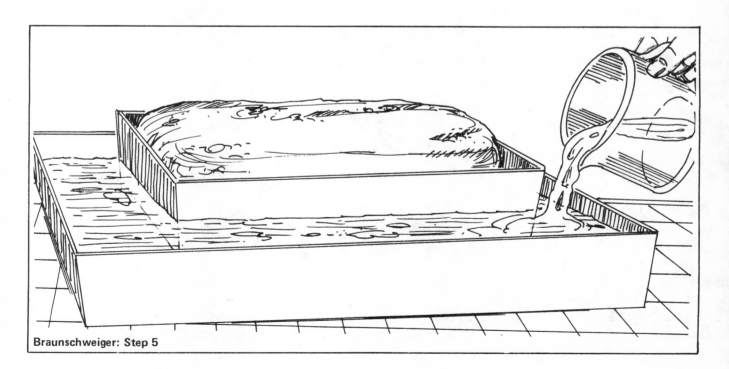

Braunschweiger: Step 5

them on a rack in the center of the preheated oven. Pour hot water in the outer pan to the depth of 1 inch.

6. Bake about 1 to 1½ hours or until the meat thermometer reaches 160°F. Check occasionally to make sure that the water in the outer pan does not boil. Lower the oven temperature if the water should boil.
7. Remove the loaf from the oven. Remove the meat thermometer. Put the loaf pan in another pan or sink of ice to cool it quickly, then refrigerate until ready to serve.
8. Remove from the pan and slice to serve. Wrap in plastic wrap or foil or seal in plastic bag and store the Braunschweiger in the refrigerator.

◆◆◆◆◆◆◆◆◆◆◆◆◆◆◆◆◆◆◆◆◆◆◆◆◆◆◆◆◆◆◆

CHORIZO

Slice this spicy Spanish sausage to serve with crackers or bread, or pan-fry it with green peppers and onions for a main dish. Chorizo is delicious with omelets, too. This recipe makes about 4 pounds of sausage.

Ingredients	Equipment
4 pounds ground pork	See Basic Equipment
½ cup vinegar	String
4 teaspoons salt	Scissors
2 teaspoons oregano	Sausage stuffer
2 teaspoons black pepper	(optional)
2 teaspoons cayenne pepper	1 11x16 baking pan (or baking utensil large
1 teaspoon garlic powder	enough to hold the 2
½ teaspoon ground cumin	loaf pans)
1 casing, 6x24 inches	

1. Preheat the oven to 275°F.
2. Follow Basic Steps 1 through 13, stuffing half the

meat mixture into the casing. Tie and cut the casing. Tie the end of the remaining casing then continue stuffing with the second half of meat mixture, tying the top.

3. Fit each filled casing into a loaf pan and press down firmly. If the sausage does not fit snugly in the pan, fill any extra space with a small metal measuring cup, crushed aluminum foil, or any other heat-proof utensil that will hold the sausage tightly in place.
4. Stick a meat thermometer in one of the sausages so that the tip of the thermometer is in center of sausage.
5. Put the filled loaf pans in the larger baking pan. Set the pan on a rack in center of your oven and pour hot water in the outer pan to a depth of 1 inch.
6. Bake about 2½ hours or until the meat thermometer reaches 160°F.
7. Remove from the oven. Remove the meat thermometer. Hold the sausages under cold running water for a few minutes to cool, then refrigerate until ready to serve.
8. Slice to serve. Cover the cut portion of sausage with plastic wrap or foil and store in the refrigerator.

COARSE CUT SAUSAGE

COUNTRY STYLE BOLOGNA

This bologna is marvelous with your own special baked beans. Or cut it into thick slices, glaze and bake as you would a ham. You can even broil or grill it over coals. If you grind your own meat, use your meat grinder's fine cutter. The recipe makes 5 pounds of bologna.

Ingredients

- 3 pounds 75% lean ground beef
- 2 pounds ground pork
- 2 cups instant nonfat dry milk
- 3 tablespoons plus 1 teaspoon salt
- 1 tablespoon white pepper
- 1½ teaspoons sugar
- 1½ teaspoons ground cardamom
- 1½ teaspoons ground coriander
- 1 teaspoon dried sage
- ¾ teaspoon ground allspice
- ¾ teaspoon ground mace
- ¼ to ½ teaspoon liquid smoke (optional)
- Few drops red food coloring (optional)
- 1 casing, 6x24 inches

Equipment

See Basic Equipment
String
Scissors
Sausage stuffer (optional)
1 11x16 baking pan (or other baking utensil large enough to hold the 2 loaf pans)

1. Preheat the oven to 275°F.
2. Put the meat in a mixing bowl; measure all the remaining ingredients except the casing into the mixing bowl.
3. Mix thoroughly with a spoon or your hands. Seasonings must be evenly distributed or you will have hot spots of pepper.
4. Tie one end of the casing with a string, then stuff half of the meat mixture into the casing using a spoon, rubber spatula, your hands, or a sausage stuffer. Pack tightly, pressing out all the air that you can.
5. Tie the top of the casing, squeezing out air at top and tying it close to the meat. Cut off the casing.
6. Tie the bottom of the remaining piece of casing and stuff it with the remaining meat. Tie top as before.
7. Fit each filled casing into a loaf pan and press them down firmly.
8. If a filled casing does not fit snugly in the pan, fill any extra space with a small metal measuring cup, crushed aluminum foil or any other heat-proof utensil that will hold the bologna tightly in place.
9. Stick the meat thermometer into one of the bologna rolls so that the tip of the thermometer is in the center of the roll.
10. Put the loaf pans in the larger baking pan. Set the pan on a rack in center of the oven and pour in hot water to a depth of 1 inch.
11. Bake about 2½ hours or until the meat thermometer reaches 160°F.
12. Remove the loaves from the oven. Remove the meat thermometer. Hold the bologna under cold running water to cool, then refrigerate until ready to serve.
13. Slice to serve. Cover the cut portion of bologna with plastic wrap or foil and store in the refrigerator.

◆◆◆◆◆◆◆◆◆◆◆◆◆◆◆◆◆◆◆◆◆◆◆◆◆◆◆◆◆◆◆◆

FRESH PORK SAUSAGE

You can pack this sausage into the casing, as directed below. Or you can package it as bulk pork sausage to use right away or to freeze as you would ground beef. You can also form patties to use right away or freeze; this sausage can be stuffed into smaller casings to make little links. Pick the method that you prefer. The recipe makes 2 pounds of sausage.

Ingredients

- 2 pounds boneless pork trimmings, ⅔ lean, cubed
- 2 teaspoons salt
- 1½ teaspoons powdered sage
- 1 teaspoon pepper
- ¾ teaspoon sugar
- ¼ teaspoon ground cloves
- 1 casing, 6x12 inches or 1 yard of smaller sausage casing

Equipment

See Basic Equipment
Meat grinder
String
Scissors
Sausage stuffer (optional)
Large saucepan or pot

1. Grind the pork through the coarse or fine cutter of the meat grinder.
2. Add all the remaining ingredients except the casing and mix thoroughly.
3. Tie one end of the casing with string and stuff, using a wooden spoon, your hands, or a sausage stuffer. Pack tightly, pressing out all the air that you can.
4. Tie the top of the casing, squeezing out the air at the top and tying close to meat.
5. Or stuff the sausage into small casing using a sausage stuffer attachment for your meat grinder and following the manufacturer's directions. Twist the filled casing every 4 inches to form links, alternating the direction you twist at end of each link.
6. Put filled casing or links in a large pan and cover them with water.
7. Cook on top of the range over very low heat for about 1 hour, checking occasionally to be sure the casing has not split. Remove if the casing splits.
8. Hold the sausage under cold running water for a few minutes to cool, then refrigerate until ready to cook.

If you wish to prepare bulk sausage or patties, skip steps 3 through 7, then refrigerate or freeze the sausage immediately. Wrap in freezer paper or heavy duty aluminum foil for freezing.

FRESH BEEF AND PORK SAUSAGE

To change this recipe to Italian sausage, replace sage and cloves with 2 teaspoons oregano, 1 teaspoon crushed red pepper and ½ teaspoon anise seed. The recipe makes about 2½ pounds of sausage.

Ingredients

1 pound lean boneless beef, cubed
1 pound lean boneless pork, cubed
½ pound boneless pork, ⅔ lean, cubed
1 tablespoon salt
2 teaspoons dried sage
1 teaspoon pepper
¼ teaspoon ground cloves
1 casing, 6x12 inches or 1 yard smaller sausage casing

Equipment

See Basic Equipment
Meat grinder
String
Scissors
Sausage stuffer
Large saucepan or pot

1. Grind meats together through fine or coarse cutter of meat grinder.
2. Follow steps 2 through 7 of Fresh Pork Sausage. Or, prepare as bulk sausage or patties, skipping steps 3 through 7. Refrigerate or freeze immediately.

KIELBASA

This is the famed sausage of Poland. Simmer it in a little red wine along with some chopped onion, then serve with boiled potatoes and asparagus spears for a magnificent meal. Or grill over hot coals and tuck the sausage slices into a bun.

If you grind the meat at home, use your meat grinder's coarse cutter. This recipe makes about 2 pounds of sausage.

Ingredients

1½ pounds coarsely ground pork
½ pound coarsely ground veal
1½ teaspoons crumbled marjoram
2 cloves garlic, minced
2 teaspoons salt
1 teaspoon pepper
⅛ teaspoon ground allspice
1 casing, 6x12 inches

Equipment

Basic Equipment
String
Scissors
Sausage stuffer (optional)
Loaf pan or baking dish large enough to hold the sausage

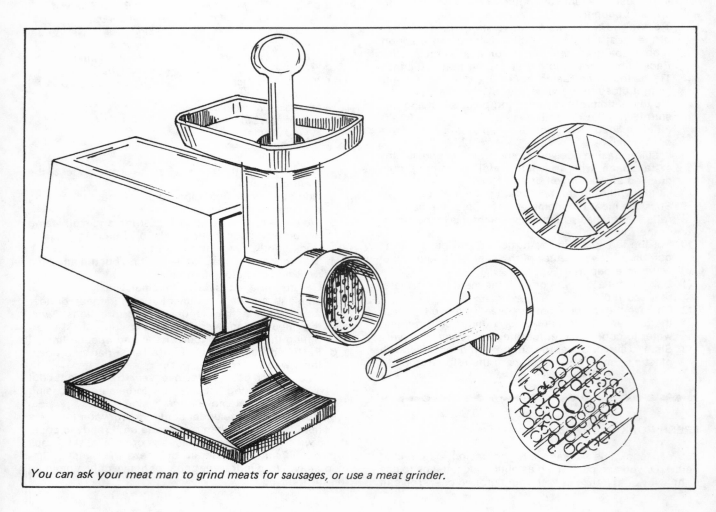

You can ask your meat man to grind meats for sausages, or use a meat grinder.

1. Preheat the oven to 325°F.
2. Combine all the ingredients except the casing in mixing bowl and mix thoroughly. The seasonings must be evenly distributed or you will have hot spots of spices.
3. Tie one end of the casing with string, then stuff it with the meat mixture using a sausage stuffer, spoon or your hands.
4. Squeeze air out at the top and tie the casing close to the meat.
5. Stick a meat thermometer into the sausage so that the tip of the thermometer is in the center of the sausage.
6. Put the sausage in a baking dish or pan and cover it with water.
7. Bake in a preheated oven about 2 hours, until the water has evaporated and the meat thermometer reaches 160°F.
8. Remove from the oven. Remove the meat thermometer and hold the sausage under cold running water a few minutes to cool, then refrigerate until ready to cook.

◆◆◆◆◆◆◆◆◆◆◆◆◆◆◆◆◆◆◆◆◆◆◆◆◆◆◆◆

SPANISH SAUSAGE

This hot sausage goes into the famous Spanish one-dish meal, *Paella*. You might also slice some into your favorite casserole recipe or Spanish rice. The recipe makes about 2 pounds of sausage.

Ingredients	Equipment
2 pounds boneless pork, ²⁄₃ lean, cubed	See Basic Equipment
1 onion, quartered	Meat grinder
1 clove garlic, crushed	String
2 teaspoons salt	Scissors
1 teaspoon paprika	Sausage stuffer
½ teaspoon crushed dried red peppers	Large saucepan or pot
½ teaspoon black pepper	
¼ teaspoon cayenne pepper	
1 casing, 6x12 inches	

1. Grind the meat, onion and garlic together using a coarse cutter.
2. Add all the remaining ingredients except the casing and mix thoroughly. Seasonings must be evenly distributed or you will have hot spots of spice.
3. Tie one end of the casing with string, then stuff in the meat mixture using a wooden spoon, your hands, or a sausage stuffer. Pack tightly, pressing out all air that you can.
4. Squeeze out air at top and tie the casing close to the meat.
5. Put the sausage in a large deep pan or pot and cover with water.
6. Cook on top of the range over very low heat at least 1 hour or until the water evaporates, adding more water during cooking time, if necessary. The sausage is done when the casing splits.
7. Remove the sausage from the pan and hold it under cold running water for a few minutes to cool. Refrigerate until ready to serve.

Smoked Foods

Smoked foods now occupy the "luxury" shelves in supermarkets and we pay extravagant prices for their unique rich flavor. But, not many years ago almost every farm in the U.S.A. had a smokehouse. Although today's modern methods of refrigeration, freezing and canning have replaced smoking as a necessary method of food preservation, you can still enjoy delectable foods smoked in your own smokehouse.

The smoking process is a combination of low heat, smoke, and brining with salt and seasonings. Once you have constructed or purchased a smoker to produce the heat and smoke, the recipes are the world's easiest. The result: smoked ribs and chops, turkey, beef, lamb, sausage, even jerky. All delicious for picnics or banquets. And, there is nothing as elegantly high-class as smoked oysters, smoked shrimp and fish. These delicacies taste like a million dollars, but cost far less than the supermarket's smoked foods.

In this chapter you will find basic, simplified directions for two kinds of smoking. Cold-smoking, which uses low temperatures, either cooks food by slowly drying it or just adds flavor without cooking the food. Smoked fish is dried by cold smoking and can be eaten without further cooking. Sausages are cold-smoked for flavor but require additional cooking. Smoke-cooking is the second kind of smoking; it uses high temperatures and produces fully cooked foods.

Basic Equipment

A special section describing different kinds of smokers and specific directions for building your own barrel smokehouse or refrigerator smoker follows the next short list of basic equipment.

1. **Smoker.** (See the following section.)
2. **Fuel.** Green, not dried, hard woods from trees that shed their leaves in the winter are the best for smoking. These include hickory, oak, beech, elm, maple, apple. Do not use wood from evergreen trees, such as pine. These woods are resinous and will make your smoked food very dark and bitter tasting. Dried corn cobs are a fine fuel for smoking. Southerners sometimes pick palmetto or cottonwood for the fire. Hickory or other hard wood chips and sawdust help to subdue the flames and to create even more smoke.

Soak the chips for half an hour before adding to the fire and dampen the sawdust before adding it.

3. **Oven thermometer.** You will want to maintain steady temperatures in your smoker.
4. **Meat thermometer.** Smoking turns meat skin dark brown; without a meat thermometer it is difficult to tell when the meat is done.
5. **Container** for the brine. A plastic pail, glass, enamel or stainless steel pan is needed for brining.

SMOKER OR SMOKEHOUSE

A smoker can be as simple as a cardboard box set over a pan of smoldering sawdust, or as elaborate as a carefully constructed smokehouse with its own fan and heat source. A smoker must have smoke, an oven or enclosure to hold the smoke, a draft or some method of letting the smoke flow, a rack or hooks to hold the food, and a source of heat that creates smoke and dries or cooks the food.

There are several small smokers, smoke ovens or smoke-cookers available at hardware or houseware stores. Covered barbecue grills can be used for smoke-cooking. Kamados (egg-shaped Japanese smoke ovens), barrel or chimney-like Chinese smoke ovens are popular, too, and can be used for other outdoor cooking besides smoking. Check labels and instruction books carefully when you shop to see what temperatures these small appliances use for smoking. Many of them will be appropriate for smoke-cooking only.

A concrete or frame smokehouse can be any old small building you happen to have available, or one you build. A slow, smoldering fire on the dirt or cement floor of the small building is all right if you watch it closely. A fire pit slightly downhill from the smokehouse, with terra cotta or stove pipe to carry smoke to the house, is the safest. (Books on smoking food and food preservation have detailed plans and diagrams for building smokehouses.)

A barrel smokehouse is relatively easy to make, can be used for low-temperature smoking and can handle a moderate quantity of food. And an old refrigerator can easily take on new life as a smoker. Directions for building a barrel smokehouse and a refrigerator smokehouse follow.

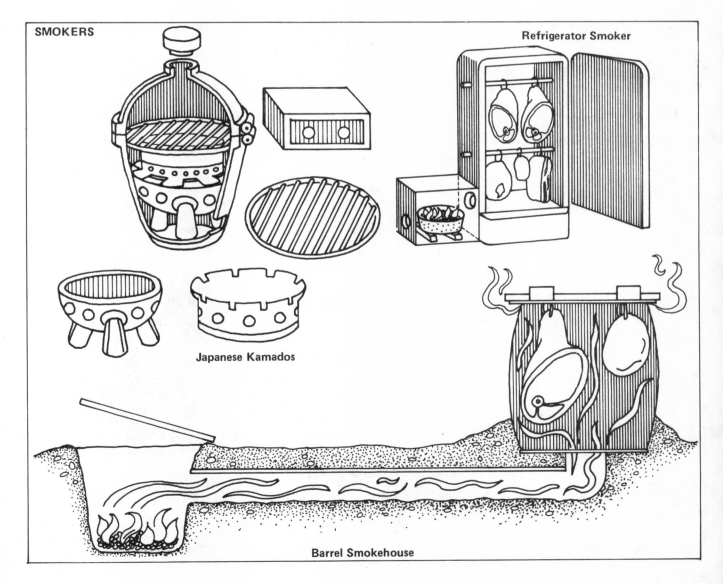

SMOKERS

Refrigerator Smoker

Japanese Kamados

Barrel Smokehouse

HOW TO BUILD A BARREL SMOKEHOUSE

Use the cleanest barrel you can find or buy, then scrub and rinse it well.

Materials Needed

50- or 55-gallon barrel or drum, metal or cardboard, ends removed

Metal cover for drum and for fire pit

Heavy metal screen cut to fit inside barrel or rack from barbecue grill that will fit inside barrel

Planks or plywood to cover fire trench

Broom handles

Cleat

"S" hooks

Equipment

Spade

Drill

Long (3-inch) stove bolts

1. Select the site for smokehouse on slight slope, if possible. The barrel will stand on top of slope with a trench running downhill from it. The trench from pit to barrel should be in the same direction as prevailing winds.
2. Dig a fire pit about 2 feet deep, 10 to 12 feet downhill from where the barrel will be.
3. Dig a trench 6 inches deep and 6 inches wide extending from the pit to where the center of barrel will be. Put a terra cotta or a stove pipe in the trench, if you wish.
4. Put the barrel in place over the end of the trench.

5. Cover the trench with planks or boards, then cover it with dirt.
6. Pile dirt around bottom of barrel to keep the smoke in, but do not block the trench entrance to barrel.
7. Attach cleats to the top of the barrel to hold the broom handles in place.
8. Hang "S" hooks over broom handles to hold the food. Or drill several holes through side of barrel about two-thirds of the way up. Insert long stove bolts and fasten them with nuts to form a support for the rack.
9. Lower a metal screen or an old barbeque grill into the barrel to rest on the stove bolts.
10. Cover the barrel with a metal cover, propping it open slightly or moving it to one side when it is necessary to let the smoke flow through.

HOW TO BUILD A REFRIGERATOR SMOKER

You can recycle any old refrigerator that is beyond repair. Check the dump, an appliance dealer or repair shop. Be sure the door will close. Buy a heavy chain and lock. Carefully lock the refrigerator so children cannot shut themselves inside. Always be sure that fire is low, otherwise insulation in refrigerator might burn.

Materials Needed

Old refrigerator

Chain and lock

Butterfly draft or vent

Cement blocks

Terra cotta or stove pipe, 1 elbow piece

Metal cover or piece of sheet metal

Equipment

Hammer

Pliers

Screw driver

Saw

Spade

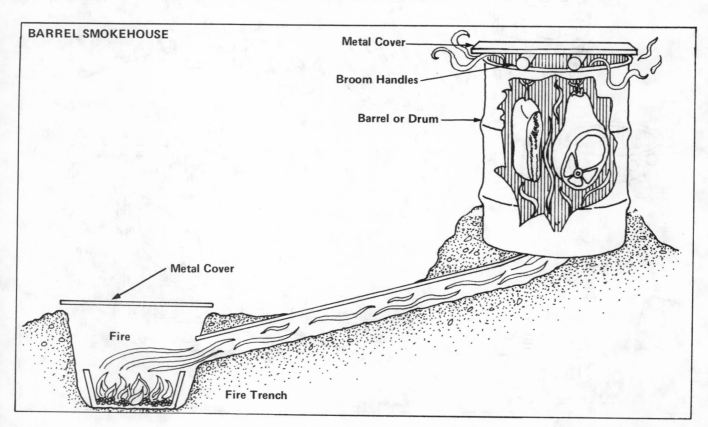

BARREL SMOKEHOUSE

Metal Cover

Broom Handles

Barrel or Drum

Metal Cover

Fire

Fire Trench

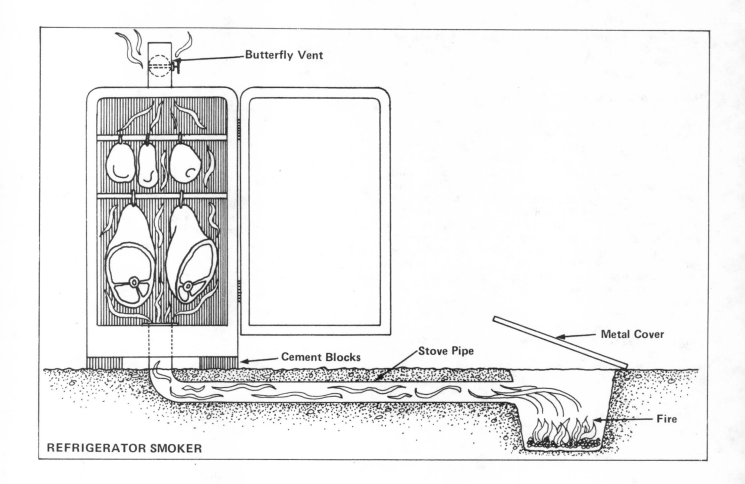

Butterfly Vent

Metal Cover

Cement Blocks

Stove Pipe

Fire

REFRIGERATOR SMOKER

1. Remove the compressor, the ice cube compartment, and any galvanized or plastic parts inside the refrigerator.
2. Block off any ducts or openings, except those in the bottom.
3. Cut a hole in the bottom, (if there isn't one) for smoke to enter, and cut another hole at top side or in top, for smoke to leave.
4. Put the butterfly draft in the hole at the top.

5. Dig a trench and a fire pit six inches deep and six inches wide, lining trench with terra cotta or stove pipe.
6. Arrange cement blocks over end of trench; set the refrigerator in place on the blocks, matching the elbow pipe to hole in the bottom of the refrigerator.
7. Use a metal cover or piece of sheet metal to cover the fire. Lift or move the cover to use it as damper to control fire.

Basic Ingredients

Besides the food you are going to smoke there is only one other ingredient, brine.

1. **Brine,** which is salt dissolved in cold water, helps preserve the foods that you smoke; it also adds salty flavor. If you plan to do a lot of smoking, and thus a lot of brine-making, buy rock salt (also known as ice cream salt or sidewalk salt). It is cheaper than table salt. The seasonings you add to the brine can be almost anything you want. Some suggestions are listed in the recipe for Smoked Fish Fillets.

How long you let food stand in the brine will determine the strength of flavor, just as the length of smoking time determines the amount of smoke flavor. A brine can be used more than once if you keep it refrigerated between uses, and if it does not have bits of meat or fish still floating in it.

Always prepare, use and keep the brine in a glass, enamel, plastic or stainless steel container. Experienced smokers like to keep a special plastic pail just for their brine.

BASIC STEPS FOR COLD SMOKING

Your smoker should produce smoke and low even temperatures without flames. Smoking most often starts at under 100°F, usually 85°F or 90°F, sometimes as low as 70°F. Smoking at this temperature can go on for hours, days or even weeks, depending on what you are smoking.

This low-temperature smoking is called cold smoking and is more a drying and flavoring process than a cooking process. Cold-smoked foods, such as bacons and hams, must be cooked before eating. Cold-smoked foods can be stored in the refrigerator for a few weeks and frozen for up to 6 months. (Bacon and hams require special curing before smoking. Instructions for curing pork are available from your county agricultural extension office, or in books devoted to smoking.)

Beef and poultry must reach an internal temperature of at least 160°F for safety's sake, and pork should reach an internal temperature of 170°F. Most of our recipes direct you to increase the smoking temperature after several hours of cooking. The food will then reach 160°F or 170° more rapidly and you will not have to stay up nights tending the fire.

Ingredients	Equipment
Food	Large bowl or plastic
Brine	pail
	Fuel
	Matches
	Smoker
	Oven thermometer
	Meat thermometer

1. Make a brine in a large bowl or plastic pail as the recipe directs. Add seasoning, if desired.
2. Put the food in the brine and place a plate on top of the food, weighting it with a jar of water or a clean rock to hold the food under the brine.
3. Refrigerate the food in the brine for the time specified in the recipe.
4. Drain the food well. Rinse, if the recipe directs. Hang up the food or put it on a rack and let it air-dry for the time given in the recipe.
5. While the food is drying, build a fire, using kindling or charcoal to start logs. Arrange green hardwood logs spoke fashion, as illustrated. Do not use paper or sawdust to start a fire — they burn to a fine ash that can coat food.
6. Soak wood chips or dampen sawdust, then add them to the fire to create dense smoke. Use chips or sawdust to smother any flames, too.
7. Adjust vents, covers or dampers so that the smoke flows slowly through the smoker and the fire stays very low.
8. Check the temperature in the smoker. Add the food when the smoker reaches the temperature given in recipe.
9. Check the smoker regularly, adding fuel, adjusting vents, dampers or covers, adding chips or sawdust when needed to maintain the temperature and smoke.

10. Check the food for doneness with meat thermometer or as the recipe directs. Remove the food from smoker when it is done.
11. Extinguish the fire by smothering (closing all covers and vents), or with water.

BASIC STEPS FOR SMOKE-COOKING

Smoking at temperatures between 150°F and 250°F is called smoke-cooking, or hot smoking. Smoke-cooked food reaches the safe temperature of 160°F more rapidly, can be eaten without any further cooking, and can be stored in the refrigerator for several days or frozen for up to six months. Most smoking done in covered barbecue grills is smoke-cooking. Temperatures inside these grills are close to oven-roasting (about 300°F), so cooking will take less time than in a smoker or smokehouse.

Ingredients	Equipment
Food	Chips or sawdust (soak
Brine	or dampen)
	Charcoal, gas or
	electric barbecue grill
	or smoker

1. To smoke-cook in a smoker or smokehouse, follow Basic Steps for Cold Smoking, but maintain a temperature of 200°F to 250°F.
2. To smoke-cook in a covered grill or small portable commercial smoker, first read manufacturer's directions for smoke-cooking and follow them exactly.
3. In a charcoal grill, briquettes are usually arranged at sides of grill with a drip pan directly under the food. On electric or gas grills adjust heat to "Low," following the manufacturer's directions.
4. Prepare the brine and food as in the recipe and Steps 1 through 4 of Basic Steps for Cold Smoking.
5. For the strongest smoke flavor, add soaked hickory chips or dampened hardwood sawdust at beginning of cooking time. For milder flavor add them for the last 15 minutes of cooking.
6. Use an oven thermometer to check the temperature inside the covered grill. (Some units have a temperature indicator on the cover.) The usual temperature for covered barbecue grills is 300°F. Add charcoal or increase heat, if necessary, to maintain that temperature, or adjust vents or dampers as the manufacturer directs.
7. Check the food for doneness with a meat thermometer or as the recipe directs and remove the food when done.
8. Extinguish the fire or turn off the unit following the manufacturer's directions.

SMOKING TIMES

What you smoke and how you smoke it determine the cooking time. This may range from minutes to hours to days. The recipes that follow give you approximate smoking times. Wherever possible, let a meat thermometer be your guide.

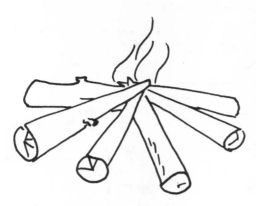

Arrange green hardwood logs spoke fashion.

SMOKED RIBS OR PORK CHOPS

The world will beat a path to your door for dinner invitations when you serve this all-time favorite.

Ingredients	Equipment
Pork chops, trimmed of fat, or spareribs or back ribs Seasoned salt Barbecue sauce	See Basic Equipment Smoker or covered grill

1. Rub the chops or ribs with seasoned salt.
2. Hang the ribs in your smoker or arrange the ribs or chops on a well-greased rack in the smoker.
3. Begin smoking at 80°F to 85°F and smoke for 1½ to 2 hours.
4. Gradually increase the temperature to 250°F and smoke for 30 to 45 minutes longer or until meat is done (it will fall from the bone).
5. Baste the ribs and chops with barbecue sauce for the last 15 minutes of cooking, if desired, and serve with additional sauce.

Follow the manufacturer's directions if you are using a covered charcoal or electric grill instead of a smoker. Check the Basic Steps for Smoke-Cooking and remember that grills have temperatures much as ovens, around 300°F. Your smoke-cooking time will be much shorter than at lower temperatures.

SMOKED BEEF, LAMB OR PORK ROASTS

Select top-quality meats and cuts that you would normally oven-roast. Smoking time depends on the size of the roast.

Ingredients	Equipment
Beef, lamb or pork roast Seasoned salt	See Basic Equipment Smoker or covered grill

1. Preheat your smoker to 225°F.

2. Rub the meat well with seasoned salt or your own blend of salt and spices.
3. Insert a meat thermometer so the tip is in center of the thickest muscle, away from fat and bone.
4. Smoke to desired doneness. Pork must reach an internal temperature of 170°F.

Follow the manufacturer's directions if you use a covered charcoal or electric grill. Check the Basic Steps for Smoke-Cooking and remember your cooking time will be shorter in a grill than in a smoker.

SMOKED OYSTERS

Serve these succulent morsels as appetizers at your next big party; when your guests rave about them casually mention that you smoked them yourself.

Ingredients	Equipment
Oysters, cleaned, shucked and washed 1 gallon water 1¼ pounds salt Salad oil	See Basic Equipment Oyster knife Measuring cup Smoker or covered grill

1. Mix the water and salt until salt dissolves.
2. Pour brine over the oysters and let stand 5 minutes.
3. Drain the oysters thoroughly.
4. Pour just enough oil over the oysters to lightly coat them.
5. Arrange them on a well-greased rack in your smoker with space between oysters for air to circulate. (Use a wire cake rack if the spaces in the smoker's rack are too wide.)
6. Smoke at 180°F for 15 minutes; turn and smoke 15 minutes longer.
7. Eat the oysters right away. Or refrigerate and eat them within a few days. Oysters can be packaged in freezer containers and frozen for up to 2 months.

SMOKED TURKEY

Smoke unstuffed birds for a stunning buffet centerpiece. Smoked turkey is extraordinarily good served cold. Smok-

ing turns the skin black, but it is not burnt. You can prepare stuffing and bake it in a casserole in your oven.

Ingredients	Equipment
Whole dressed unstuffed turkey or turkey pieces	See Basic Equipment
1 gallon water	Paper towels
1 pound salt	Smoker or covered grill
⅓ cup honey	
¼ cup sherry	

1. Check the weight of turkey and note it. Put the turkey in a large container that can hold enough brine to cover the bird.
2. Mix the water and the salt and pour over the turkey. If you need more brine to cover turkey, make more using these same proportions. Cover and place a weight on the cover to hold turkey under brine.
3. Refrigerate at least 8 hours, preferably overnight.
4. Lift the turkey from the brine, gently press out the liquid and pat dry, inside and out, with paper towels.
5. Hang the turkey in a cool, drafty place and let it air-dry about 1 hour.
6. Insert a meat thermometer in the thigh with the tip in center of the flesh, away from the bone.
7. Hang the turkey in a smoker or put it on a well-oiled rack in the smoker.
8. Start smoking at 90°F with dense smoke and smoke for 1 hour per pound.
9. Gradually increase the temperature to 200°F-225°F and smoke for 1 hour per pound or until the meat thermometer reaches 185°F.
10. Combine honey and sherry and use them to baste turkey during the last few hours of cooking.

If using a covered charcoal or electric grill instead of smoker, follow manufacturer's directions for smoking. Temperatures inside covered grill will always be higher, more like regular oven temperatures, so cooking time will be much less.

SMOKE-FLAVORED SALT

Smoke some salt while you are smoking other food; then store salt so you can add smoke flavor any time you want it.

Ingredients	Equipment
Table salt	Shallow pan
	Smoker

1. Spread the salt in shallow pan.
2. Put the pan on rack in the smoker while you are smoking other foods at 85°F or so.
3. Smoke about 3 to 4 hours or until golden in color.

SMOKED FISH FILLETS

Marinate fish only a few hours if you prefer mild salt-spice flavors, but 6 hours or overnight for pronounced spiciness.

Ingredients	Equipment
10 fillets (about 1 pound each) lean, white firm-fleshed fish	See Basic Equipment
1 quart water	Paper towels
½ cup salt	Wire rack
½ cup sugar	Smoker
Any 1 or 2 of the following: white or black pepper; onion or garlic salt; molasses, honey or brown sugar; bay, tarragon or dill	

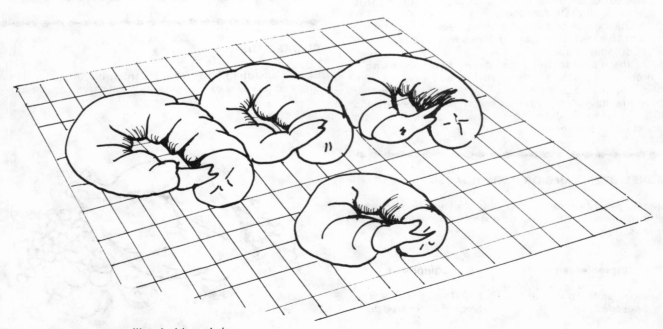

Use a screen over your grill to hold up shrimp.

*leaves; ground ginger
or mace; grated lemon
peel or lemon wedges
or slices; hot pepper
sauce or dried red
pepper flakes.*

1. Combine the water, salt, sugar and seasonings in a large bowl, pan or plastic bag and mix until the sugar and salt dissolve.
2. Add the fish fillets, cover and weight the cover with a plate or jar of water to hold the fish under brine.
3. Refrigerate for several hours or overnight.
4. Drain the fish and rinse well with cold water.
5. Pat the fillets dry with paper towels; then arrange on a wire rack and let them air-dry about 30 to 60 minutes.
6. Oil or grease the racks in the smoker and arrange the fish on them, skin side down, with space between the pieces for smoke to circulate.
7. Start smoking at 90°F. After 15 minutes gradually increase temperature to 135°F-140°F and smoke until the fish is golden brown and flakes when cut with a fork, about 1 to 2 hours.
8. Eat the fish right away, or refrigerate and eat within a few days. The fish can be wrapped tightly and frozen.

◆◆◆◆◆◆◆◆◆◆◆◆◆◆◆◆◆◆◆◆◆◆◆◆◆

FISH THAT SMOKE WELL. Freshwater: walleye or Northern pike, bass, catfish, perch, whitefish, trout.
Saltwater: pompano, cod, flounder, whitefish, halibut, pollock, mullet, mackerel.

◆◆◆◆◆◆◆◆◆◆◆◆◆◆◆◆◆◆◆◆◆◆◆◆◆

SMOKED SHRIMP

Smoked shrimp are among the most elegant appetizers or main dishes you can serve.

Ingredients	Equipment
10 pounds peeled raw shrimp	*See Basic Equipment*
1 quart water	*Paper towels*
½ cup salt	*Wire rack*
½ cup sugar	*Smoker*
1 tablespoon mixed pickling spice or 1 packet prepared spices for crab and shrimp or any of the spices listed under Smoked Fish Fillets	

1. Prepare a brine from water, salt, sugar and spices as directed in recipe for Smoked Fish Fillets.
2. Refrigerate the shrimp in brine 30 minutes to 2 hours, depending on the strength of flavor you prefer.
3. Drain the shrimp and rinse well with cold water.
4. Pat dry with paper towels, then arrange them on a wire rack and let them air dry about 30 minutes.
5. Oil or grease the racks in your smoker and arrange the shrimp on the racks with space between for smoke to circulate. Use a wire cake rack if the spaces in the smoker's rack are too wide.
6. Start smoking at 90°F. After 15 minutes gradually in-

crease the temperature to 135°F to 140°F and smoke until the shrimp are done, about 1 to 1½ hours. Taste the shrimp to check doneness and smoke for a longer time, if necessary.

◆◆◆◆◆◆◆◆◆◆◆◆◆◆◆◆◆◆◆◆◆◆◆◆◆

JERKY

The meat for jerky must be very lean because any fat left on is likely to become rancid, so shop wisely and trim carefully. The recipe makes about 1 pound of jerky. Season it generously for appetizers, but season moderately for back pack or camping meals or snacks.

Ingredients	Equipment
3 to 5 pounds lean beef cut 1½ inches thick (round or flank steak)	*See Basic Equipment* *Very sharp knife* *Smoker*
⅓ cup soy sauce	
3 tablespoons vinegar	
2 tablespoons sugar	
2 tablespoons sherry or lemon juice	
1 teaspoon onion powder	
1 teaspoon seasoned salt	

1. Put the meat in the freezer until partly frozen. Then slice it very thin (across the grain if you use flank steak).
2. For mildly-seasoned jerky sprinkle the meat with seasoned salt and pepper and smoke right away. For stronger flavor, combine all the remaining ingredients in a bowl or plastic bag.
3. Add the meat, cover or tie the bag, and refrigerate for several hours or overnight. Turn the meat in the marinade once or twice.
4. Drain the meat well.
5. Arrange the meat on well-greased racks in your smoker with space between the pieces for air to circulate.
6. Smoke at 85°F to 90°F until meat is dry and brittle, about 24 hours.

◆◆◆◆◆◆◆◆◆◆◆◆◆◆◆◆◆◆◆◆◆◆◆◆◆

SMOKED SAUSAGE

Any of the recipes in the chapter on sausages can be smoked, if you wish. Smoking flavors the food but does not cook it.

◆◆◆◆◆◆◆◆◆◆◆◆◆◆◆◆◆◆◆◆◆◆◆◆◆

Sausages in casing:
1. Hang the uncooked sausages from hooks in your smoker.
2. Smoke at about 70°F for 1 to 2 hours.
3. Cook them in the oven or on top of range as directed in the recipe.

◆◆◆◆◆◆◆◆◆◆◆◆◆◆◆◆◆◆◆◆◆◆◆◆◆

Sausage in loaf pans:
1. Put the loaf pan in the center of the rack in your smoker.
2. Smoke at about 70°F for 1 to 2 hours.
3. Then cook in the oven as directed in the recipe.

Dried Foods

The summer's harvest can cheer your menu all year if you take advantage of the oldest and simplest method of preserving food — drying. Pilgrims and early settlers survived thanks to the Indians who taught them how to dry their provisions. Today, the thought of dried foods conjures up nostalgic visions: herb bouquets perfuming country kitchens; jewel-like dried fruits stored in the pantry waiting to sweeten holiday cakes; vegetables, beans and corn safely gathered inside for a comfortable winter.

When you dry herbs, vegetables, and fruits you will be adding nothing to them — only removing water. The low water content prevents bacteria from spoiling the dried foods. Dried foods, of course, are shriveled up; their nutritional content is concentrated, but vitamins C and A are usually lost.

All of the food in this chapter could be dried outside in direct sunlight if you live in a hot arid area. But, oven-drying should be used if you live where it is the least humid or cool. Our recipes all use the oven-drying method.

By following a few simple steps you can garner a cornucopia of goodies: full-flavored herbs, not supermarket herbs tasting like dust; handy, colorful vegetables that retain their distinctive tastes; a full provider of dried peas and beans to turn into hearty main dishes for mere pennies; and dried fruits for a fraction of what they cost at the supermarket. The fruits are sulpher-free and nourishing. Cooked, they make piquant compotes or fruit-soups. Uncooked, they are perfect in granola, cookies and cakes. Dried fruits are energy-packed snacks both kids and grownups love. Arranged in wicker baskets or glass jars, they turn into handsome gifts.

Basic Equipment

1. **Oven thermometer.** An oven temperature no higher than 120°F must be evenly held for 12 to 24 hours.
2. **Knife.** A very sharp knife is absolutely necessary for slicing foods paper thin. Uniform, thin slices make the most successful dried foods. A wide-bladed Oriental cleaver is efficient and accurate.
3. **Cookie sheet.** Select a perfectly flat large sheet; a sheet with a lip or edge slows down the drying process.
4. **Steamer.** Vegetables must be blanched before drying and steam blanching preserves more vitamins than blanching by boiling. You can make a steamer from a large deep pot with a tight-fitting lid, a colander, wire basket or rack, and some blocks to hold the rack above the water. There should be two to three inches of water to boil and produce steam, so the rack will need to stand five or six inches above the bottom of the pot.
5. **Spatula.** To make sure the sliced foods are drying evenly, you will have to stir them from time to time. A long-handled spatula is especially efficient.
6. **Clean airtight containers.** Dried herbs can be stored

in baby food jars, old spice jars, half-pint canning jars, jelly jars. Other dried foods can be stored in coffee cans, large canning or freezing jars, peanut butter jars or canisters with tight lids to keep out moisture and vermin. Plastic bags, tightly closed with rubber bands or twist ties also work.

Basic Ingredients

Herbs should be disease-free. Fruit should be without blemish, fresh as possible and fully ripened so that the sugar content is at its peak. Carefully pick over any of the foods to be dried; one bad slice can ruin an entire drying tray.

OVEN TEMPERATURES

The ideal temperature for drying is 90°F to 115°F. If you have a gas oven, the pilot light should keep the heat at this ideal temperature. Use an oven thermometer to check the temperature. If you have an electric oven, turn its temperature to "Warm" and check the oven thermometer after half an hour. You can leave the door ajar to sustain an even heat. If your electric oven has no warm setting, try leaving on the oven's light, checking to see if the tem-perature is adequate. The maximum temperature for dry-ing is 120°F.

Basic Steps

1. Prepare the food. Preparation will vary with the type of food being dried. Each recipe will tell how to wash, drain, and then peel, slice or chop the food.
2. Pre-treat the food as the recipe directs. Vegetables must be steam-blanched to stop the action of spoil-age-causing enzymes. Fruits can be treated with ascorbic acid solution to prevent discoloration.
3. Spread food in a single even layer on a cookie sheet.
4. Put the tray in the oven and dry for 12 to 24 hours, checking the oven temperature from time to time. (Corn may take longer than 24 hours.)
5. Stir occasionally during drying, using a spatula to lift, turn and move pieces at the center to the outside.
6. Check for doneness as the recipe directs. Vegeta-bles should be brittle and rattle on the tray. Fruit should feel leathery. Do not under-dry or the food will spoil.
7. Remove foods from the oven and let them stand until completely cooled, stirring occasionally.
8. When completely cooled, package foods for storage in clean airtight containers.

STORAGE

Dried foods long to recapture the water they lost, so they must be kept in dry, airtight containers. A cool, dark, dry

Vegetables must be steam blanched before drying.

Food dries best spread in a single layer.

storage place is best. Flavors and colors change in the sunlight and heat. If you notice moisture on the inside of the container, quickly remove the food and return it to the oven for further drying.

REHYDRATION

Dry vegetables, except onions and finely chopped peppers, need to soak before cooking. Pour 1½ cups of boiling water over each cup of dried food. Most vegetables need to soak for about two hours. Fruit to be stewed will need to soak from 2 hours to overnight, depending on the thickness of the slices and the degree of dryness.

RECIPES

HERBS

Both seeds and leaves of herbs can be dried to add zest to any dish — from breakfast eggs to midnight snacks.

Herb seeds. Drying is the natural way a plant suspends its seeds' germination. Dill, caraway, anise, fennel, cumin and coriander perform the seed drying process automatically, all you have to do is gather the seeds before the wind scatters them. Pick the pods or flower heads when they are almost dry and spread them on a tray to dry completely at room temperature, then shake the heads to loosen the seeds. A tidier method of seed collecting is to pick the entire plant and hang it upside down inside a paper bag. Punch a few holes around the top of the bag for air circulation and hang up the herb. The seeds drop off into the bag as they dry. Store seeds in airtight containers in a cool, dark, dry place. They can be used whole or finely ground.

Herb leaves. The pungent essence of herbs is carried in the plant's oils. Herb leaves brim with their essential oils right before the plant blooms — this is the best time to harvest the leaves.

Ingredients	Equipment
Any of the following: *chives, marjoram, basil, thyme, parsley, oregano, mint, dill, celery leaves, tarragon, chervil, or savory.*	*Paper towels* *Cookie sheet* *Oven thermometer* *Storage containers*

1. Wash the leaves quickly with cold water; pat them dry with paper towels.
2. Pull leaves from top two-thirds of plant. Spread them evenly in single layer on a cookie sheet.
3. Dry in the oven at no higher than 120°F until the leaves are brittle and will crumble when pinched. If the leaves do not crumble readily, return them to the oven for a few more hours.
4. Store the leaves whole, or crumble.

◆◆◆◆◆◆◆◆◆◆◆◆◆◆◆◆◆◆◆◆◆◆◆◆◆◆◆

CARROTS AND PARSNIPS

Select mature, but not woody, vegetables for the best results.

Ingredients	Equipment
Carrots or parsnips	*See Basic Equipment* *Paper towels*

1. Wash the carrots or parsnips thoroughly.
2. Steam them whole for 20 minutes. Spread them on paper towels to dry.
3. Peel and slice ⅛-inch thick, or shred.
4. Spread the vegetables not more than ½-inch thick on a cookie sheet.
5. Dry in the oven at no higher than 120°F until the pieces are very brittle. Carrots will be a deep orange.

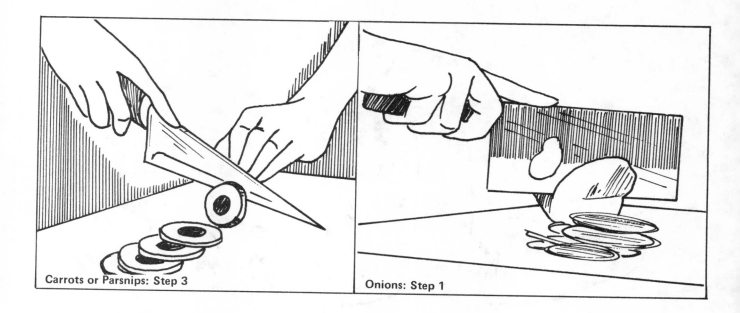

Carrots or Parsnips: Step 3

Onions: Step 1

PEAS AND BEANS

Here is the basis for old-fashioned baked beans or long-simmered bean soups.

Ingredients	Equipment
Any of the following:	*See Basic Equipment*
Shelled green beans	*Steamer*
Shelled lima beans	*Cookie sheet*
Edible green soybeans	

1. Steam blanch for 15 to 20 minutes. Shell the soybeans after blanching.
2. Spread them on paper towels to dry.
3. Spread the peas or beans on a cookie sheet in single layer.
4. Dry in the oven at no higher than 120°F until a single pea or bean will shatter when tapped with a hammer.

MUSHROOMS.

You will enjoy having mushrooms on hand to add to sauces, soups and stews. There is no need to blanch mushrooms.

Ingredients	Equipment
Mushrooms	*Sharp knife or cleaver*
	Cookie sheet
	Thermometer
	Storage containers

1. Wash the mushrooms well; pat them dry with paper towels.
2. Slice the mushrooms if they are large, or leave them whole. Slice the stems, too, if they are not tough.
3. Spread them on a cookie sheet in a single layer.
4. Dry in the oven at no higher than 120°F until the large pieces are leathery and the small pieces are brittle.

ONIONS

You can buy onions when they are plentiful and cheap, then dry enough to season your meals for many months. There is no need to steam blanch onions.

Ingredients	Equipment
Onions	*Sharp knife or cleaver*
	Cookie sheet
	Thermometer
	Storage containers

1. Peel the onions and slice them very thin. Separate them into rings.
2. Spread the slices on a cookie sheet in a single layer.
3. Dry in the oven at no higher than 120°F until they are very crisp.
4. Crumble and store in airtight containers.

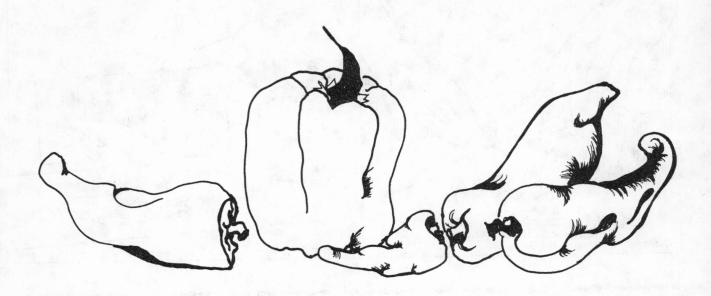

GREEN AND RED PEPPERS

A peck or bushel of peppers bought at the end of the summer can be dried and used all winter. A pinch or a handful adds flavor and color to casseroles, stews and egg dishes.

Ingredients	Equipment
Green or red bell peppers or hot green or red peppers	*See Basic Equipment Paper towels*

1. Wash the peppers; remove the tops and seeds.
2. Slice them into thin rings or strips.
3. Steam-blanch them for 10 minutes. Spread the strips or rings on paper towels to dry.
4. Spread them on a cookie sheet in a single layer.
5. Dry in the oven until the pieces are shriveled but pliable.

◆◆◆◆◆◆◆◆◆◆◆◆◆◆◆◆◆◆◆◆◆◆◆◆◆◆◆◆◆

PUMPKIN AND WINTER SQUASH

Dried pumpkin and winter squash can be freshened in warm water and then baked just as you would fresh winter squash, glazing the slices with cider and brown sugar during the last minutes of cooking. Or, you can simmer the refreshed slices until they are tender, whip them with butter, brown sugar, salt and pepper, and top with a dash of nutmeg.

Ingredients	Equipment
Pumpkin or squash	*See Basic Equipment Paper towels*

1. Cut the pumpkin or squash in quarters, remove the seeds and peel.

2. Cut them into 1-inch strips, then cut each strip crosswise into thin slices.
3. Steam-blanch 8 to 10 minutes, until the slices are sticky but not soft.
4. Spread them on paper towels to dry.
5. Spread the slices on a cookie sheet in a single layer.
6. Dry in the oven at no higher than 120°F. The pieces will be leathery.

◆◆◆◆◆◆◆◆◆◆◆◆◆◆◆◆◆◆◆◆◆◆◆◆◆◆◆◆◆

PUMPKIN SEEDS

If you are planning to dry pumpkins, you can scoop out the seeds and enjoy them too. Toasted lightly in oil and salted, pumpkin seeds are a favorite fall treat.

Ingredients	Equipment
Pumpkin seeds	Cookie sheet
1 or 2 tablespoons oil or butter (optional)	
Salt	

1. Preheat the oven to 325°F.
2. Thoroughly rinse the pumpkin seeds.
3. Butter or oil the cookie sheet, if you want.
4. Spread the seeds on the cookie sheet.
5. Toast the seeds in the preheated oven for 10 to 12 minutes, watching closely so the seeds do not burn.
6. Remove from the oven and salt to taste.

CORN

Commercial cornmeal will taste bland once you have tried your own nutrition-packed dried corn. Grind the dried corn in a nut or seed grinder or in a heavy-duty blender. Then use the finely ground meal for corn bread, johnnycake, spoon bread or for coating foods before frying.

Ingredients	Equipment
Ears of corn	See Basic Equipment

1. Husk corn and trim ears, if necessary.
2. Steam-blanch for 12 to 15 minutes. Drain.
3. Cut kernels from cob and spread on cookie sheet in single layer.
4. Dry in oven at no higher than 120° until a single kernel will shatter when tapped with a hammer. Corn may take up to 48 hours to dry completely.

DRIED FRUIT

Most of our dried fruit recipes call for crystalline ascorbic acid to preserve the fruit and prevent discoloration. Ascorbic acid is vitamin C. Commercially dried fruits have been treated heavily with sulpher fumes. The sulpher treatment helps repel insects during outdoor drying, preserves the fruits' color and prevents deterioration. While there are some books available that describe the complicated process of sulphering, we think that the ascorbic acid treatment is the easiest for our oven-dried fruit. The result is not as acid-tasting as commercial fruit. The apricots, in particular taste more like fresh fruit when treated only with ascorbic acid. Fruit treated with ascorbic acid lasts for around eight months; but sulpher-treated fruit lasts sometimes for years. However, an eight-month's supply of chewy, sweet, fruit-snacks should see you through the winter and back into the fresh fruit season.

APPLES OR PEARS

Choose flawless, tart cooking apples to dry for a special,

sweet snack. Pears are the one exception to the rule that fruit for drying should be fully ripe. Pears should be slightly underripe to make the choicest dried fruit.

Ingredients	Equipment
Apples or pears	Peeler
Crystalline ascorbic acid	Sharp knife or cleaver
Water	Measuring spoons and cup
	Cookie sheet.
	Thermometer
	Storage containers

1. Combine the ascorbic acid with the water (2½ teaspoons of ascorbic acid with 1 cup water is enough for 5 quarts of cut fruit).
2. Pare and core the fruit and cut it into ¼-inch slices, rings or cubes.
3. Sprinkle the fruit with the ascorbic acid mixture as you pare and cut, turning gently to coat each piece.
4. Spread them on a cookie sheet in a single layer.
5. Dry in the oven at no higher than 120°F. The pieces will be pliable and feel springy.

PLUMS (PRUNES)

Chop your dried prunes and mix them with cream cheese for a simple sandwich spread. Or stew them with a slice of lemon, a stick of cinnamon and a few whole cloves.

Ingredients	Equipment
Prune plums	Sharp knife
	Cookie sheet
	Thermometer
	Storage containers

1. Cut plums in halves and remove pits.
2. Spread in single layer on cookie sheet, cup side up.
3. Dry in the oven at no higher than 120°F until the prunes feel pliable and leathery.

FRUIT LEATHER

This chewy confection was probably the first all-day sucker. You make the leather by cooking the fruit until it is soft, then you puree it, sweeten it, and spread it out to dry. Cut the fruit leather into strips or squares to tuck in backpacks, lunch boxes, tackle boxes or bike bags. This is a good way to use less-than-perfect fruits.

Ingredients	Equipment
1 gallon pitted apricots, peaches or prunes	Measuring cups and spoons
1½ cups pineapple juice, water or any other complementary fruit juice	Large pot with cover
	Strainer or colander lined with cheesecloth
Honey	Strainer or food mill
1 tablespoon almond extract, (optional)	Large mixing bowl
Cornstarch	Cookie sheet
	Wire racks
	Small sifter or strainer
	Plastic wrap or waxed paper
	Thermometer
	Sharp knife

1. Measure the fruit and juice into a large pot, cover and heat slowly over low heat until the fruit is tender. Cook slowly, watch carefully and stir occasionally to prevent sticking.
2. Pour the cooked fruit into a strainer or colander lined with cheesecloth. Set the colander over a large mixing bowl and drain well. Stir gently to help it drain. (Save the juice and pour it in another container. You can use the juice for fruit drinks or in other recipes.)
3. When as much juice as possible has drained, set the

PEACHES AND APRICOTS

Peaches will take longer to dry than apricots. You can make mid-winter jams or conserves with the dried fruit. Or, stew some of them in orange juice with a cinnamon stick and a little vanilla. Stir in just a bit of orange liqueur, then chill and top with whipped cream. Simply elegant!

Ingredients	Equipment
Peaches or apricots	Sharp knife
Crystalline ascorbic acid	Measuring spoons and cup
Water	Cookie sheet
	Thermometer
	Storage containers

1. Cut the fruit into halves and remove the pits.
2. Combine the ascorbic acid and water (2½ teaspoons of ascorbic acid disolved in a cup of water is enough for 5 quarts of cut fruit).
3. Spread the halves cup side up on a cookie sheet.
4. Dry them in the oven at no higher than 120°F until they feel pliable and leathery.

GRAPES

In case you have not guessed, the result is raisins.

Ingredients	Equipment
Thompson seedless grapes	Colander or wire basket
	Large saucepan or pot
	Cookie sheet

1. Wash and stem the grapes. Place them in a colander and lower into rapidly boiling water for just a few seconds to split the skins.
2. Lift out and spread them on paper towels to dry.
3. Spread in a single layer on cookie sheet.
4. Dry in the oven at no higher than 120°F until pliable.

Blanching grapes in boiling water stops enzyme activity and makes drying easier.

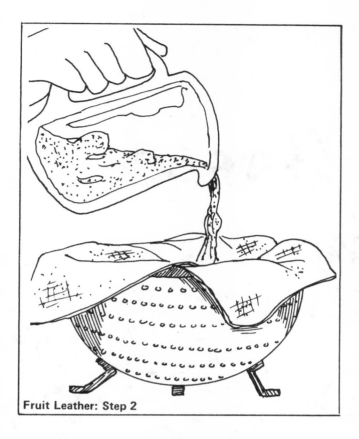

Fruit Leather: Step 2

8. Dry it in the oven at no higher than 120°F until the leather is stiff enough to lift off the cookie sheet.
9. Put the leather on wire racks in a warm dry place for a few hours to finish drying on both sides.
10. Put a few tablespoons cornstarch in a small strainer and sift a very light coating over each side of the leather.
11. Stack the sheets of leather with plastic wrap or waxed paper between and cover with a sheet of plastic wrap. Store in a cool, dry place.
12. Cut the leather into strips, squares, diamonds or rectangles to eat.

APPLE LEATHER

If you are tired of making applesauce from windfalls, make apple leather.

Ingredients	Equipment
1 gallon whole apples	Peeler
3 cups cider or apple juice	Sharp knife
Honey	Electric grinder, food chopper or blender
1 to 2 teaspoons each ground cloves and cinnamon, if desired	Measuring cups and spoons
	Large pot
	Cookie sheets
	Plastic wrap or waxed paper

1. Peel and core the apples and chop them with a knife; run the fruit through the coarse cutting blade of an electric grinder or manual food chopper, or chop in a blender, saving all the juice.
2. Heat the apples and juice in a large pot as in Fruit Leathers, but cook uncovered, stirring occasionally to prevent sticking, until mixture is consistency of apple butter. (Do not drain the liquid, but cook until it evaporates.)
3. Stir in honey to taste and the spices.
4. Spread ¼-inch thick on greased cookie sheets.
5. Dry and store as in Fruit Leathers.

strainer over a large mixing bowl. Press the fruit through the strainer (or food mill).
4. The fruit skins can be stirred back into the pulp to be a part of the leather or you can discard them, as you wish. Prune skins are usually discarded.
5. Add honey, a tablespoon at a time, tasting as you go, until the mixture is as sweet as you like.
6. If you wish, stir in 1 tablespoon almond extract.
7. Spread the fruit, which should be at least the consistency of apple butter or thicker, about ¼ inch thick on lightly greased cookie sheets.

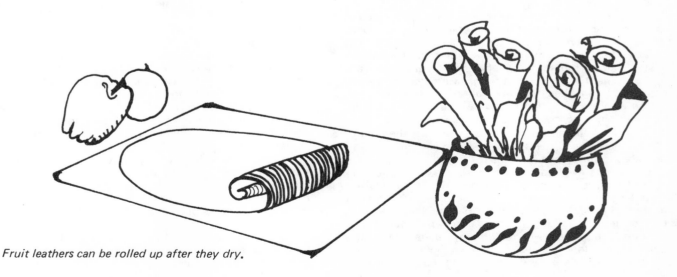

Fruit leathers can be rolled up after they dry.

Bread

Nothing evokes the essence of home, hearth and secure happiness like bread baking in the oven. Its rich, warm smell makes an ordinary day worth remembering. One ancient Greek philosopher (Democritus) supposedly prolonged his life for three days merely by inhaling the odor of freshly baked loaves. The word "bread" itself means: life, food, money, spirit, the fruit of civilization, hospitality, sincerity, truth.

Bread symbolizes humankind's evolution from tribes of hunters and gatherers that lead a perilous hand-to-mouth existence, to permanent farming communities. The first known cities arose only in regions where grain was harvested. Most religious beliefs, myths and festivals followed the rhythm of the grain growing season. Moses commanded the Feast of the Tabernacles to be celebrated with grains, bread and wine — symbols of a permanent homeland after years of wandering.

Life-giving, life-sustaining, bread was truly the staff of life for the ancient world. At first bread was nothing but pounded grain pressed into cakes and dried in the sun. Baking ovens eventually evolved; the baking profession ranked high in ancient civilizations. The Egyptians are credited with baking the first leavened bread. These first leavened loaves were sourdough breads, leavened with bits of fermented dough saved from previous bread batches. The workers who built the pyramids were paid a daily wage of three loaves of bread and two jugs of beer; Egyptian taxes were collected in bread loaves.

The Roman army conquered most of Europe and Asia on a diet of mixed grain bread — the original Roman meal bread. Roman bakers united in a Society of Pistors and held a seat in the Roman senate. Even the shapes of breads have long histories: the pretzel, for instance, is a Roman invention that was eaten only on religious occasions. The pagans passed the custom of pretzel-eating to the Christians. Up until this century the pretzel was eaten only during Lent.

Breads for rituals, breads for daily life — bread still plays a major role in most of the world's diet. Almost every country or ethnic group has its own special bread. Bagels, Polish Pickle Rye, Pumpernickel, and Pita are some of the ethnic favorites included in this chapter.

In the United States, the nutritional importance of bread diminished as a large variety of foods became readily accessible. The invention of the steel roller for milling white flour made white breads cheap and easy to produce. The custom of eating special breads on special occasions is observed less and less. Lately, though, there has been a renewed interest in homemade breads and specialty breads. The bread-baking tradition is enjoying a welcome revival and you can take advantage of modern bread-making techniques used in this chapter to bake superior loaves.

Bread-making is an amazing sequence of events. You take what seem to be simple ingredients, mix them together in a certain way and you create a living thing that grows and changes as you watch.

Yeast, tiny single-celled organisms, feeds on sugar and liquid. The yeast cells give off gas as they grow and reproduce. Flour, mixed with liquid, forms gluten that traps these tiny bubbles of gas within the dough. Baking expands these air bubbles and, at the same time, sets the protein of the gluten. Sugar browns and forms the crust. Oil or shortening tenderizes the crumbs.

These steps are a simplification of a complex series of chemical and physical reactions. But describing them helps explain why bread-making is such a popular, creative activity. The mixing is fun. Kneading bread is a marvelous way to work off energy, frustrations, or anger. Watching the dough expand until it doubles its size is, if you stop to think about it, awesome. And, best of all, you can smell the bread baking in your own oven and you can eat warm slices of your delicious loaves. Nothing can substitute for "homemade" when it comes to bread.

Basic Equipment

1. **Glass and metal measuring cups.** Standard measuring cups with clear markings are best. Use the glass measuring cup for liquids, it is easier to see the ounces, The metal measuring cup is fine for dry ingredients.
2. **Measuring spoons.** Metal or plastic standard measuring spoons for ¼ teaspoon, ½ teaspoon, 1 teaspoon and 1 tablespoon should should be used. All measurements are for level spoonfuls.
3. **Mixing bowls.** No matter what size bowl you are using, the heavier it is the easier mixing will be.
4. **Electric mixer or egg beater.** Most bread recipes can be mixed by hand, but you have to have a strong arm to beat a stiff dough 300 strokes at a time. An electric mixer makes the job easier.
5. **Rubber scraper.** Use a rubber scraper for efficient scraping of your mixing bowl.
6. **Cutters.** A sharp knife is always useful. Round biscuits can be cut with a drinking glass.
7. **Pastry brush.** Use a pastry brush with soft bristles for spreading melted butter or egg whites on the top of breads and rolls before baking.
8. **Baking pans.** Muffin tins are good for dinner rolls as well as muffins. The standard size bread pan is around 9x5x3 inches and holds a one to one-and-a-half pound loaf of bread. Cookie sheets are called for in some recipes.
9. **Bread board or kneading area.** A wooden cutting board or bread board at least 16x16 inches is best for kneading, rolling and cutting bread dough. A formica counter or table top will do, but be careful not to damage it when you cut or slice.

Basic Ingredients

Bread commonly contains flour, yeast, liquid, a sweetener, oil or butter, and salt. Eggs, additional sweeteners, fruit, nuts, meat or cheese and other grains can go into bread, too.

1. **Flour.** Flour made from wheat contains a magical substance, gluten. Gluten forms long elastic strands, giving bread its volume and texture. White flour has more gluten than any other flour. Most bread recipes call for some white flour to lighten the loaf. Breads made from all whole wheat or all rye flours are smaller and heavier than breads made from white flour.

    Unbleached whole wheat flour, sometimes called whole grain flour, gives you all the nutritional benefits of the grain. A whole grain contains protein, the B-complex vitamins (thiamin, niacin and riboflavin) and iron; it also has a tough outer layer, the bran, that provides roughage. Whole wheat flour is hard to knead and slow to rise.

    Bleached or unbleached enriched flours have fewer nutrients than whole wheat flour, but both are commonly used and they meet the United States Federal Drug Administration's standards of nutrition. Bleached enriched flour has been treated with a maturing agent, not with laundry bleach as you might think. Unbleached enriched flour usually requires more kneading than bleached flour because it has not been aged or matured.

Some ethnic breads, like Pita, are more authentic if you use unbleached or whole wheat flour. At other times you will want a light, fine-textured loaf that needs bleached enriched flour. Never substitute "self-rising" flour or biscuit mixes for the flour in the recipes that follow.

If you plan to bake a lot of bread, buy flour in a 25 pound bag. Millers blend flours with higher protein content into the bigger bags. High-protein flour makes the best bread. You will save money by buying a large quantity.

Almost all flours are pre-sifted for you at the mill so you do not need to sift at all. Stir the flour in the bag or canister. Spoon it, do not scoop it, into a dry measuring cup and level it off. If you substitute soy flour for some of the wheat flour, sift the soy flour to remove any lumps.

2. **Yeast.** Yeast is leavening. It makes the bread rise. Quick breads are leavened with baking powder or baking soda and an acid. As the name implies, they work almost instantly. Yeast needs liquid, sugar, warmth and time. You can use active dry yeast or compressed yeast. Our recipes call for active dry yeast because it is so much easier to mix. Buy dry yeast in a strip of 3 packets, or look for small jars that contain the equivalent of several packets. Some natural food stores sell large packages of dry yeast. Or perhaps your local baker will sell you a big chunk of his compressed yeast. Remember that compressed yeast must be softened in lukewarm water or any liquid given in the recipe before it is added to the other ingredients.

3. **Liquid.** The liquid used in bread making can be water, milk, potato water, fruit or vegetable juice, even beer.

4. **Sweetener.** Sugar is the usual sweetener, but you can use honey, molasses or brown sugar.

5. **Oil or butter.** Most of the recipes in this chapter call for butter or oil. Melted shortening, margarine or lard can also be used.

6. **Salt.** Use ordinary table salt.

NUTRITION

Bread, if made with whole wheat (whole grain) or enriched flours, provides several grams of protein, the B-complex vitamins, iron and — if milk is used in the recipe — calcium. Whole grain flours provide additional vitamins and trace minerals, as well as necessary roughage. The carbohydrates in bread are an important source for energy. You can add even more nutrition to bread by mixing in other ingredients. Substitute a cup or two of sifted soy flour for part of the wheat flour; add an extra half-cup or more of nonfat dry milk powder; stir in a half-cup or more of wheat germ. Breadmaking, once you have mastered the basics, is a kitchen art that lends itself to improvisations.

BASIC STEPS

This method of bread making combines the yeast and flour, saving you a step. For another shortcut, double the amount of yeast and cut both rising times in half. Whole wheat flour (also called whole grain flour) can replace the enriched all-purpose flour. A whole wheat loaf will be harder to knead, slower to rise and smaller, coarser and denser than a white flour loaf — but it is more nutritious. You can make a loaf with half white and half whole wheat flour, or exchange any portion of white flour for whole wheat flour. The recipe makes 2 loaves.

Basic Ingredients

5½ to 6½ cups whole wheat
    or enriched all-
    purpose flour
1 cup milk
1 cup water
2 tablespoons sugar
2 tablespoons oil
1 tablespoon salt
  Oil

Basic Equipment

Glass and metal
  measuring cups
Measuring spoons
Saucepan
Electric mixer with large
  bowl or large mixing
  bowl and wooden
  spoon
Rubber spatula
Large clean board or
  counter
Pastry brush
Sharp knife
Rolling pin (optional)
2 (8½ x 4½-inch) loaf
  pans
Wire racks

1. Stir together 2 cups of flour and the yeast in a large mixing bowl.
2. Measure milk, water, sugar, oil and salt into a saucepan and heat them over low heat only until warm (120°F to 130°F), stirring to blend.

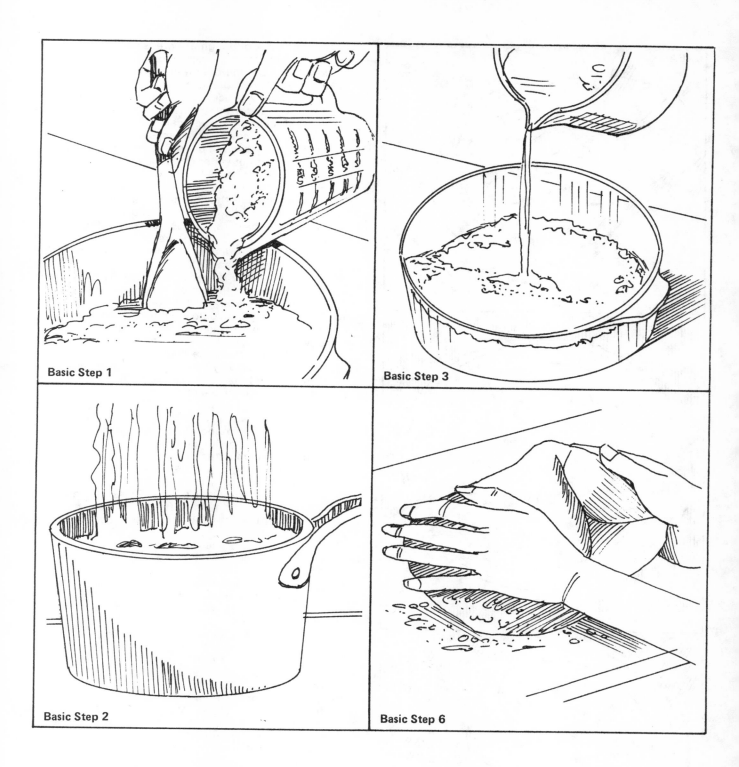

Basic Step 1

Basic Step 3

Basic Step 2

Basic Step 6

3. Add the liquid ingredients to the flour-yeast mixture and beat until smooth, about 2 minutes on the medium speed of your electric mixer or beat 300 strokes by hand.
4. Add 1 cup of flour and beat 1 minute on medium speed or 150 strokes by hand.
5. Stir in more flour to make a moderately stiff dough.
6. Turn out onto a lightly floured surface and knead by pressing ball of the dough away from you with the heels of your hands. Fold the dough over toward you,

making a half circle with its rounded edges toward you. Push down firmly on these edges, then give the dough a quarter turn, fold again and push. Repeat the quarter turn, fold and push for about 8 to 10 minutes more. The dough will be smooth and satiny. Gently press two fingers into the dough. If it springs back, leaving only a slight indentation, you have kneaded it enough. If not, knead more.
7. Shape the dough into a ball. Grease a large mixing bowl and put the ball of dough in bowl, turning so

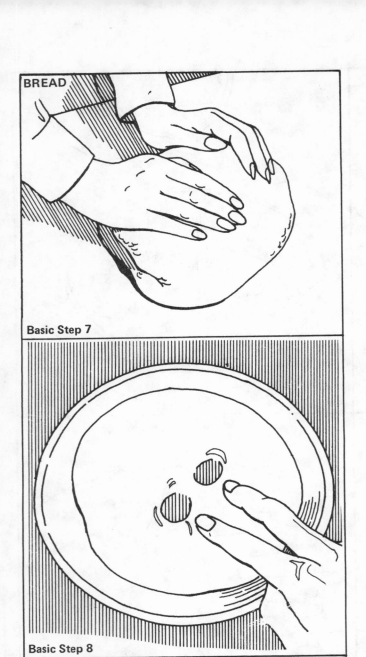

BREAD

Basic Step 7

Basic Step 8

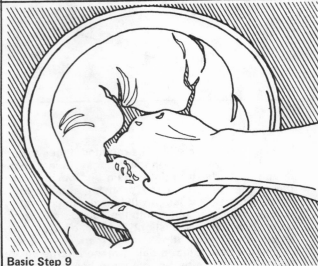

Basic Step 9

that all sides of dough are greased too.

8. Cover with plastic wrap, waxed paper or a clean towel and put the dough in a warm place (80°F to 85°F) until it doubles in size. There are many adequately warm places for dough to rise: a sunny, draft-free window; a spot near the radiator; the top of your refrigerator. Or, you can use your oven (do not turn it on) by moving both racks to their lowest positions. Put the bowl of dough on the upper rack, then put a pan of hot water on the lower rack and close the door. Some cooks fill a large bowl with hot water, put a rack over it and put the bowl of dough on the rack. Be careful that the temperature does not go over 85°F or the dough will rise too rapidly and the bread will have a coarse texture. Whole wheat dough will take 1 to 1½ hours to rise. Gently press 2 fingers into the dough. If indentations remain, the dough has risen enough.

9. Punch down the dough. Push your fist right down into the center of the dough in the bowl, then fold the outside edges over into the center "crater."

10. Turn the dough out onto a lightly floured surface: cut the dough in half and shape the halves into balls. Cover with plastic wrap and let them rest 10 minutes. Resting helps make the dough easier to handle.

11. Shape the loaves by either of the following methods.
    Conventional Flatten or roll each ball of dough to form a rectangle 9 inches wide. Fold the rectangle in half, lengthwise. Seal the edges by pressing them firmly with your fingertips. Roll the loaf under your palms to round it out, then put it in a greased loaf pan, seam side down.
    Roll-Up Method Flatten or roll each ball of dough to form a rectangle 9 inches wide. Starting at a 9-inch end roll it up jelly roll fashion. Seal the seam by pinching it with your fingers. Press the ends with the side of your hand to seal. Fold the ends under the loaf, then put it in a greased loaf pan, seam side down.

12. Brush the tops of the loaves with oil.

13. Let them rise in a warm place until doubled in bulk, about 1 hour.

14. Bake in a preheated 400°F oven 30 to 35 minutes. If the tops of the loaves start to get too brown before the baking time is up, cover them lightly with a piece of aluminum foil.

15. Check the bread for doneness by tipping it out of the pan and thumping the bottom. The loaf should sound hollow. Remove it from the pan immediately, brush with oil if you want a soft crust, and cool on a wire rack.

16. Store the cooled bread in a cool, dry place away from any source of heat. Wrapping in plastic wrap or plastic bags helps keep the bread soft. If you want, you can freeze the bread. Wrap it tightly or seal it in a plastic bag for the freezer. Thaw it at room temperature.

Recipes

ALL GRAIN BREAD

Rye, wheat and oats combine in this bread for superb eating.

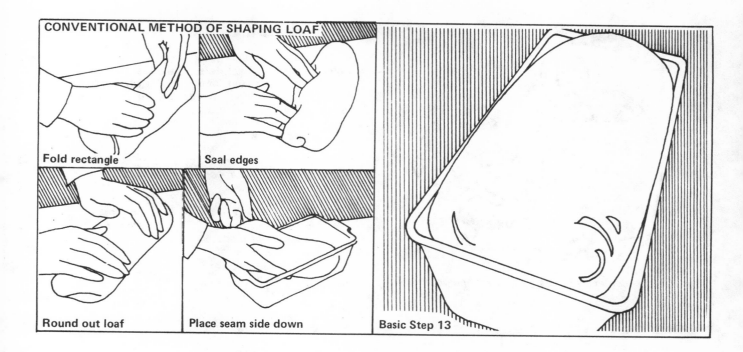

CONVENTIONAL METHOD OF SHAPING LOAF

Fold rectangle

Seal edges

Round out loaf

Place seam side down

Basic Step 13

Ingredients

1½ cups rye flour
1 cup enriched all-purpose flour
1 cup wheat germ
1 cup rolled oats
2 packages dry yeast
1½ cups milk
1 cup water
3 tablespoons butter or oil
3 tablespoons honey
2 tablespoons molasses
2 teaspoons salt
1 egg

Whole wheat flour, as needed

Equipment

See Basic Equipment

All Grain Bread: Step 5

1. Stir together the flours, wheat germ and oats.
2. In large mixing bowl stir together 2 cups of the flour mixture and the yeast.
3. Measure the milk, water, butter, honey, molasses and salt into a saucepan and heat only until warm (120°F to 130°F), stirring to blend.
4. Add the liquid ingredients to the flour-yeast mixture and beat until smooth, about 2 minutes on the medium speed of your electric mixer or 300 strokes by hand.
5. Add the egg and beat until blended.
6. Add 1 cup of the flour mixture and beat 1 minute on the medium speed or 150 strokes by hand.
7. Add the remaining flour and stir in enough whole wheat flour to make a moderately stiff dough.
8. Turn out on a lightly floured surface and knead.
9. Follow Basic Steps 7 through 16.

Pumpernickel contains molasses, chocolate and potatoes.

PUMPERNICKEL BREAD

Aromatic, coarse and so dark you might think both molasses and chocolate were in the dough. And they are! Top slices of Pumpernickel Bread with some of your own sausage, cheese and cream mustard and pickles, pour a glass of your own beer, then have some homemade ice cream for dessert. Now you are truly self-sufficient!

Ingredients	Equipment
4 cups whole wheat or enriched all-purpose flour	See Basic Equipment Cookie sheet
1½ cups rye flour	
¼ cup corn meal	
2 packages dry yeast	
1¼ cups water	
2 tablespoons dark molasses	
1 square (1 ounce) unsweetened chocolate, chopped	
1 tablespoon oil	
2 teaspoons salt	
1 cup mashed potatoes	
1 tablespoon caraway seed	

1. Combine the enriched all-purpose and rye flours.
2. Measure 1¾ cups of the blended flours, the corn meal and yeast in a large bowl and stir together.
3. Measure the water, molasses, chocolate, oil and salt into a saucepan and then heat over low heat only until warm (120°F to 130°F), stirring to blend. The chocolate does not need to be completely melted.
4. Add the liquid ingredients to the flour-yeast mixture and beat until smooth, about 3 minutes on the high speed of your electric mixer, or 300 strokes by hand.
5. Add 1 cup of the blended flour and the potatoes; beat another 2 minutes, or 300 strokes.
6. Stir in the caraway seeds and enough of the blended flour to make a soft dough.
7. Follow Basic Steps 6 through 16.

POLISH PICKLE RYE

If you make only one other bread recipe in addition to white or whole wheat, this should be the one! This extraordinary bread will improve your whole repertoire of sandwiches — especially sandwiches with pickles. The recipe makes 2 round loaves.

Ingredients	Equipment
4 cups whole wheat or enriched all-purpose flour	See Basic Equipment Saucepan Custard cup
2 cups rye flour	2 (1-quart) round glass casseroles
2 packages dry yeast	Sharp Knife
1 cup water (in 2 parts)	
2 teaspoons dill seeds	
½ cup liquid from jar of Polish-style pickles	
½ cup buttermilk	
2 tablespoons sugar	
2 tablespoons oil	
2 teaspoons salt	
2 teaspoons caraway seeds	
Oil or 1 egg, beaten	

1. In a large mixing bowl stir together the white and rye flours.
2. Measure 2 cups of the blended flour into a large bowl of your electric mixer; stir in the yeast.
3. In a saucepan, heat ½ cup of the water to boiling. Measure the dill seeds into a custard cup; pour boiling water over them and let stand for 10 minutes.
4. Rinse the saucepan, then use it to heat the remaining ½ cup water, pickle juice, buttermilk, sugar, 2 tablespoons oil and salt over low heat until warm (about 120°F to 130°F).
5. Stir in the dill seeds, water and caraway seeds.
6. Add the liquid and seed mixture to flour-yeast mixture and beat until smooth, about 3 minutes on the high speed of an electric mixer, or 450 strokes by hand.

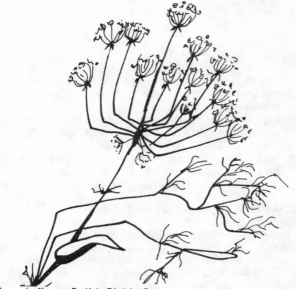

Dill seeds flavor Polish Pickle Rye.

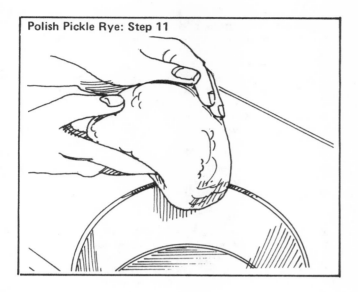

Polish Pickle Rye: Step 11

1. Stir together 2½ cups flour and the yeast in a large mixing bowl.
2. Measure the milk, water, ¼ cup oil, sugar and salt into a saucepan and heat over low heat only until warm (120°F to 130°F), stirring to blend.
3. Add the liquid ingredients to the flour-yeast mixture and beat 3 minutes on the high speed of your electric mixer or 300 strokes by hand.
4. Add the whole wheat flour, then gradually stir in more enriched all-purpose flour to make a stiff dough.
5. Turn out the dough on a lightly floured surface and knead 5 to 10 minutes.
6. Cover the dough with a bowl or pan and let it rest 20 minutes.
7. While the dough is resting, grease 2 (4½x8½-inch) loaf pans.
8. Divide the dough in half; roll each half into a 7x14-inch rectangle.
9. Roll up each rectangle, starting with narrow side, as in the roll-up method, Basic Step 11.
10. Put the loaves in greased pans. Brush their tops with oil.
11. Cover them with plastic wrap and refrigerate 2 to 24 hours.
12. Remove from the refrigerator and let them stand at room temperature 10 minutes while preheating the oven to 400°F.
13. Prick any gas bubbles on surface of loaves with a skewer or toothpick.
14. Bake in the preheated oven for 40 minutes.
15. Immediately remove the loaves from the pans and brush with oil. Cool on wire racks.

7. With a wooden spoon stir in more flour to make a soft dough.
8. Turn out the dough onto a lightly floured surface and knead *gently* until smooth, about 5 to 8 minutes.
9. Cover the dough with a bowl or plastic wrap and let it rest for 40 minutes.
10. Grease the casseroles.
11. Divide the dough in half. Shape into balls by tucking the edges underneath and pinching to hold them in place. Put each ball in a greased casserole.
12. With a sharp knife, cut 3 shallow slits in the top of each ball of dough.
13. For a soft crust, brush with oil. For a shiny, firm crust, brush with a beaten egg.
14. Let the loaves rise in a warm place until doubled, about 40 minutes.
15. Bake them in a preheated 350° oven 50 to 55 minutes. Cover the tops of loaves with foil during last 10 minutes of baking to prevent overbrowning. Remove the loaves from casserole dishes and cool on wire racks.

◆◆◆◆◆◆◆◆◆◆◆◆◆◆◆◆◆◆◆◆◆◆◆◆◆◆◆◆◆◆

REFRIGERATOR WHEAT BREAD

Mix and shape the dough when it's convenient, then refrigerate it for 2 to 24 hours, until you are ready to bake. The recipe makes 2 loaves.

Ingredients	Equipment
3½ to 4 cups enriched all-purpose flour	See Basic Equipment
2 packages dry yeast	Plastic wrap
2 cups milk	
¾ cup water	
¼ cup oil	
3 tablespoons sugar	
1 tablespoon salt	
4 cups whole wheat flour	
Oil	

BOLILLOS (MEXICAN HARD ROLLS)

Most crusty rolls require a special step to give a crisp crust. Commercial bakers shoot steam into ovens while their hard rolls bake. This recipe gets its thick "skin" from a simpler trick — a brush of cornstarch and water before baking. The recipe makes 18 rolls.

Ingredients	Equipment
5½ to 6 cups enriched all-purpose flour	See Basic Equipment
1 package dry yeast	Cookie sheets
2 cups water	Small saucepan
2 tablespoons sugar	Very sharp knife
2 tablespoons butter	
1 tablespoon salt	
¼ cup water	
½ teaspoon cornstarch	

1. Follow Basic Steps 1 through 10.
2. Divide the dough into 18 equal portions; shape each portion into a ball.
3. Shape each ball into a 5-inch oval by rolling it with your hands; then gently pull the ends into points.
4. Place the rolls on greased cookie sheets and let them rise in a warm place until doubled, about 30 minutes.
5. In a small saucepan, heat ¼ cup water and cornstarch to boiling; cool slightly.
6. Brush each roll with the cornstarch mixture.
7. With a very sharp knife cut a slash 2 inches long and ¾ inch deep in each roll.
8. Bake them in preheated 400°F oven 35 to 40 minutes or until golden brown.

◆◆◆◆◆◆◆◆◆◆◆◆◆◆◆◆◆◆◆◆◆◆◆

ENGLISH MUFFINS

You bake these muffins on a griddle or in a skillet instead of in the oven, then split and toast them. If you want to be particularly British, serve the muffins with bangers (sausages) for breakfast. You can add ¼ to ¾ cup raisins or chopped dried apricots, dates or apples to the dough just before kneading. The recipe makes 20 muffins.

Ingredients	Equipment
4 to 5 cups enriched flour	See Basic Equipment
1 cup whole wheat flour	3-inch cookie cutter
¾ cup wheat germ	Cookie sheets
1 package dry yeast	Skillet or griddle
1 cup milk	Turner or spatula
1 cup water	
3 tablespoons butter or oil	
2 tablespoons sugar	
1 teaspoon salt	
Corn meal	

1. Stir together the flours and wheat germ.
2. Follow Basic Steps 1 through 10, dividing the dough in half.
3. Sprinkle the cutting board generously with corn meal. On the corn meal surface, roll or pat each half of the dough to make a square about ½ inch thick.
4. Cut the muffins with the floured cookie cutter.
5. Arrange the muffins on ungreased cookie sheets, leaving an inch between each muffin.
6. Cover the muffins and let them rise in warm place until doubled, about 45 minutes to 1 hour.
7. Place the muffins on a preheated medium-hot skillet that has been lightly greased and sprinkled with corn meal. Cook them about 15 minutes per side. Watch carefully so the muffins do not burn.
8. Cool the muffins, then split, toast and butter.

◆◆◆◆◆◆◆◆◆◆◆◆◆◆◆◆◆◆◆◆◆◆◆

BAGELS

Bagels are unique. They look like a shiny doughnut, but they are cooked by broiling, boiling *and* baking. Split and toast them, then spread with cream cheese and top with lox (smoked salmon) for a traditional Jewish treat. The following recipe is for egg-bagels. Eliminate the eggs and you have the original water-bagel. The recipe makes 16 bagels.

Bagels are boiled before they bake.

Ingredients

5 to 6 cups wholewheat or
    enriched all-purpose
    flour
2 packages dry yeast
¼ cup sugar
2 teaspoons salt
1⅓ cups hot (120°F to 130°F)
    water
⅓ cup oil
2 eggs
1 gallon water
3 tablespoons sugar

Equipment

See Basic Equipment
Saucepan
2 cookie sheets

1. Follow Basic Steps 1 through 3.
2. Blend in the eggs, one at a time.
3. Add 1 cup of the flour and beat 1 minute on the medium speed of your electric mixer or 150 strokes by hand.
4. Stir in more flour to make a moderately stiff dough.
5. Turn out the dough onto a lightly floured surface and knead 2 minutes.
6. Shape into a ball, then cover and let it rise until doubled — about 1 ½ hours.
7. Punch down cover and let it rise again in a warm place until doubled, about 45 minutes.
8. Punch down, then turn out onto a lightly floured surface and knead until smooth and satiny, about 8 to 10 minutes.
9. Preheat the broiler. Put 1 gallon water and 3 tablespoons sugar on top of the range to boil.
10. Divide the dough into sixteen portions. Form each portion into a rope 11 inches long.
11. Moisten the ends of each rope with water, then press together, forming a ring.
12. Arrange the bagels on lightly floured cookie sheets and broil 5 to 6 inches from the heat for 1½ minutes on each side.
13. Drop the bagels into the boiling sweetened water, 2 or 3 at a time so that the bagels do not touch, and simmer 4 to 5 minutes.
14. Lift the bagels from the water with a slotted spoon and place them on wire racks to drain.

15. When all bagels have simmered, arrange them on lightly greased baking sheets and bake in a pre-heated 350°F oven 40 to 45 minutes.
16. If desired, let the bagels dry on a rack overnight.

◆◆◆◆◆◆◆◆◆◆◆◆◆◆◆◆◆◆◆◆◆◆◆◆◆◆◆

PITA (Pocket Bread)

These flat buns form a pocket inside as they bake. Just slit them and tuck in any sandwich filling you like. A traditional Middle Eastern bread, they go well with shish kabobs. The recipe makes 16 little flat loaves.

Ingredients

5 to 6 cups whole wheat or
    unbleached enriched
    all-purpose flour
2 packages dry yeast
2 cups water
¼ cup oil
1 tablespoon sugar
2 teaspoons salt

Equipment

See Basic Equipment
Rolling pin
Cookie sheets

1. Follow Basic Steps 1 through 3.
2. Stir in more flour to make a moderately soft dough.
3. Turn out on lightly floured surface and knead until smooth and satiny, about 5 to 10 minutes.
4. Cover the dough with a bowl or pan and let it rest 30 minutes.
5. Cut the dough into 16 equal portions and shape each portion into a ball.

Pita makes tasty sandwiches.

6. Roll the balls out into circles 5 inches in diameter.
7. Place them on greased cookie sheets and let them rise in warm place until puffy, about 30 to 45 minutes.
8. Bake in a preheated 400°F oven on bottom rack about 10 minutes or until very lightly browned.

CRACKED WHEAT BREAD

Cracked Wheat Bread is shaped into flat round loaves, much like the biblical "staff-of-life" bread. This hearty bread is perfect for picnics. Or, you can eat it while hot — split and butter it for a chewy and flavorful treat. The recipe makes 3 round loaves.

Ingredients	Equipment
1 cup cracked wheat	See Basic Equipment
1 cup water	Saucepan
1 cup milk	2 cookie sheets
2 tablespoons sugar	
2 tablespoons butter	
2 teaspoons salt	
2 cups whole wheat flour	
1 package dry yeast	
2 to 2½ cups enriched all-	
purpose flour	
Oil	

1. Combine the cracked wheat and the water in the saucepan. Heat to boiling, then remove from the heat.

2. Stir in the milk, sugar, butter and salt; cool to lukewarm.
3. Stir together the whole wheat flour and yeast in large mixing bowl.
4. Add the cracked wheat mixture and beat until smooth, about 2 minutes on the medium speed of your electric mixer or 300 strokes by hand.
5. Add 1 cup of enriched flour and beat 1 minute or 150 strokes.
6. Stir in more enriched all-purpose flour to make a moderately stiff dough.
7. Turn out onto a lightly floured surface and knead 10 to 12 minutes.
8. Shape into a ball and place in lightly greased bowl, turning to grease all sides.
9. Cover and let it rise until doubled, about 1½ hours.
10. Punch down then divide the dough into thirds, shape into balls and let them rest for 10 minutes.
11. On greased cookie sheets press each ball into a circle ½ inch thick. Brush each circle with oil.
12. Let them rise in warm place until doubled, about 45 minutes.
13. Bake in a preheated 400°F oven 12 to 15 minutes. Cool on wire racks.

CHEDDAR-BACON BREAD

Nothing can match the fragrance of this bread! Keep the kitchen windows closed unless you want to draw a crowd. The recipe makes 2 loaves.

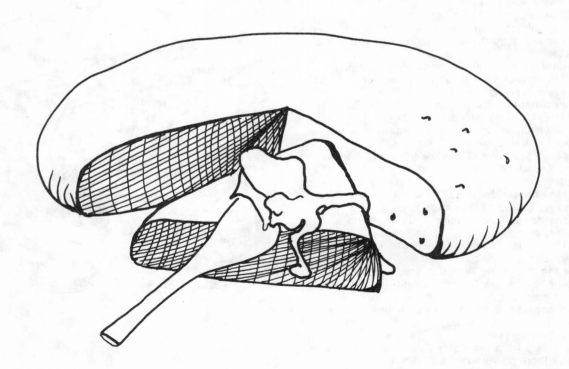

Ingredients	Equipment
5 cups whole wheat or enriched all-purpose flour 1 package dry yeast 1 cup milk ¾ cup water 3 tablespoons oil 2 tablespoons sugar 1 teaspoon salt 12 ounces (3 cups) shredded sharp cheddar cheese 3 slices bacon, crisp-cooked and crumbled	See Basic Equipment 2 (9x5x3-inch) loaf pans.

1. Stir together 2 cups flour and yeast in the large bowl of your electric mixer.
2. Heat the milk, water, oil, sugar and salt in a saucepan over low heat only until warm (120°F to 130°F), stirring to blend the ingredients.
3. Add the liquid ingredients to the flour-yeast mixture and beat until smooth, about 2 minutes on medium speed or 300 strokes by hand.
4. Stir in more flour, cheese and bacon to make a moderately stiff dough.
5. Turn out onto a lightly floured surface and knead until smooth, about 5 to 8 minutes.
6. Cover and let it rise in warm place until doubled, about 45 minutes to 1 hour.
9. Punch down the dough, turn out on a lightly floured surface and divide it in half. Cover and let it rest 10 minutes.
10. Shape the loaves by either method as directed in Basic Step 11.
11. Cover and let the dough rise until doubled.
12. Bake in a preheated 350°F oven about 30 to 35 minutes. Remove from pans and cool on racks.

WELSH RABBIT BREAD

The liquid in this braided cheese-bread is a surprise — beer.

Ingredients	Equipment
5 to 6 cups whole wheat or enriched all-purpose flour 2 packages dry yeast 2 tablespoons sugar 2 teaspoons salt 1 teaspoon dry mustard Dash cayenne pepper 1 can (12 ounces) beer, or 1½ cups milk ½ cup water 8 ounces (1¾ cups) cubed pasteurized processed cheese 2 tablespoons butter 1 tablespoon Worcestershire sauce	See Basic Equipment 2 (9x5x3-inch) loaf pans

1. Measure 2 cups of flour, the yeast, sugar, salt, mustard and pepper into a mixing bowl and stir together.
2. Measure the beer, water, cheese and butter in a saucepan and heat them over low heat, stirring constantly until the cheese is melted. Cool the mixture until it is warm (120°F to 130°F).
3. Add the liquid ingredients to the flour-yeast mixture and beat until smooth, about 3 minutes.
4. Stir in the Worcestershire sauce and add enough flour to make a soft dough.
5. Shape the dough into a ball. Put the ball in a large greased bowl.
6. Cover and let it rise until doubled, about 45 minutes to 1 hour.
7. Punch down and divide the dough in half.
8. Roll each half into a 5x11-inch rectangle. Cut each rectangle into 3 (11-inch) strips, leaving the strips joined at one end.
9. Braid the three strips of each rectangle. Tuck the ends under. Put each braid in a greased 9x5x3-inch loaf pan.
10. Brush them with oil and let them rise in warm place until doubled, 45 minutes to 1 hour.
11. Bake in a preheated 350°F oven 45 to 55 minutes or until deep golden brown. Cover the tops of the loaves with foil to prevent overbrowning, if necessary.
12. Remove them from their pans immediately and cool on wire racks.

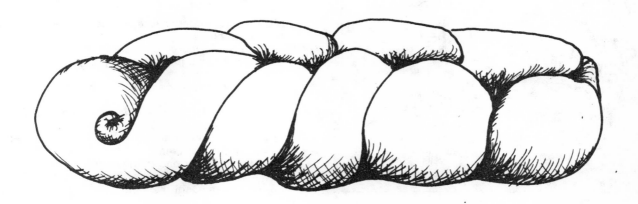

ONION BREAD

This is a batter bread — you beat instead of knead and bake it in a casserole instead of a loaf pan. Serve fragrant wedges of this bread served with your own cheese or cold cuts — what a splendid combination.

Ingredients	Equipment
5 cups whole wheat or enriched all-purpose flour	See Basic Equipment 2-quart casserole Small skillet Fork
2 packages dry yeast	
½ cup milk	
½ cup water	
½ cup butter	
3 tablespoons sugar	
1 teaspoon onion salt	
1 teaspoon celery salt	
½ teaspoon minced dried onion	
2 eggs	
2 tablespoons butter	
1 medium onion, chopped	
1 egg yolk	
1 teaspoon water	

1. Stir together 2 cups flour and the yeast in large mixing bowl.
2. Heat the milk, ½ cup water, ½ cup butter, sugar, onion salt, celery salt and dried onion in saucepan over low heat only until warm (120°F to 130°F) stirring to blend.
3. Add the liquid ingredients to the flour-yeast mixture and beat until smooth, about 2 minutes on the medium speed of your electric mixer or 300 strokes by hand.
4. Blend in the eggs and 1 cup flour and beat 1 minute on medium speed or 150 strokes by hand.
5. Add the remaining flour and beat to make a very thick batter.

6. Cover the mixing bowl and let the dough rise in warm place until bubbly, about 30 to 45 minutes.
7. Stir down the dough with a wooden spoon and beat briefly.
8. Turn it into a greased 2-quart casserole.
9. Bake in a preheated 375°F oven about 30 minutes or until firm.
10. Meanwhile, melt 2 tablespoons butter in skillet; add the onion and cook, stirring often, for about 5 minutes or until tender and golden. Remove from the heat and cool to room temperature.
11. Beat the egg yolk with 1 teaspoon water and stir it into the cooled, cooked onion.
12. Using a pastry brush or tablespoon, spread the onion mixture over the top of the bread.
13. Return the bread to the oven for 20 to 25 more minutes. Cover with foil if the top begins to get too brown.
14. Cool it in its casserole for 10 minutes before removing. Then cool the loaf on a rack.

◆◆◆◆◆◆◆◆◆◆◆◆◆◆◆◆◆◆◆◆◆◆◆◆◆

BROWN BREAD

Rich, dark, moist and studded with currants, you will love this brown bread spread with your homemade cream cheese or with a crock of baked beans. This is a quick-bread; it uses no yeast. Baking containers for Brown Bread are 2 (1-pound) coffee cans. Save the cans so you can make this recipe again, or use them to change the shape of other breads. The recipe makes 2 loaves.

Ingredients	Equipment
1½ cups whole wheat or enriched all-purpose flour	See Basic Equipment 2 (1-pound) coffee cans Cake tester or small skewer Spatula
⅓ cup sugar	
2 teaspoons soda	
1½ teaspoons salt	
1 cup wheat germ	
1 cup fine graham cracker crumbs	
½ cup currants	
2 eggs	
1½ cups buttermilk	
¾ cup light molasses	
¼ cup oil	

1. Measure the flour, sugar, soda and salt into a large bowl. Stir to blend.
2. Add the wheat germ, crumbs and currants and mix well.
3. Mix the egg, buttermilk, molasses and oil in another bowl until blended.
4. Add the liquid ingredients all at once to the dry ingredients and stir just until all the dry ingredients are moistened.
5. Grease the coffee cans well and then flour them lightly.
6. Divide the batter between the two coffee cans.
7. Bake in a preheated 350° F oven for 55 to 60 minutes, or until the cake tester or small skewer inserted in center comes out clean.
8. Cool the Brown Bread in the cans on a rack for 5 to 10 minutes, then loosen the bread with a spatula and tip out of can. Cool them on a rack.

Onion Bread: Step 5

OATMEAL BATTER BREAD

Cottage cheese is the special ingredient in this no-knead bread. Serve the slices or wedges warm with cream cheese and apple butter. Unbelievably good! The recipe makes two medium sized loaves.

Ingredients	Equipment
3½ cups whole wheat or enriched all-purpose flour	See Basic Equipment Saucepan
2 packages dry yeast	2 (1½-quart) casseroles or souffle dishes
2 cups cream-style, small-curd cottage cheese	
⅓ cup molasses or honey	
¼ cup water	
3 tablespoons butter or margarine	
2 teaspoons salt	
½ teaspoon soda	
2 eggs	
1 cup uncooked, rolled oats	
Melted butter	
Sugar	

1. Stir together the flour and yeast in a large mixing bowl.
2. Measure the cottage cheese, honey, butter, water, salt and soda into the saucepan and heat only until warm (120°F to 130°F), stirring to blend.
3. Add the cottage cheese mixture to flour-yeast mixture and beat until smooth, about 2 minutes on the medium speed of your electric mixer or 300 strokes by hand.
4. Add the eggs and beat until blended.
5. Add 1 cup of flour and beat 1 minute on medium speed or 150 strokes by hand.
6. Stir in the oats and remaining flour.
7. Cover the mixing bowl and let the dough rise in a warm place until doubled, about 1 hour.
8. Stir the batter down with a wooden spoon and beat it briefly.
9. Turn the batter into 2 greased 1½-quart casseroles.
10. Brush the tops with melted butter.
11. Let the bread rise, uncovered, in warm place until nearly doubled, about 45 minutes.

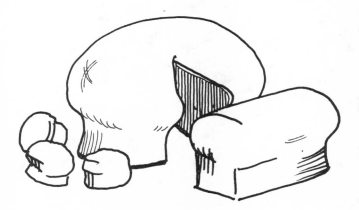

Batter rolls are irregular in shape, but taste delicious.

12. Bake in preheated 350°F oven for 35 minutes.
13. Let the loaves cool in the casseroles 10 minutes, then remove from the casseroles and cool on racks.
14. Brush the tops of the loaves with melted butter and sprinkle lightly with sugar.

PARMESAN BATTER ROLLS

It is hard to find a simpler method for homemade rolls, and it is hard to find a better roll than a Parmesan Batter Roll. The recipe makes 2 dozen rolls.

Ingredients	Equipment
3¼ cups whole wheat or enriched all-purpose flour	See Basic Equipment Tablespoon
2 packages dry yeast	Cookie sheet
½ cup milk	
½ cup water	
½ cup butter	
¼ cup sugar	
2 teaspoons salt	
1 egg, room temperature	
1 cup grated Parmesan cheese	
Oil	
Sesame seeds	

1. Stir together 1 cup of flour and the yeast in a large mixing bowl.
2. Measure the milk, water, butter, sugar and salt into a saucepan and heat over low heat only until warm (120°F to 130°F), stirring to blend.
3. Add the liquid ingredients to the flour-yeast mixture and beat until smooth, about 3 minutes.
4. Blend in the egg, 1 cup flour and the Parmesan cheese; continue to beat for 2 minutes.
5. Add the remaining flour to make a thick batter.
6. Cover the mixing bowl and let it stand in a warm place about 1 hour.
7. Stir down and beat briefly.

8. Drop rounded tablespoonsful of batter onto the greased cookie sheets.
9. Brush the tops with oil and sprinkle with sesame seeds.
10. Let them rise in a warm place until doubled, about 30 minutes.
11. Bake in a preheated 325°F oven 20 to 25 minutes or until golden. Cool briefly on a rack. Serve warm.

5. Turn out the dough onto a lightly floured surface and knead until smooth, about 3 to 5 minutes.
6. Divide the dough into 12 pieces; roll each piece into a rope about 15 inches long.
7. Sprinkle coarse salt on the kneading surface and roll the ropes in salt.
8. Tie the pretzels by holding ends, looping to center, twisting and gently pressing ends in place.
9. Place the pretzels on greased cookie sheets.
10. Bake in a preheated 425°F oven for 20 minutes, or until lightly browned.

SOFT PRETZELS

Kids love to make bread, and they will especially enjoy rolling and tying pretzels. You may find every child in the neighborhood in your kitchen. The recipe makes 12, double or repeat if necessary.

Ingredients	Equipment
2 cups enriched all-purpose flour	See Basic Equipment
2 cups whole wheat flour	Sharp Knife
1 package dry yeast	2 cookie sheets
1 teaspoon salt	
1 1/3 cups hot (120°F to 130°F) water	
3 tablespoons oil	
1 tablespoon honey	
Coarse salt	

1. Stir the flours together.
2. In a large mixing bowl combine 1½ cups flour, yeast and salt.
3. Add the water, oil and honey to the flour-yeast mixture and beat until smooth, about 2 minutes.
4. Add enough more flour to make a moderately stiff dough.

BREAD STICKS

This is one bread product that is better crisp than soft. When the baked sticks have cooled, wrap them in foil and set them aside for a few days. Then heat them in foil in a 400°F oven for just a few minutes before serving. The recipe makes about 2 dozen long sticks.

Ingredients	Equipment
1 cup plus 2 tablespoons lukewarm water (80°F to 90°F)	See Basic Equipment
1 package dry yeast	Rolling pin
3 cups whole wheat or enriched all-purpose flour	Sharp knife
2½ tablespoons sugar	2 cookie sheets
2 teaspoons caraway seeds	
1½ teaspoons salt	
½ teaspoon garlic powder	
1 tablespoon oil or melted butter	
Caraway seeds or coarse salt (optional)	

1. Sprinkle the yeast over the water in a glass measur-

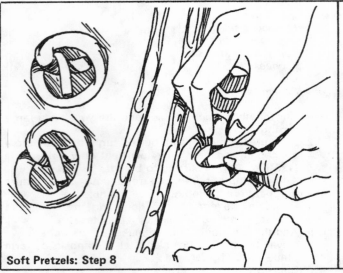

Soft Pretzels: Step 8

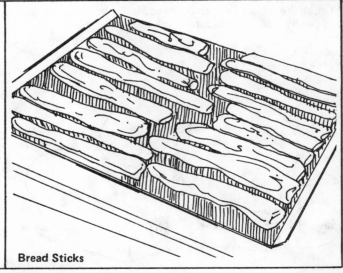

Bread Sticks

ing cup and let it stand a few minutes to soften.
2. Meanwhile, stir together the flour, sugar and seasonings in a large mixing bowl.
3. Add the softened yeast and oil and stir until well mixed; add more flour if necessary to make a moderately stiff dough.
4. Turn out onto a lightly floured surface and knead until smooth and elastic, about 5 minutes.
5. Proceed as in Basic Steps 4 through 7. Rising will take at least 1 hour.
6. Turn the dough out of the bowl onto a lightly floured surface and divide it in half.
7. Roll or pat each half into a rectangle about 12 inches long.
8. Cut the rectangle lengthwise into 1-inch strips with a sharp knife.
9. Roll each strip under your hands to form a stick. (Cut the sticks in half if you prefer shorter ones.) Place the sticks on greased cookie sheets.
10. Sprinkle them with additional caraway seeds or coarse salt, if desired.
11. Cover with plastic wrap and let them rise in warm place until doubled, about 1 hour.
12. Bake in a preheated 400°F oven about 15 minutes or until they are lightly browned. Remove from the cookie sheets and cool on wire racks.

◆◆◆◆◆◆◆◆◆◆◆◆◆◆◆◆◆◆◆◆◆◆◆◆

HONEY GRAHAM CRACKERS

Spread with homemade peanut butter or cream cheese and served with milk, Honey Graham Crackers make a satisfying snack. Graham Crackers are named after Sylvester Graham; early in the 19th century he objected to milling off the wheat grain's outer layer (called bran). Whole wheat flour, sometimes known as Graham flour, retains the bran as well as the wheat germ. This recipe makes 24 crackers; double it if you wish.

Ingredients	Equipment
2 cups whole wheat flour	Large mixing bowl
½ cup sugar	Measuring cups and
1 teaspoon baking powder	spoons
¼ teaspoon salt	Pastry blender or two
½ cup (1 stick) butter or	table knives
margarine	Fork
1 egg	Rolling pin
¼ cup honey	2 cookie sheets
2 tablespoons cold water	

1. Measure the flour, sugar, baking powder and salt into a mixing bowl and stir together.
2. Cut in the butter with a pastry blender or two knives until the mixture is of the consistency of small peas.
3. Beat the egg, honey and water together.
4. Add them to the flour mixture and mix with a fork until the mixture will hold together, adding a few drops of cold water, if necessary.
5. Turn out the dough onto a well-floured surface and knead until the dough holds together.
6. Roll out to ⅛-inch thickness.
7. Cut the dough into squares or rectangles and arrange on greased cookie sheets. Prick the tops of the crackers with a fork.
8. Bake in a preheated 350°F oven for 15 minutes.
9. Remove from the cookie sheets and cool on a rack.

◆◆◆◆◆◆◆◆◆◆◆◆◆◆◆◆◆◆◆◆◆◆◆◆

SOURDOUGH

Although the Egyptians discovered the secret of leavening bread with a fermented piece of leftover dough, the term sourdough brings to mind the prospectors of the West and Northwest. These hardy souls carried a crock of sourdough starter as a standard piece of equipment — as important as a pick and shovel. Sourdough cookery seemed to wane for many years, but the revival of baking bread at home and the rediscovery of sourdough's delightful tang have brought the crock of sourdough starter back to American kitchens.

◆◆◆◆◆◆◆◆◆◆◆◆◆◆◆◆◆◆◆◆◆◆◆◆◆◆

SOURDOUGH STARTER

Ingredients	Equipment
2 cups enriched all-purpose flour 1 package dry yeast 2 cups warm water	Large glass or plastic mixing bowl Measuring cups Wooden spoon Crock or glass or pottery container

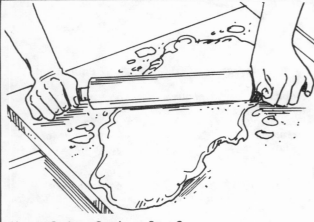

Honey Graham Crackers: Step 6

Sourdough Starter: Step 3

1. Combine all the ingredients in a large mixing bowl and mix until well blended.
2. Let the starter stand uncovered in a warm place (80°F to 85°F) for 48 hours. Stir it from time to time.
3. Stir well before using.
4. Pour out the amount you need, then replenish the remaining starter by mixing in 1 cup each of flour and warm water.
5. Let the starter stand uncovered in a warm place a few hours until it bubbles again.
6. Pour it into a crock or other non-metal container, cover it loosely and refrigerate until needed.
7. When ready to bake sourdough bread again, take the starter out of the refrigerator the night before you plan to use it, so it can warm up and start working.
8. You must use the starter at least once every two weeks and replenish what you have used. You can use it daily — that's even better.

◆◆◆◆◆◆◆◆◆◆◆◆◆◆◆◆◆◆◆◆◆◆◆◆◆◆

SOURDOUGH BREAD

Form this dough into long loaves, like French bread, or make bread sticks, following shaping directions in the Bread Sticks recipe. The recipe makes 2 long loaves.

Ingredients	Equipment
3 cups whole wheat or enriched all-purpose flour 1 cup sourdough starter 2 cups warm water 2 tablespoons sugar 1 tablespoon salt 1 teaspoon baking soda 3½ cups enriched unbleached all-purpose flour (approximately) Corn meal Melted butter	Measuring cups (glass and metal) Measuring spoons Large mixing bowl (not metal) Wooden spoon Waxed paper Cookie sheets Very sharp knife Pastry brush Wire racks

1. Measure the first 3 cups of flour, starter, water, sugar, salt and soda into large mixing bowl and beat until smooth.
2. Cover the dough loosely with waxed paper and let it stand in a warm place (80°F to 85°F) at least 18 hours.
3. Stir down the batter. Mix in the remaining flour until you make a moderately stiff dough.
4. Turn out the dough onto a lightly floured surface and knead until smooth and satiny, about 8 to 10 minutes.
5. Divide the dough in half. Form each half into a ball.
6. Roll each ball under your hands to form a long, thick rope, about 12 inches long.
7. Arrange the loaves on greased cookie sheets that have been sprinkled with corn meal. Make shallow slashes on top of each loaf with a very sharp knife, if desired.
8. Brush the tops of the loaves with butter.
9. Cover with plastic wrap and let them rise in a warm place until doubled, about 1½ hours.
10. Bake in a preheated 400°F oven about 40 to 50 minutes.
11. Brush tops with melted butter. Cool on a rack.

SOURDOUGH BISCUITS

Remember that you start these biscuits the night before, but you eat them right away. You have to plan ahead with sourdough! This recipe makes 18 biscuits.

Ingredients	Equipment
½ cup whole wheat or enriched all-purpose flour	Measuring cups (glass and metal)
1 cup sourdough starter	Measuring spoons
⅔ cup milk	Large mixing bowl (not metal)
1 tablespoon sugar	Wooden spoon
1½ cups enriched flour	Mixing bowl
2 teaspoons baking powder	Waxed paper
1 teaspoon baking soda	Pastry blender or two table knives
¾ teaspoon salt	Biscuit cutter
½ cup shortening	Cookie sheet

1. Measure ½ cup flour, starter, milk and sugar into mixing bowl and beat until smooth.
2. Cover loosely with waxed paper and let stand in warm place (80°F to 85°F) at least 18 hours.
3. Stir the batter down.
4. In another mixing bowl stir together 1½ cups flour, baking powder, soda and salt.
5. Cut in shortening until mixture resembles coarse crumbs.
6. Blend in the starter mixture.
7. Add more flour, if necessary, to make a soft dough.
8. Turn out onto lightly floured surface and knead gently 30 seconds.
9. Roll or pat out ½ inch thick.
10. Cut out the biscuits with a floured cutter and place them on an ungreased cookie sheet.
11. Bake in preheated 450°F oven 10 to 12 minutes.
12. Eat the biscuits right away or they become very hard.

◆◆◆◆◆◆◆◆◆◆◆◆◆◆◆◆◆◆◆◆◆◆◆◆◆◆◆◆◆◆

SOURDOUGH PANCAKES

Feast on these and you will know why prospectors guarded their sourdough starter with their lives. The recipe makes 5½ dozen small pancakes.

Ingredients	Equipment
2 cups whole wheat or enriched all-purpose flour	Large mixing bowl (not metal)
2 cups sourdough starter	Measuring spoons
1 cup milk	Measuring cups (metal and glass)
2 eggs, beaten	Wooden spoon
¼ cup sugar	Waxed paper
¼ cup oil	Fork or egg beater
1 tablespoon baking powder	Griddle or skillet
1 teaspoon salt	Turner
1 teaspoon baking soda	

1. Measure the flour, starter and milk into a large mixing bowl and beat until smooth.
2. Cover loosely with waxed paper and let it stand in warm place (80°F to 85°F) at least 18 hours.
4. Add the remaining ingredients and stir until smooth.
5. Bake on a lightly greased preheated 400°F griddle or skillet, using 1 tablespoon of batter for each pancake.

CHEESE

Cheese, along with bread, ranks as the most dramatic food you can create at home. Cheese is nothing but the solid particles of milk (called curd) separated from the liquid portion (called whey). The solid curd is drained, salted and pressed. The dramatic action comes when the curds coagulate. Like bread dough miraculously doubling in bulk, the startling curds-and-whey separation has to be seen to be believed.

The first cheese, the story goes, was accidentally discovered when a desert nomad stored milk in a calf's belly canteen. The calf's belly contained the enzyme rennet that coagulated the milk in the desert heat. Roquefort cheese was also an accidental discovery. A piece of cheese was left in a cave in Roquefort, France; the cave harbored mold spores which grew on the cheese, making distinctive blue veins. Unlike most molds, Roquefort mold is not harmful. Still, it must have taken courage or dire hunger to have bitten into the first Roquefort. Perhaps the most infamous cheesemaker was Polyphemus, the cyclops. Homer describes him in a cave separating the curds and whey of his goats' milk.

The Romans brought the art of making cheese to Europe and England. From England the Pilgrims brought cheeses to the New World. Making cheese was a normal part of farm production for most American rural families. The first cheese factory did not open until 1851, in New York. New York had ideal cheese-making conditions — good weather, extensive grazing land, prosperous farms. Until 1900 it led American cheese production. The industry spread westward and Wisconsin now produces the most American cheese. There are also some outstanding cheese factories that sell regionally: Vermont is famous for its Cheddar, and a factory in California rivals French Camembert with its soft, crusted cheese.

Cheese seems to go with everything, from apple pie to wine. A simple course of cheese and fruit, served with your own homemade cordial, makes an elegant dessert. Or, you can serve cheese as an appetizer.

In addition to the basic cheese recipes, this chapter includes recipes for cheese balls and cheese spreads. They are made with a combination of hard and soft cheeses. There is a superb recipe for cream cheese made from yogurt in the yogurt chapter; you can use homemade cream cheese as the base for many of the cheese balls and cheese spreads. Or, you can combine commercially made cheeses — either way, these cheese balls and spreads are far tastier than any you can buy, and much cheaper, too. Nut-crusted cheese logs and wine spreads are just two of the next recipes that make lovely gifts as well as handsome appetizers.

The first part of this chapter is devoted to making natural hard cheese — a Colby type and Cheddar. The basic steps for the miraculous cheese-making process are carefully spelled out before the recipes. Next you will find recipes for two kinds of cottage cheeses. Homemade cottage cheese has a fresh tang; you will be delighted with its delicate taste and amazed at how easy it is to make.

Your finished cheese is determined by several things: the kind of milk used; the kind of starter used; the method of preparation; salting; and ripening conditions. The natural cheese you can make at home ripens with the action of enzymes and micro-organisms. Ripening may take several weeks, producing a mild flavor, or several months, giving a rich, sharp flavor. Natural cheese is a living thing — it continues to ripen as long as it is stored. The protein content of homemade natural cheese equals meat ounce for ounce, sometimes even surpassing it. In addition, cheese is high in calcium and riboflavin. Unless made from skim milk, cheese does contain saturated fats.

Because the cheeses in this chapter are natural cheeses with no preservatives added, they should be handled with care. Cook or heat them at very low temperatures. Cheese, because it is a protein, can become tough and rubbery if cooked at too high a temperature.

You can add cheese toppings to casseroles or other baked dishes at the very last moments of baking time. Your own cheeses will make any meal special. Fresh cheeses (cottage or cream) are best served cold, right from the refrigerator. The other cheeses will grate or shred easiest directly from the refrigerator, but they will mellow and reach their full flavor at room temperature.

Basic Equipment

1. **Glass measuring cup**
2. **Measuring spoons and large wooden spoon**
3. **Saucepot or kettle,** 4- to 6-quart size
4. **Large kettle or roaster** that can accommodate a 4- to 6-quart pot.
5. **Thermometer.** A floating or immersion dairy thermometer with reading starting at 70°F. is a must. Some candy-making thermometers have reading as low as 70°F, but most start higher, so check yours. Hardware, farm supply or home wine-making shops should have thermometers of this type. The home cheese-making kits include dairy thermometers and a cheese press.
6. **Long-handled knife or spatula**
7. **Colander** (footed is best)
8. **Cheesecloth**
9. **Fork**
10. **Cheese press** made from a well-and-tree platter, cake rack and something heavy to weigh down the cheese (an iron or book, for instance). Or, a commercial cheese press. Our recipes tell you how to make cheese without a press, but a cheese press does simplify the process and they are not expensive.
11. **Plastic wrap or wax paper**
12. **Very clean hands**

Basic Ingredients

1. **Milk.** Homogenized fresh milk works best for making cheese at home. Nonfat dry milk could be used, but you would have to add whipping cream for the proper fat content.

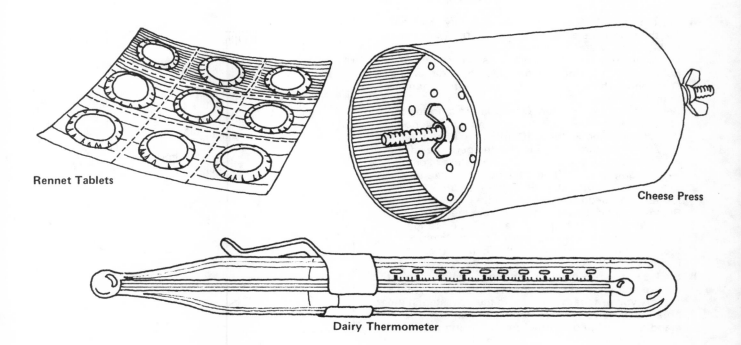

Rennet Tablets

Cheese Press

Dairy Thermometer

2. **Buttermilk.** Fresh milk is low in acidity so you have to add a "starter" to begin the curdling process. Commercial cultured buttermilk gives the milk its proper lactic acid content.
3. **Water**
4. **Rennet.** Rennet is also known as Junket. Rennet is an enzyme from the stomach of unweaned calves. It curdles the milk. Once curdled, you separate the liquid whey from the solid curds and press the curds into cheese.
5. **Coloring.** Cheese coloring and rennet tablets, in batches of 12, are included in the cheese making kits. You can also mail order them. Directions for dissolving coloring and rennet tablets are included in their package.
6. **Salt.** Add ordinary table salt to the curds just before pressing them.

Basic Steps

1. Measure the milk and buttermilk into a 4- to 6-quart pot or kettle and mix. Cover, place out of direct sunlight and let stand undisturbed at room temperature for 6 hours. The mixture can stand for up to 12 hours.
2. Mix coloring with water, following manufacturer's directions.
3. Put the pot or kettle of milk in the larger pot, then pour hot water into that larger pot to make a "double boiler." Or, use a thermostatically controlled burner or asbestos pad on top of the burner to hold a constant low heat.
4. Put the "double boiler" of milk over very low heat. Put the thermometer in the milk mixture. Slowly heat milk to 86°F, watching closely.
5. When milk reaches about 86°F, dissolve the rennet in cold water, following the manufacturer's directions. (The rennet should not stand in the solution for more than 30 minutes.)
6. Stir in the rennet solution. Or, if you are coloring the cheese, stir the color solution into milk at this point, then stir in rennet solution. Continue to heat and stir for 2 to 3 minutes, keeping the temperature of the milk between 86°F and 90°F. (Temperature is crucial — any cooler than 86°F and the curd will take longer to form; much hotter than 86°F and the curd will form too fast and become hard to handle.)
7. Remove the pot or kettle of milk from the water bath to a warm place. (Leave the water bath on range for step 10, but turn the heat off for now.) Remove the thermometer. Cover and let the milk stand for 30 minutes.
8. Stick a spoon or a clean finger into the milk; it should be like a thick pudding by now. If the curd breaks cleanly you are ready to go on to the next step. If the break is not clean, cover the pot or kettle and let it stand a few minutes longer before testing it again.

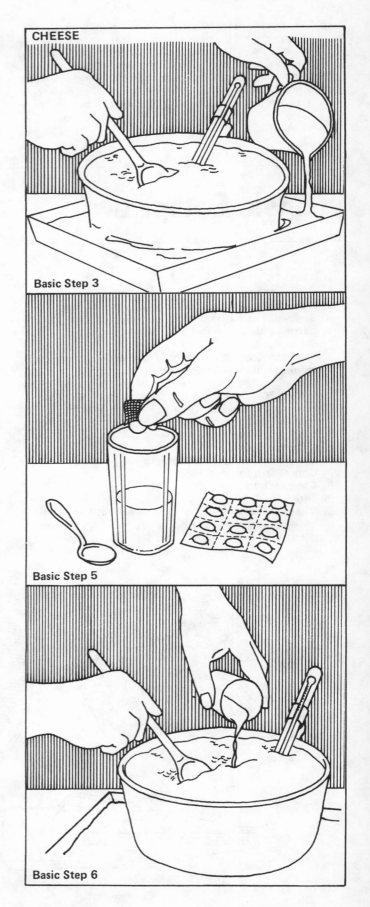

CHEESE

Basic Step 3

Basic Step 5

Basic Step 6

Basic Step 8

Basic Step 9

Basic Step 10

Basic Step 11

Basic Step 12

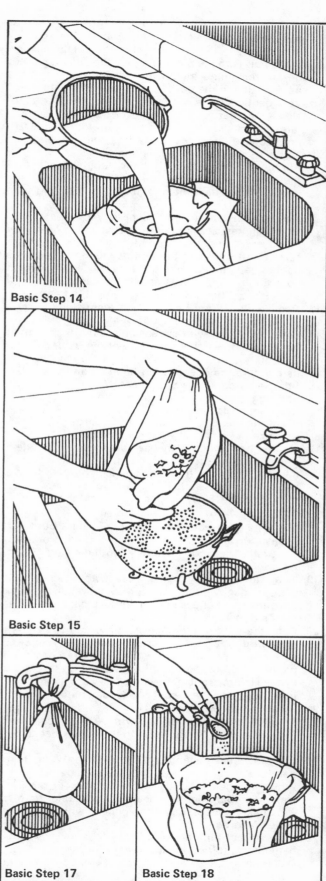

Basic Step 14

Basic Step 15

Basic Step 17

Basic Step 18

9. Cut the curd in the pot with a long-bladed knife or spatula by holding the knife at a 45° angle and cutting rows ½ to 1 inch apart across half of the mixture in the pot. Turn the pot and repeat the cutting pattern on the remaining half. Turn the pot again and cut across, slicing the curd into ½- to 1-inch cubes.
10. Very gently stir the curd with a spoon or your hand, slowly and carefully turning over the curds. Lift any large chunks to the top and cut them with a knife. Do not squeeze the curds. The curds will now begin to shrink as they separate from the whey.
11. Put the pot of curds back in the "double boiler" on the range, placing the thermometer back in the curds. Slowly heat them to 100°F. This should take about 30 minutes.
12. Keep the mixture at 100°F. over very low heat, for 30 to 45 minutes, stirring gently with a spoon every few minutes. (A stool and a good book can make this a restful half hour.) At the end of this time the curds should be firm and not stuck together. Hold some in your hand — the curds should fall apart, not be a solid mass. They will look like scrambled eggs.
13. Remove curd from heat and let them stand in their pot for 1 hour, stirring occasionally.
14. Line a colander with cheesecloth cut big enough to hang well down over the sides of the colander. Put the colander in the sink. Pour the curd mixture from its pan into the cheesecloth-lined colander.
15. Stir the curds with a spoon or your hands, then lift and jiggle the cheesecloth to help drain the whey from the curds.
16. Wrap the cheesecloth around the curds and gently squeeze out as much whey as possible.
17. Gather the top of the cheesecloth together and tie it to the kitchen faucet; let it hang and drain about 45 minutes. (You can hang the cheesecloth bag from a cupboard door handle if you need to use the sink. Be sure to put a bowl or pan underneath the bag to catch the whey.)
18. Open the cheesecloth bag and sprinkle the curd with 1 teaspoon of salt. Mix it in with a fork. Taste and add more salt, 1 teaspoon at a time, until the flavor is just right for you.
19. Wrap the cheese in the cheesecloth again and squeeze gently but firmly to press out whey. Or, pack the curd into a cheese press, following the manufacturer's directions.
20. Form the curd in the cheesecloth into a roll or ball and put it on a well-and-tree platter, or a wire cake rack over a pan or plate. Put plastic wrap or waxed paper on top of the ball. Put a weight on top of the cheese to press out more whey. The weight can be an iron, a big book, a heavy bookend, whatever.
21. Press the cheese at least 12 hours.
22. Remove the weight, plastic wrap and cheesecloth. Be sure to pour off any whey that may have accumulated on the platter.
23. Let the cheese stand on the rack at room temperature about 1 hour or until the surface is dry.
24. Wrap the cheese tightly in plastic wrap or dip it in wax (use paraffin or beeswax, available from a winemaking shop). Label the cheese with its proper variety and date.
25. You can eat the cheese now, but the flavor will be better if you refrigerate it at least 2 to 3 weeks to age. (You can age it several months, if you can wait that long!)

Basic Step 21

Basic Step 24

STORAGE

The refrigerator is the best storage spot for your freshly made cheeses. Wrap them well in plastic wrap, plastic bags, or foil to keep them from drying out. Mold may grow on the cheese if it is not carefully wrapped. Mold has roots that may penetrate deeply, so you are safer to throw out any moldy cheese rather than try and cut away the mold. Only an expert with a microscope can distinguish a harmful mold from a harmless one.

Cheese can be frozen, but it will become crumbly when thawed. Frozen cheese is better for cooking than for sandwiches or snacks. If you cut the cheese into pieces no thicker than 1 inch before you freeze it, you will be able to store it for up to 6 months. Be sure you wrap it tightly in moisture and vapor proof wrappings. Frozen cheese ought to be thawed in the refrigerator and used as soon as possible because it deteriorates rapidly.

Recipes

COLBY CHEESE

Colby-type cheese has a softer body and a milder flavor than cheddar. Without added coloring, this cheese is much like Monterey Jack cheese. The recipe makes about 1 pound of cheese.

Ingredients	Equipment
1 gallon homogenized milk	See Basic Equipment
3 tablespoons buttermilk	
1 rennet tablet	
1 coloring tablet	
4 teaspoons salt, or to taste	

Follow the Basic Steps

◆◆◆◆◆◆◆◆◆◆◆◆◆◆◆◆◆◆◆◆◆◆◆◆◆◆◆◆◆◆◆

CHEDDAR CHEESE

When you make this cheese, you allow the curd to knit or mat together, then turn and pile it to push out the whey. This process is called cheddaring, and thus the name cheddar. Recipe makes about 1 pound of cheese.

SPECIAL NOTE: The curd MUST stay at 98°F to 100°F for the cheddaring process, so before starting to make cheddar Cheese, Check your oven to be certain it can maintain that temperature. Put a pan of water on the top rack of the oven and put the dairy thermometer in the water. A gas oven may have enough heat from its pilot light, but you may need to leave the door ajar to keep the heat low enough to hold temperature of water (or curd) at 98°F to 100°F. If your oven is electric, test its "Warm" setting to see if the water temperature in the pan will stay at 98°F. As with a gas oven, adjusting the door may help.

Ingredients	Equipment
1 gallon homogenized milk	See Basic Equipment
3 tablespoons buttermilk	Wire cake rack
1 rennet tablet	Jelly roll pan (10x15x2-inch)
1 coloring tablet	Turner or wide spatula
4 teaspoons salt, or to taste	

1. Prepare the cheese following the Basic Steps up to and including Step 16.
2. Put the cake rack on the jelly roll pan and spread a fresh piece of cheesecloth over it.
3. Turn the drained curd out on the cheesecloth, spreading it evenly, about 2 inches thick.
4. Put it on the top shelf of your oven: put a thermometer in the curd and maintain the temperature at 98°F to 100°F. The temperature must not vary or the curd will be ruined.
5. After about 15 to 20 minutes the curd will begin to mat together. Remove the cheese from the oven. Remove the thermometer and cut the curd into strips 1 or 2 inches wide with a sharp knife or poultry shears.
6. Replace the thermometer so you can check the temperature and return the cheese to the oven for 10 to 15 minutes. Then reach in and turn the strips with a wide spatula or turner.
7. Continue cheddaring the strips in oven at 98°F to 100°F for 1 hour, turning every 15 minutes or so. Never let the temperature drop below 98°F.
8. By now the cheese should look something like cooked white meat of chicken. Cut the solid strips of curd into ½-inch cubes.
9. Sprinkle curd cubes with salt. (You can eat at this point, if you wish.)
10. Return to Basic Steps at Step 18; press and age the cheese as directed.

COTTAGE CHEESE

This cheese received its name because it was made in cottages. Cottage Cheese came to this country on the Mayflower. The recipe makes 1 cup.

Ingredients	Equipment
½ gallon skim milk	Double boiler or 2
6 tablespoons homogenized milk (or you may use sour milk and omit the vinegar)	saucepans (one to fit inside the other to form a double boiler)
	Measuring spoons
1½ teaspoons vinegar	Dairy thermometer
½ rennet tablet	Clean dishtowel
1 tablespoon cold water	Colander
½ to 2 teaspoons salt	Fork

1. Pour the milk and vinegar into top of double boiler. Put it over hot water and then turn on the heat. Slowly warm the milk until it reaches 70°F to 75°F — no higher.
2. Turn off the heat; remove the top of the double boiler.
3. Dissolve ½ rennet tablet in 1 tablespoon cold water and stir it into the warm milk.
4. Cover the milk mixture and set it aside in a warm place (75°F to 80°F) for 12 to 16 hours. Do not disturb.
5. Check it after 12 hours. You should be able to see some whey on top of the milk. Tip the pan slightly; the curd should split or cleave. If you do not see these signs, let it stand a few hours longer.
6. Line a colander with a towel; put it into the sink.
7. Pour the mixture from the pan into the colander and let the whey drain off. Help the draining by gently stirring the curd with a fork every now and then and by lifting the cloth to roll cheese from side to side.
8. When all whey has drained off, stir in the salt to taste.
9. For creamed cottage cheese, stir in 1 to 2 tablespoons milk or cream.

SOUR CURD COTTAGE CHEESE

This cheese has a little more tang than regular cottage cheese, and more closely resembles the old-fashioned cottage cheese because it does not use rennet. "Clabber" is another word for this product.

Ingredients	Equipment
½ gallon skim milk	See Equipment for
2 tablespoons buttermilk	Cottage Cheese
½ to ¾ teaspoon salt	

1. Pour the skim milk in the top of a double boiler, put it over hot water, then turn on the heat. Slowly warm the milk until it reaches 75°F to 80°F — no hotter.
2. Turn off the heat, remove the top of double boiler and let milk cool, if necessary, to 75°F.
3. Stir in the buttermilk, mixing well.
4. Cover and set aside in warm place as in Step 4 of Cottage Cheese.
5. Finish as in Steps 6 through 8 of Cottage Cheese.

NOTE: Sour Curd Cottage Cheese may not have as firm a curd as regular Cottage Cheese. It will become firmer after a day or two in the refrigerator.

CHILI CHEESE BALL

Here is a spicy gift for any occasion. Make 1 large ball, or divide mixture in thirds and make three small balls.

Ingredients	Equipment
1 cup cottage cheese	Measuring cup and spoons
3 ounces cream cheese	Mixing bowl
1 or 2 cloves garlic, crushed	Rotary or electric beater
2 teaspoons chili powder	Rubber spatula
2 teaspoons Worcestershire sauce	Plastic wrap or waxed paper
½ teaspoon salt	
Few drops to ¼ teaspoon hot pepper sauce	
8 ounces (2 cups) shredded cheddar cheese, at room temperature	
1 cup coarsely chopped pecans	

1. Beat the cottage cheese, cream cheese and seasonings together at high speed until fairly smooth.
2. Gradually beat in the cheddar cheese until smooth.
3. Mound the mixture on a piece of plastic wrap or wax paper; chill it for 1 hour in the refrigerator, or 15 to 20 minutes in the freezer for easier handling.
4. Shape the cheese into a ball and roll it in the pecans. Wrap the ball well and store it in the refrigerator until ready to use or give away.

CHEDDAR AND COTTAGE CHEESE DIP

You can pack this tasty dip in handsome coffee mugs to give as gifts. Keep the dip refrigerated until gift time, though. The recipe makes about 3 cups. Double it, if you wish.

Ingredients	Equipment
2 cups cottage cheese	Measuring cup
2 teaspoons instant minced onion or your own dried crumbled onion	Measuring spoons
1 teaspoon celery salt	Mixing bowl
1 teaspoon Worcestershire sauce	Rotary or electric beater
8 ounces (2 cups) shredded cheddar cheese	Rubber spatula

1. Combine all the ingredients and beat them with an electric beater until blended.
2. Cover and refrigerate the dip for several hours to blend the flavors.

SPICED COTTAGE CHEESE SPREAD

Super-sophisticates enjoy this cheese spread on thin slices of French or pumpernickel bread, accompanied by fresh fruit and wine.

Ingredients	Equipment
2 cups cottage cheese	Measuring cup
8 ounces cream cheese, softened	Sieve or strainer
2 tablespoons drained sweet pickle relish	Mixing bowl
2 tablespoons hot mustard	Measuring spoons
1 tablespoon caraway seed	Rotary or electric beater
1 tablespoon paprika	Rubber spatula
½ teaspoon salt	Small crocks, mugs or other containers for storing and giving

1. Press the cottage cheese through sieve into mixing bowl.
2. Add all remaining ingredients and beat well.
3. Cover and chill several hours to blend flavors.

WISCONSIN DIP

Here is a great dip for assorted crackers or cocktail rye bread. Or you can use apple slices, pear slices, fresh carrots, zuchinni or cauliflower as dippers. The recipe makes about 2½ cups.

Ingredients	Equipment
8 ounces (2 cups) shredded cheddar cheese	Measuring cup
8 ounces cream cheese, softened	Measuring spoons
¾ cup beer	Mixing bowl
2 tablespoons poppy seed	Rotary or electric beater
½ to 1 teaspoon seasoned salt	Rubber spatula

1. Beat all the ingredients together until smooth and blended.
2. Cover and refrigerate for several hours to blend flavors.

SWISS CHEESE DILLY SPREAD

Cocktail rye slices are the perfect partner for this zesty spread. This recipe makes a little more than 2 cups.

Ingredients	Equipment
1½ cups cubed Swiss cheese	Measuring cup
⅓ cup sour cream	Blender
⅓ cup milk	Measuring spoons
1 tablespoon parsley flakes	Rubber spatula
1 teaspoon dill seed	Crock or serving container
1 teaspoon seasoned salt	
¼ teaspoon garlic powder	
¼ cup bacon-flavored bits	

1. Measure ¾ cup cheese into your blender's container.
2. Add all the remaining ingredients except the cheese and bacon bits; blend at medium speed until smooth.
3. Add the remaining cheese and blend until smooth.
4. Turn the spread into a crock or other container, cover and refrigerate until ready to serve.
5. Stir in the bacon-flavored bits just before serving.

CHERRY HEERING CHEDDAR SPREAD

Pack this elegant cheese spread in a crock, bowl, mug or other pretty container, and bring it out with a tray of crackers when guests drop in. The recipe makes about 2 cups.

Ingredients	Equipment
2 cups cubed cheddar cheese	Blender
¾ cup milk	Measuring cup
⅓ cup Cherry Heering	Rubber spatula
½ cup chopped ripe olives	Knife
	Crock or container

1. Measure 1 cup of the cheese into your blender's container.
2. Add the milk and liqueur; blend them at a medium speed until smooth.
3. Add the remaining cheese and blend until smooth.
4. Remove the blender jar from blender. Stir in olives with a rubber spatula.
5. Turn the spread into a crock or other container, cover and refrigerate until ready to serve.

COCONUT CHEESE BALLS

These balls are a slightly sweet addition to a cheese tray or a delightful garnish for fruit salads or cold-cut plates. One ball will just fit in the center of a pineapple slice.

Ingredients	Equipment
1 cup cottage cheese, sieved	Measuring cup
8 ounces cream cheese	Sieve or strainer
½ cup finely chopped nuts	Mixing bowl
2 teaspoons sugar	Rotary or electric beater
1 teaspoon ground ginger	Measuring spoons
1 can (3½ ounces) flaked coconut	2 cookie sheets
	Plastic wrap or waxed paper

1. Preheat oven to 350°F.
2. Beat the cottage cheese and cream cheese until blended; beat in the nuts.
3. Cover 1 cookie sheet with waxed paper. Drop heaping measuring teaspoons of the cheese mixture onto the waxed paper. Chill at least 1 hour for easier handling.
4. Meanwhile, combine the sugar and ginger; add the coconut and toss to mix.
5. Spread the coconut mixture on a cookie sheet and toast in the oven until golden, stirring occasionally.
6. Shape the cheese mounds into balls; roll them in the coconut.
7. Chill until serving time.

CHEDDAR-PEPPER HOT SPREAD

You can turn this versatile cheese spread into spicy sand-wiches or party appetizers. This recipe makes about 2½ cups of spread.

Ingredients	Equipment
2 cups cubed cheddar cheese	Measuring cup
½ cup milk	Blender
¼ cup butter or margarine	Measuring spoons
2 tablespoons dried green pepper	Rubber spatula
1 whole canned pimiento	Crock or serving container
¼ teaspoon hot pepper sauce	

1. Measure 1 cup of cheese into your blender's container.
2. Add all remaining ingredients except the cheese and blend at medium speed until smooth.
3. Add the remaining cheese and blend until smooth.
4. Turn the spread into a crock or other container, cover and refrigerate until ready to serve.

CHEESE AND BEEF BALL

Chipped beef gives this cheese ball a rosy coating. Sur-rounded with crackers and celery chunks, it makes a handsome centerpiece for a smorgasbord. The recipe makes one 2-pound ball.

Ingredients	Equipment
2 pounds cream cheese, softened	Large mixing bowl
½ cup chopped pimiento-stuffed green olives	Wooden spoon
2 teaspoons garlic powder	Knife
1 cup chopped chipped beef	Measuring cup
Dried parsley flakes or freshly chopped parsley	Measuring spoons
	Plastic wrap or waxed paper

1. Mix the cheese, olives and garlic powder until blended.
2. Mound on plastic wrap or waxed paper; chill the cheese 1 hour in the refrigerator, or for 15 to 20 minutes in the freezer for easier handling.
3. Shape the cheese into a ball and roll it in the chipped beef. Sprinkle it with parsley.
4. Wrap well and store in the refrigerator until ready to serve.

WHITE BRICK CURRY SPREAD

Try this unusual spread on sesame seed crackers, or even on a pineapple chunk — exotic! The recipe makes about 2½ cups of spread.

Ingredients	Equipment
2 cups cubed white brick cheese	Measuring cup
½ cup milk	Blender
½ cup mayonnaise	Measuring spoons
2 tablespoons curry powder	Rubber spatula
2 tablespoons horseradish	Crock or serving container
2 tablespoons vinegar	
1 tablespoon garlic powder	
1 tablespoon grated onion	

1. Measure 1 cup of cheese into your blender's container.
2. Add remaining ingredients except the rest of the cheese and blend at medium speed until smooth.
3. Add the remaining cheese and blend until smooth.
4. Turn into a crock or other container, cover and refrigerate until ready to serve.

NUTTY BLEU CHEESE LOG

Put this log on a party table with some homemade crackers, your own wine and a few pears and your reputa-tion as a host is made! The recipe makes 1 log, about 2 pounds.

Ingredients

1 pound cheddar cheese,
    shredded
1½ pound bleu cheese,
    crumbled
2 tablespoons finely
    chopped onion
1 tablespoon
    Worcestershire sauce
8 ounces cream cheese,
    softened
   Milk (1 or 2 tablespoons)
½ cup chopped pecans or
    walnuts

Equipment

Measuring cup
Shredder
Large mixing bowl
Rotary or electric beater
Measuring spoons
Knife
Plastic wrap or waxed
    paper
Rubber spatula

1. Beat the cheddar cheese and bleu cheese, onion and Worcestershire together until well mixed.
2. Turn out onto piece of waxed paper and form the mixture into a log. Roll it up in waxed paper or plastic wrap and chill until firm, about 1 hour.
3. Beat the cream cheese until soft, adding a tablespoon or two of milk until cheese is of frosting consistency.
4. Remove the log from the refrigerator, unwrap and frost with the cream cheese.
5. Roll the log in the chopped nuts or sprinkle the nuts on it. Rewrap and chill it until ready to serve.

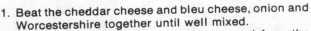

PARSLEY CHEESE BALL

This recipe makes one enormous ball, enough for a big party. You can divide the recipe in half or in fourths and make 2 or 4 smaller balls, if you wish.

Ingredients

4 pounds cheddar cheese,
    shredded
1 cup chopped parsley
1 teaspoon garlic powder
12 ounces cream cheese
   Milk

Equipment

Shredder
Knife or scissors (to
    chop parsley)
Measuring cup
Measuring spoons
Clean hands
Mixing bowl
Rotary or electric beater
Rubber spatula
Plastic wrap or waxed
    paper

1. Work the cheese, ¼ cup of the parsley and the garlic powder together with your hands until mixed, then form it into a large ball, pressing firmly into shape.
2. Cover the ball with plastic wrap and chill until firm, about an hour.
3. Beat the cream cheese until soft, adding a tablespoon or two of milk until the cheese is of frosting consistency.
4. Remove the cheese ball from refrigerator and remove the wrap. Spread the cream cheese frosting all over the ball.
5. Sprinkle the remaining parsley over the ball, or roll the ball in the parsley. Re-wrap and chill it until ready to serve.

PORT WINE SPREAD

Here is the perfect gift for the VIP who has everything. This recipe makes about 2 cups. If you want more, repeat the recipe rather than doubling it. A blender can handle smaller amounts better.

Ingredients

2 cups cubed cheddar or
    colby cheese
¾ cup milk
½ cup Port wine

Equipment

Measuring cup
Blender
Rubber spatula
Mixing bowl
Fork
Crock or serving
    container

1. Measure 1 cup of cheese into your blender's container.
2. Add the milk and blend until smooth.
3. Add the remaining cheese and blend until smooth.
4. Turn into a mixing bowl and pour in the wine.
5. Stir with a fork or rubber spatula just enough to swirl the wine through cheese to make streaks. Do not blend in the wine.
6. Turn into a crock or other container, cover and refrigerate until ready to serve.

Cheese Glossary

ASIAGO. Made from whole milk; imported, it is made from partly-skimmed milk. *Characteristics:* Dark surface, creamy inside; hard, granular texture; piquant flavor. *Uses:* Eating; Cooking.

BAKER'S CHEESE. Made from skim milk. *Characteristics:* White, resembles Cottage Cheese, however is softer and finer grained; slightly sour flavor. *Uses:* Eating; Cooking (its more common use).

BEL PAESE (a trade name). Made from whole milk. *Characteristics:* Gray-brown surface, light-yellow inside; soft texture; delicate flavor. *Use:* Eating.

BLUE: Made from whole milk. *Characteristics:* White interior with blue veins; semisoft, crumbly; piquant flavor that gets stronger with age; usually foil-wrapped. *Uses:* Eating; Cooking.

BRICK. Made from whole milk. *Characteristics:* Yellow-brown surface, creamy yellow inside; semisoft; mild but pungent flavor, midway between Cheddar and Limburger. *Use:* Eating.

BRIE. Made from whole milk, sometimes skimmed. *Characteristics:* Brown, edible crust, creamy yellow inside; soft; resembles Camembert; mild to pungent. *Use:* Eating.

CACIOCAVALLO. Made from whole milk. *Characteristics:* Light-brown, glossy surface, yellowish-white color; smooth, firm body; without eyes; slightly salty, smoky flavor; spindle-shape, cord bound. *Uses:* Eating; Grating when old and dry.

CAMEMBERT. Made from whole milk. *Characteristics:* Gray-white, edible crust; soft, creamy interior; full flavor. *Use:* Eating. (Before serving store at room temperature until runny.)

CANTELLE (a trade name). Made from whole milk. *Characteristics:* Red waxed surface, yellow interior; mild flavor; similar to Trappist cheese. *Uses:* Eating; Cooking.

CHEDDAR. Made from whole milk. *Characteristics:* Yellow-brown surface, cream to deep-orange color; firm cheese; mild flavor when fresh; sharper the more cured and aged; English Cheddar is generally a little drier and milder than the American. *Uses:* Eating; Cooking.

CHESHIRE. Made from whole milk. *Characteristics:* Yellow surface, cream to deep-yellow color; firm, more crumbly than Cheddar; sharp flavor the more aged. *Uses:* Eating; Cooking.

COLBY. Made from whole milk. *Characteristics:* Deep yellow; softer body and more open texture than Cheddar (it contains more moisture and for this reason won't keep as well as Cheddar). *Uses:* Eating; Cooking.

COON. Made from whole milk. *Characteristics:* Cheddar-type cheese with dark surface; crumbly texture; sharp tangy flavor. *Uses:* Eating; Cooking.

COTTAGE CHEESE. Made from skim milk with cream and salt added. *Characteristics:* White; soft; pleasant sour taste. *Uses:* Eating; Cooking.

   SKIM-MILK COTTAGE CHEESE. A form of Cottage Cheese with no cream added.

   POT CHEESE. A form of Skim-milk Cottage Cheese with a larger, dry curd; neither cream nor salt added.

CREAM CHEESE. Made from cream and milk. *Characteristics:* White; smooth, soft texture; delicate, slightly acid taste. *Uses:* Eating; Cooking.

EDAM. Originally made of whole milk but now the fat content is reduced. *Characteristics:* Red waxed surface, yellowish inside; semisoft to hard; mild flavor. *Uses:* Eating; Cooking.

FARM. (Farmer's or Pressed): Made from whole or partly skimmed milk. *Characteristics:* White, dry form of Cottage Cheese; pressed into parchment paper packages. *Use:* Cooking.

FETA. Made from ewe's milk; sometimes goat's milk. *Characteristics:* White; soft; salty cheese. *Uses:* Eating; Cooking.

FONTINA. Made from whole milk; imported may be made from ewe's milk. *Characteristics:* Slightly yellow with oiled surface; semisoft to hard; delicate, nutty flavor. *Uses:* Eating; Cooking; Grating when aged.

GAMMELOST. Made from skimmed, sour milk. *Characteristics:* Golden brown; semisoft to hard. *Use:* Eating.

GJETOST. Made from cow's and goat's milk whey or goat's milk whey, only. *Characteristics:* Golden brown; semisoft to hard; sweet uncheeselike flavor. *Use:* Eating.

GORGONZOLA. Made from whole milk. *Characteristics:* Clay-colored exterior, white with blue veins inside; semisoft, crumbly texture; piquant flavor. *Use:* Eating.

GOUDA. Made from whole or partly-skimmed milk. *Characteristics:* Usually red surface, yellow interior; semisoft to hard; similar to Edam but milk is skimmed; mellow flavor; Irish Blarney cheese is similar, but has holes like Swiss; domestic (Baby) Gouda is softer and often has a slightly sour flavor. *Use:* Eating.

GRUYERE. Made from whole milk. *Characteristics:* Light yellow, firm with small holes; tastes like Swiss only slightly sharper; U.S. Gruyere is a foil-wrapped process cheese. *Uses:* Eating; Cooking.

HAND CHEESE. Made from sour milk and skim milk. *Characteristics:* Soft; pungent, sour-milk cheese; so named because originally it was molded into final shape by hand. *Use:* Eating.

JACK (*Monterey*). Made from whole, partly-skimmed, or skim milk. *Characteristics:* Mild, Cheddar-type cheese; whole-milk Jack is semisoft; Jack made from partly-skimmed or skim milk is called grating-type, dry Jack, or dry Monterey. *Uses:* Eating; Cooking; Grating.

LIEDERKRANZ (a trade name). Made from whole milk. *Characteristics:* Russet surface, creamy inside; soft, robust taste and aroma, like a mild Limburger. *Use:* Eating.

LIMBURGER. Made from whole milk. *Characteristics:* Grayish-brown surface, creamy white inside; semisoft; full, aromatic taste. *Use:* Eating.

LIPTAUER. Made from ewe's milk and some cow's milk. *Characteristics:* Pickled pot cheese; can be prepared at home. *Use:* Eating.

MOZZARELLA. Made from whole milk or partly-skimmed milk. *Characteristics:* White; semisoft, mild cheese. *Uses:* Eating; Cooking.

MUENSTER. Made from whole milk. *Characteristics:* Yellow-tan surface, white to light-yellow interior; semisoft; tastes like Brick only milder. *Uses:* Eating; Cooking.

NEUFCHATEL, NEUCHATEL. Made from whole or skim milk or mixture of milk and cream. *Characteristics:* White; soft; mild cheese. Bondon, Malakoff, Petit Suisse, and Petit Carré are other French cheeses that differ from Neufchatel mainly in fat content, size, and

shape. The spelling "Neuchâtel" without the "f" is used for this cheese when it originates in Switzerland. *Use:* Eating.

PARMESAN. Made from partly-skimmed milk. *Characteristics:* Dark-green or black surface, whitish inside; hard, granular texture; flavor gets stronger with age; very old Parmesan is a delicacy. *Uses:* Eating when fresh; Grating when older.

PEPATO. Made from mixture of whole cow's and goat's milk. *Characteristics:* Light, grayish color; hard and dry; peppercorns added. *Use:* Grating.

PETIT SUISSE. Made from fresh, whole milk with cream. *Characteristics:* Soft, rich unripened French cheese. *Use:* Eating.

PINEAPPLE. Made from whole milk. *Characteristics.* A Cheddar type, shaped like a pineapple and usually hard. *Uses:* Eating; Cooking.

PONT L'EVEQUE. Made from whole or slightly-skimmed milk. *Characteristics:* Yellow; soft; sharp-flavored. *Use:* Eating.

POONA. Made from whole milk. *Characteristics:* Pale; soft; aroma like mild Limburger. *Use:* Eating.

PORT SALUT. Made from whole or partly-skimmed milk. *Characteristics:* Russet surface, creamy inside; elastic curd, semisoft; mild flavor like Gouda; aroma like Limburger (Made by Trappist monks). *Use:* Eating.

PRIMOST. Made from whey. *Characteristics:* Light brown; soft; mild flavor. *Use:* Eating.

PROVOLONE. Made from whole milk. *Characteristics:* Yellowish; hard; smoky flavor; link-shape or round and hangs from strings; Provoloncini is a smaller version of the same cheese. *Uses:* Eating; Cooking.

REGGIANO. Made from whole milk. *Characteristics:* Very hard; sharp, pungent flavor; granular; nearly the same as Parmesan. *Use:* Grating.

RICOTTA. Made from whey. *Characteristics:* White, soft; like Cottage Cheese. *Uses:* Eating; Cooking.

ROMADUR. Made from whole milk or partly-skimmed milk. *Characteristics:* Soft; whole-milk Romadur is similar to Liederkranz; aroma like Limburger only milder. *Use:* Eating.

ROMANO (*Incanestrato*). Made from partly-skimmed cow's, goat's or ewe's milk. *Characteristics:* Greenish-black surface, whitish inside; granular and hard texture; sharp flavor. *Use:* Grating.

ROQUEFORT. Made from ewe's milk (A French regulation limits use of the word Roquefort to cheese made in the Roquefort area from ewe's milk). *Characteristics:* White, blue-green veins; crumbly, semisoft to hard; sharp flavor. *Uses:* Eating; Cooking.

SAGE. Made from whole or partly-skimmed milk. *Characteristics:* Green, mottled appearance throughout; sage flavored (At one time, green sage leaves were added to the curd before it was hooped. Now sage extract is added for flavor). *Uses:* Cooking; Grating.

SAPSAGO. Made from slightly sour, skim milk. *Characteristics:* Light-green color; very hard; pungent, flavored with powdered clover leaves; small, conical shape. *Uses:* Eating; Grating.

SARDO. Made from whole cow's milk. *Characteristics:* Cream to gray color; firm and smooth. *Uses:* Eating; Cooking.

SBRINZ. Made from whole or partly-skimmed milk. *Characteristics:* Gray-green surface, white inside; hard, granular texture; medium-sharp flavor. *Use:* Grating.

STILTON. Made from whole milk. *Characteristics:* Cream-colored with blue-green veins; wrinkled surface; crumbly; sharp flavor. *Use:* Eating.

SWISS (*Emmentaler*). Made from whole milk. *Characteristics:* Light-yellow interior with holes that develop in the curd as the cheese ripens; elastic body; mild, nutty flavor. *Uses:* Eating; Cooking; Grating.

TILSITER (*Ragnit*). Made from whole or skim milk. *Characteristics:* Slightly yellow; medium firm, similar to Brick cheese; medium-sharp taste, similar to mild Limburger. *Uses:* Mostly eating; Sometimes cooking.

TRAPPIST. Made from whole cow's milk; ewe's or goat's milk may be added. *Characteristics:* Pale yellow; semisoft; mild flavor; similar to Port Salut. *Use:* Eating.

VACHERIN. Made from whole milk. *Characteristics:* Firm, hard rind and very soft interior; aromatic. *Use:* Eating.

YOGURT

Contrary to popular opinion, yogurt was not recently discovered in a health food store in Greenwich Village. It has been around for thousands of years. One story says that an angel brought it to Abraham. Nearly every village in ancient Asia, Europe and Africa made yogurt under one name or another.

The ancient Persians served *mast*, a spicy yogurt sauce, over their shish kebabs. Restaurants that serve Middle Eastern dishes today usually sauce their kebabs and gyros with *mast*. The Persians also invented the first ice cream soda: they beat yogurt with cool spring water until it foamed. Marco Polo reported he was served yogurt by the Mongolians. Indian cooking uses yogurt extensively, too. Next time you order hot curry dishes in an Indian restaurant, ask for a bowl of yogurt to cool your palate between courses.

Yogurt is milk fermented by certain bacteria growing under controlled conditions of time and temperature. Perfect yogurt is smooth, creamy, almost custard-like, rich and slightly tart. Yogurt, at the very least, is as good for you as milk. Probably better, some experts claim. It provides valuable bacterial flora that help keep your digestive system functioning happily; it is a good source of protein and calcium, especially for people who cannot digest milk.

Try it over fruit and over cereal. Yogurt can turn into a vegetable topping, a curry sauce, a dip. You can bake it in casseroles, cakes, cookies and bread recipes. It can replace mayonnaise, sour cream and ice cream. Yogurt becomes a low-calorie dessert when you flavor it with fruit, honey or molasses, cinnamon or nutmeg, vanilla or almond extract, instant coffee or cocoa. It becomes a salad dressing when seasoned with herbs or dry soup mixes. Stir in wheat germ, chopped nuts, chopped fruits, chopped vegetables, chicken, tuna, olives, jam, jelly, preserves, or almost anything you want. In fact, yogurt is so versatile you can even spell it four different ways and be absolutely correct — yogurt, yoghurt, yoghourt or yogourt.

BASIC EQUIPMENT

Everything you use to make yogurt must be exceptionally clean. Run all the equipment through the dishwasher or wash in hot suds, then rinse thoroughly first with hot water and then with boiling water.

1. **Thermometer.** You will need a dairy thermometer, or any other thermometer that can be put into the milk.

It has to register as low as 90°F. Temperature is just as important in yogurt making as in cheese making.

2. **Containers.** Containers for incubating and storing the yogurt can be anything you like: peanut butter jars with lids, plastic refrigerator dishes or cups with lids, small crocks with lids, whatever.

3. **Incubator.** Because yogurt needs several hours at a constant low temperature of 90°F to thicken, you will need to buy or construct an incubator. There are electric yogurt makers available in houseware and hardware stores that do a fine job. Other possibilities are:

- Heating pad, set on low, wrapped around quart jar of yogurt and fastened in place with string or rubber bands.
- A cardboard box, lined with newspapers or old blankets, with a heating pad set on low in the bottom and more newspapers or blankets to cover.
- Cardboard box, insulated as above, with a 40 watt bulb fixed on a long cord inside. Cover with papers or blankets.
- A styrofoam picnic cooler with a heating pad set on low in the bottom.
- A large pan filled with an inch or two of hot water and set in a warm place. Put in the containers of yogurt and place the thermometer in the water and add more hot water when necessary to maintain 90°F.
- A sunny windowsill, gas oven, radiator top or refrigerator top — even a closed car.
- A large thermos container.

Every yogurt *aficionado* has his own special incubator — a particular baby blanket, the second section of the Sunday newspaper, a box that held canned peaches, whatever. Undoubtedly, you will come up with an arrangement that is uniquely yours.

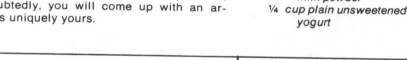

Basic Ingredients

1. **Cultured starter.** The starter supplies the special bacteria that thickens the milk. For your first batch of yogurt buy a carton of plain unflavored, unsweetened yogurt — not ''swiss-styled'' yogurt with gelatin in it. After you make your own first batch, just save ¼ cup of it to start the next batch. Use homemade yogurt that is five days old or less as a starter. Older cultures sometimes turn stringy or lumpy.

2. **Milk.** Any type of milk from any animal can be made into yogurt, except condensed or raw milk. We recommend a combination of low-fat or skim milk and nonfat dry milk powder. The fresher the milk the better. Whole milk makes a richer, thicker yogurt than skim milk, but it is more expensive.

YOGURT

Ingredients	Equipment
1 quart low fat (2%) or skim milk	See Basic Equipment
1 cup instant nonfat dry milk powder	
¼ cup plain unsweetened yogurt	

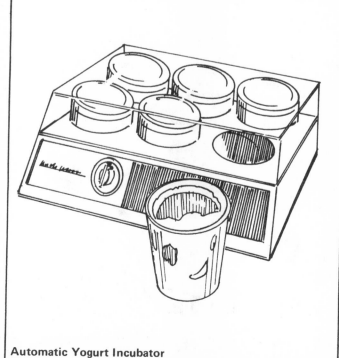

Automatic Yogurt Incubator

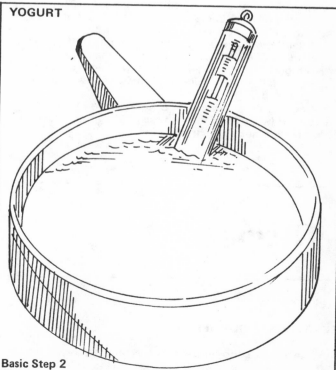

YOGURT

Basic Step 2

YOGURT

Basic Step 6 *Yogurt can incubate in a blanket.*

1. Measure the milk and nonfat dry milk into a saucepan and stir to blend.
2. Put the thermometer in the pan. Heat the milk over low heat to about 180°F. DO NOT BOIL.
3. Remove from heat and cool to 100°F to 115°F.
4. Stir in the yogurt until well blended.
5. Rinse the bowl or containers with hot water to warm them. Then pour in the milk mixture. Cover it tightly.
6. Put the bowl or containers in an incubator and keep it at 90°F for at least 3 hours. Do not disturb!
7. After three hours test a spoonful for flavor. If you like mild yogurt, remove it from the incubator and refrigerate. For a tarter taste incubate longer, testing every half hour. Refrigerate. The yogurt will thicken as it chills.
8. Yogurt will keep at least a week in the refrigerator. Liquid (whey) may form on top of the yogurt. Just let it be and eat as is, or stir it in.

Ingredients

1 *pint tomato juice*
1 *pint yogurt*
2 *cucumbers, peeled, seeded and cut in chunks*
1 *sprig fresh dill or tarragon*
  Salt or seasoned salt to taste

Equipment

Pint measuring cup
Knife
Blender

1. Combine all the ingredients in a blender container and blend until smooth.
2. Chill until ready to serve. Stir, if necessary, before pouring the soup into chilled soup cups or mugs.
3. Garnish with additional fresh herb sprigs.

Recipes

SENSATIONAL SUMMER SOUP

Keep this cool soup on hand in the refrigerator, or let it star at a summer brunch or luncheon.

YOGURT SPREAD OR CREAM CHEESE

In the Middle East they prepare yogurt this way to use as a spread. It is a superior, tangy cream cheese for dips, spreads or in recipes.

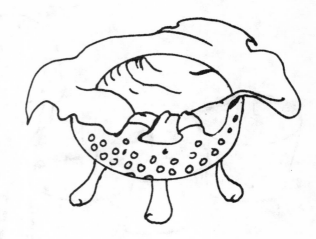

Ingredients	Equipment
Freshly made yogurt	Cheesecloth
	Colander or strainer
	Bowl or pan

1. Line the colander or strainer with several thicknesses of cheesecloth and put it in the sink.
2. As soon as the yogurt has finished incubating, before you refrigerate it, pour it into the cheesecloth-lined colander and let drain.
3. Gather up the corners of the cheesecloth and tie them together or with a string to form a bag.
4. Hang the bag from a faucet or cupboard door handle. Place a bowl underneath to catch the whey and let it drain 8 hours or overnight.
5. Turn the spread out of bag into another container and refrigerate until ready to use.

TART AND TANGY DILL DRESSING

For Jerusalem Salad, thinly slice tomatoes, cucumber and green peppers, pour on this dressing and chill several hours. Spoon the salad into lettuce cups to serve. The dressing recipe makes 1 cup. If you prefer a sweet, rather than tart dressing, stir in 2 tablespoons sugar.

Ingredients	Equipment
1 cup yogurt	Measuring cup and
2 tablespoons vinegar	spoons
½ small onion, finely diced	Blender
½ teaspoon salt	Refrigerator container
½ teaspoon dill weed or	Rubber spatula
seed	
¼ teaspoon dry mustard	
¼ teaspoon garlic powder	

1. Combine all the ingredients in a blender container and blend until smooth.
2. Pour the dressing into a refrigerator container and refrigerate for several hours to blend the flavors.

YOGURT DRESSING

Add almost any herb or seasoning you like to this all-purpose low-calorie dressing: chopped fresh or dried mint, dill, tarragon, basil, celery seeds or caraway seeds, dried soup mixes or salad dressing mixes. Serve over tossed green salads, sliced cucumbers, cole slaw, sliced tomatoes, cooked and chilled green and waxed beans, hot or cold sliced potatoes. The recipe makes about 1½ cups dressing.

Ingredients	Equipment
1½ cups plain yogurt	Measuring cup and
2 teaspoons soy sauce	spoons
1 teaspoon celery or	Mixing bowl or
seasoned salt	refrigerator container
½ teaspoon each onion and	Spoon or rubber spatula
garlic powder or 1	
teaspoon grated onion	
and 1 clove garlic,	
minced	

1. Mix all the ingredients until blended.
2. Cover and refrigerate at least 1 hour to blend the flavors.
3. Store in the refrigerator.

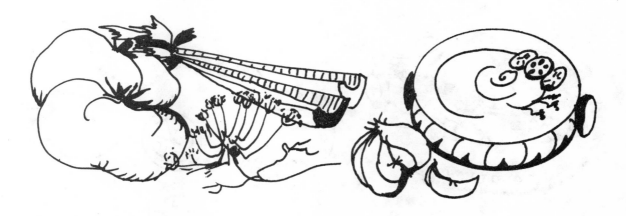

YOGURT SHERBET

Serve this tangy sherbet on warm days for real refreshment. You can even freeze it in small paper cups with wooden sticks in them to make frozen yogurt popsicles for the kids. The recipe makes 1 or 2 pints, depending on what you add to the yogurt.

Ingredients

1 pint yogurt
1 cup chopped cooked, dried, or fresh apricots, peaches, plums or berries. Or ¾ cup apricot, strawberry, pineapple, grape or cherry preserves. Or 1 ripe avocado, peeled, seeded and mashed

Equipment

Measuring cup
Mixing bowl
Wooden spoon or rubber spatula
Ice cube tray

1. Mix the yogurt with your choice of other ingredients.
2. Turn into an ice cube tray and freeze. Eat when just frosty or freeze longer and cut the sherbet into cubes and pile them in sherbet glasses.
3. Sprinkle with chopped nuts, wheat germ or additional fruit or preserves to garnish.

YOGURT DRESSING FOR FRUIT

Fix a platter of seasonal fruits, spoon this delightful dressing over them and garnish with additional grated citrus peel or fresh mint leaves. The dressing makes a perfect topper for gelatin salads or canned fruit, too. This recipe makes about 1 cup.

Ingredients

1 cup yogurt
1 tablespoon shredded citrus peel (use lime, lemon or orange or any combination)
2 to 3 tablespoons citrus juice
2 to 3 tablespoons sugar or honey
½ teaspoon ground nutmeg or mace
½ teaspoon vanilla

Equipment

Measuring cup and spoons
Shredder or grater
Knife
Juicer
Small mixing bowl or refrigerator container

1. Combine all the ingredients and mix well.
2. Cover and refrigerate until ready to serve.
3. Store the dressing in the refrigerator.

ICE CREAM

History students may have trouble remembering dates, but ice cream lovers are likely to remember these events:

2nd Century B.C. — The Romans eat sherbet.

1533 — Catherine de' Medici brings ice cream from Italy to France.

1670 — The first ice cream parlor opens in Paris.

1812 — Dolly Madison serves strawberry ice cream at Inaugural Ball.

1846 — Nancy Johnson invents hand-cranked ice cream freezer.

1904 — St. Louis World's Fair ice cream vendor creates the ice cream cone.

1923 — The Good Humor bar is born.

I scream, you scream, we all scream for ice cream! A quick look in the yellow pages will show you that ice cream is becoming more and more popular. Ice cream stores are everywhere. You can buy good ice cream at the supermarket, or at any of the burgeoning ice cream parlors. But, for the most fun and for a flavor that commercial ice cream can not duplicate, make it yourself.

If you want to pinch pennies, you can save by using only milk, little or no cream, or evaporated milk. But if it is rich, thick texture and flavor you are after, splurge and buy cream.

Once you have mastered the basic steps for making ice cream, endless variations are possible. You do not have to go as far as truffled ice cream, a dessert served at an Edwardian extravaganza, but you can be wildly creative with fruits, nuts, flavorings, candy. For birthday parties, homemade ice cream is one of the most memorable gifts you can share with your guests. Pale pink frosting, sugar roses, a rich chocolate cake and homemade ice cream — even adults need birthday parties like that. After all, happiness is fulfilling a long-deferred childhood dream, isn't it? Have as much cake and ice cream as you want!

BASIC EQUIPMENT

1. **Freezer.** Freezing makes ice cream, and it requires special steps and equipment. You can pour a mixture of cream, sugar and flavorings into an ice cube tray and let your food freezer do the work. But the result will be a hard, crystalline product, often referred to as still- or quiet-frozen ice cream. It is Nancy Johnson's invention — a container with paddles constantly churning the ice cream mixture, surrounded by ice and salt — that gives us the smooth, light, frosty mixture we like today. The constant motion of the paddles keeps ice crystals small and beats in air.

There are many home ice cream freezers available. Some have wooden tubs, some plastic, some fiberglass. Either works well, but we prefer the fiberglass tub or bucket. You can choose manual (the old-fashioned crank-type) or electric freezers. There is also a small electric freezer that you place inside your food freezer, but we will limit our directions to the ice-and-salt models.

If you have plenty of strong-armed help then select the crank-type. But, if you are going to do it yourself, pick the electric. The cranking can take a half hour or more and, especially at the end of that time, it is really hard work.

Always read through the Use and Care Booklet that comes with your freezer before you start, learning the different parts of the freezer, where they go and how they work. Then study the basic steps for that particular model. The possibilities of errors are almost nil, if you follow the instructions.

2. **Ice.** Ice and rock salt are really equipment, rather than ingredients. They work together to freeze the ice

cream. Salt melts the ice. As it melts it absorbs heat from the ice cream, lowering its temperature and causing it to freeze. The proportions of ice and salt are very important. Too much salt means the ice cream will freeze too rapidly and be coarse-textured. Too little salt slows down the freezing and the ice cream will be spongy and buttery in texture.

Always use crushed ice. It melts evenly and freezes the ice cream more evenly than chunks of ice. You can buy crushed ice, or crush ice by putting it in a heavy cloth or burlap bag and whacking it soundly with a mallet or hammer — or use an ice crusher.

If you have room in your food freezer you can save some money by stashing extra ice instead of buying it. Emply ice cube trays into heavy plastic or brown grocery bags and keep them in the freezer, adding more ice cubes everytime you think of it until you have accumulated enough for your ice cream freezer.

If you buy milk in cardboard cartons, use those cartons for ice-making. When empty rinse them well, then fill with water and freeze solid. Whack the containers with a hammer, or pound them hard on cement to get chunks. Crush the chunks. You will need 20 pounds of ice to freeze and ripen a gallon of ice cream.

3. **Rock salt.** Use rock salt, also called ice cream salt or sidewalk salt, to layer with the ice. Table salt is too fine, also too expensive. Always weigh or measure the salt. You will need about 3 cups or 2 pounds of salt for a gallon of ice cream. Use a glass measuring cup rather than metal to measure salt because the salt will pit a metal cup. Salt is so corrosive you must take other precautions. Always work on several layers of newspapers, whether inside or out, so any spilled brine will not damage your floor or lawn. Discard the brine and the left over salt and ice away from trees or grass. Salt will kill grass. Rubber gloves help protect your hands from the cold and the salt.

Basic Ingredients

1. **Milk.** Milk and/or cream, along with sweetening and flavorings, is the basic ingredient of ice cream. You can use homogenized whole milk, evaporated or sweetened condensed milk, reconstituted instant non-fat dry milk or skim milk, half and half or light cream, whipping cream or heavy cream. Fruit juices replace part or all of the milk or cream for sherbets and ices.

2. **Sweetener.** Granulated sugar is the most common sweetener, but brown sugar, honey, molasses, corn syrup or artificial sweeteners can replace it. If you want to change ingredients, first follow a proven recipe to the letter. Then, when you have perfected your basic ice cream skills, begin varying sweeteners, as well as other ingredients.

3. **Flavorings.** When it comes to flavoring, anything is possible. Use pure extracts for richer flavor. Vanilla, almond, cognac, rum, maple, mint, and fruit-flavored liqueurs are just a few of the liquid flavorings possible. Ice cream making is one of the few times you can be a little heavy-handed with your addition of flavorings. Flavors need to be stronger for ice cream, because when the ice cream hits your taste buds it is so cold it numbs them a little. Remember, when you sample the unfrozen mixture, if it tastes a little too strong it will probably be just right when frozen.

4. **Fruits and nuts** were made for ice cream. You can start at A, with avocado, apricot or almond and go almost all the way through the alphabet: banana or blueberry; cherry, cashew, cantaloupe or coconut; date; elderberry; fig or filbert; grape or guava; huckleberry; lemon or lime; kumquat; mango, maraschino cherry or mandarin orange; nectarine; orange; pineapple, persimmon, pecan, peanut or prune; quince; raspberry or raisin; strawberry; Tutti Frutti; ugli fruit; and walnut (black or California).

5. **What else might you add?** Chocolate, of course, or instant coffee or tea, marshmallows, crushed peppermint, toffee or other candy, macaroons, pumpkin, spices. Or swirl in sundae sauces or jams to make your own ripple.

Eggs are sometimes added to make a rich, golden frozen custard or French ice cream.

STORAGE

Homemade ice cream does not last long — it is usually eaten immediately. But, its flavor and texture are actually better if it is stored in your refrigerator's freezer at 0°F for up to a month. Homemade ice cream is harder than commercially made ice cream. It dips best if you move it to the refrigerator for 10 minutes or so. Be sure to cover the surface of the ice cream with a piece of plastic wrap and then seal the container tightly. This double cover helps prevent ice crystals from forming on the surface.

ICE CREAM FREEZER

Hand Crank or Motor Unit

Lid

Dasher

Can

Drain Hole

Bucket

BASIC STEPS

Remember to read and follow the instructions that come with your ice cream freezer. Some freezers may require different proportions of ice and salt than are given in these Basic Steps.

Ingredients

Milk and ice cream
Sugar
Flavorings

Equipment

Measuring cup
Measuring spoons
Large mixing bowl
Rotary or electric beater
Wooden spoon
Rubber spatula
2 to 3 pounds rock salt
Glass measuring cup
20 to 25 pounds ice
Ice crusher
*1 quart saucepan for
    measuring ice*
Ice cream freezer

1. Prepare the ice cream mixture as the recipe directs and chill thoroughly. Overnight chilling is best.
2. Wash the can, dasher and cover of the ice cream freezer in hot suds, rinse thoroughly in hot water and dry. Chill them in the refrigerator or freezer. You do not need to wash the bucket and should not wash the crank or motor assembly.
3. Crush the ice.
4. Replace the can and dasher in the freezer bucket; pour in the ice cream mixture. The can should be ½ to ⅔ full.
5. Put the cover on the can; fit the motor or crank assembly into the cover and fasten it to the bucket as the manufacturer directs.
6. Put the freezer on several thicknesses of newspaper. An electric mixer will have to be near an outlet.
7. Warm up the motor for 1 minute.
8. While the motor is running, begin adding ice and

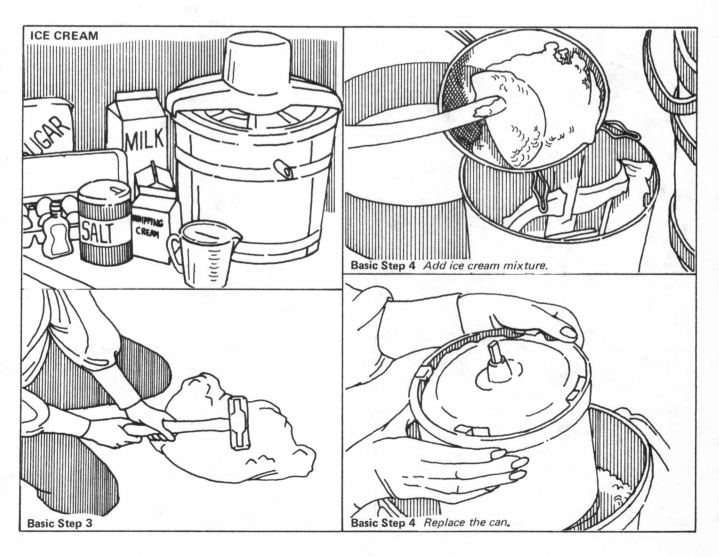

ICE CREAM

Basic Step 4 *Add ice cream mixture.*

Basic Step 3

Basic Step 4 *Replace the can.*

salt. Start with 6 cups crushed ice, or about 2 inches of crushed ice. Sprinkle ¼ cup rock salt evenly over the ice. Repeat these layers until the can is surrounded and covered with layers of ice and salt.

9. Be sure the hole in top side of the freezer bucket is free so the salt-water brine can drain off. Put a plastic container underneath the hole to catch any drips.

10. Crank a hand freezer evenly and quickly, turning more rapidly as you feel mixture thicken so you can whip air into the ice cream. When you can not crank any more (because the mixture is so thick, not because your arm has given out), it is time to stop. This may be about half an hour, but freezing times can vary widely, so go by consistency rather than time.

    Run an electric mixer until the motor labors heavily or stops. Immediately unplug the freezer (with dry hands!).

11. Drain the brine into a bucket, driveway or non-grassy place by tilting the freezer carefully.

12. Remove the ice and salt to about 2 inches below the cover.

13. Remove the motor or cranking assembly.

14. Wipe the cover and top of the can with paper towels

to remove ice and salt. Carefully remove the cover and lift out the dasher.

15. Using a rubber spatula, scrape ice cream off the dasher and into the can (or hand the dasher to the hungry crowd that is probably now pressing in on you and let them clean off the dasher).

16. With a rubber spatula push the ice cream from the top sides of the can to the center and stir briefly to blend.

17. Cover the top of the can with several thicknesses of foil, plastic wrap or waxed paper, then replace the cover. Plug the hole in the cover with a cork, wad of paper towels or foil.

18. Now add more layers of ice and salt, this time using about ⅓ to ½ cup salt for each 6 cups or two inches of crushed ice. Layer the ice and salt up to and cover the top of the can.

19. Wrap the freezer in several thicknesses of newspaper, cover with a heavy towel or old blanket and move to a cool place to ripen for 2 to 3 hours.

20. Drain off the brine and remove ice and salt as in steps 11, 12 and 14. Have a serving spoon or scoop and dishes ready.

21. Lift the can from the freezer and serve at once.

22. If you have any ice cream left (unlikely) or if you are not going to eat it all right then (also unlikely) transfer the ice cream to a plastic freezer container; cover top of ice cream with a plastic wrap, seal the container and store it in your food freezer.

NOTE: you may skip the ripening stage, Basic Steps 17 through 20, if you wish. Instead, put the can of ice cream in your food freezer to ripen. Or you can transfer the ice cream immediately to plastic freezer containers, seal and let them ripen in the food freezer.

Recipes

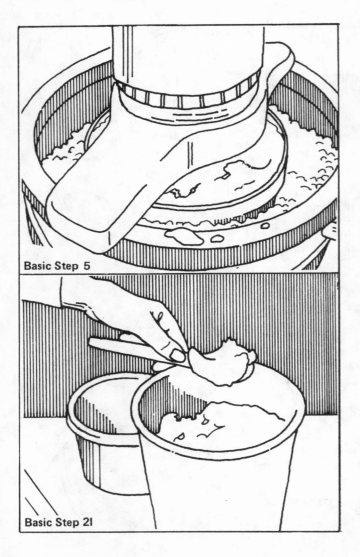

Basic Step 5

Basic Step 21

BASIC VANILLA ICE CREAM

Add almost anything you like to the ice cream mixture just before freezing. See Basic Ingredients for suggestions. The recipe makes 1 gallon.

Ingredients	Equipment
2 quarts light cream (half and half)	See equipment under Basic Steps
1 quart milk	
3 cups sugar	
2 tablespoons pure vanilla extract	
1 teaspoon salt	

1. Stir all the ingredients together until the sugar dissolves.
2. Chill thoroughly.
3. Pour into the can of an ice cream freezer and freeze as directed in Basic Steps.

CHOCOLATE ICE CREAM I

Ingredients

4 ounces melted
    unsweetened
    chocolate
4 cups sugar
2 quarts light cream (half
    and half)
2 tablespoons pure vanilla
    extract
1 teaspoon salt

Equipment

See equipment under
    Basic Steps
Saucepan

1. Heat the quart of milk until just hot to the touch.
2. Stir in 4 ounces of melted unsweetened chocolate and 1 cup of sugar.
3. Stir in all the remaining ingredients and chill thoroughly.
4. Pour the chilled mixture into the can of your ice cream freezer and freeze following the Basic Steps.

DOUBLE CHOCOLATE ICE CREAM

Prepare Chocolate Ice Cream as directed. Just before pouring into the freezer can, stir in 1 package (6 ounces) of coarsely chopped unsweetened chocolate.

CHOCOLATE ICE CREAM II

Cocoa and corn syrup are the unusual ingredients in this rich recipe. The recipe makes about 1 gallon.

Ingredients

1 quart milk
1 cup cocoa
1 cup light corn syrup
5 eggs
2 cups sugar
1 quart whipping cream
1 tablespoon pure vanilla
    extract

Equipment

See equipment under
    Basic Steps
Saucepan

1. Combine 2 cups of the milk, cocoa and corn syrup in a saucepan. Heat over medium heat until boiling, stirring constantly. Cool.
2. Beat the eggs in a mixing bowl until foamy.
3. Gradually beat in the sugar.
4. Beat in the cocoa mixture, then stir in the remaining milk, cream and vanilla.
5. Chill thoroughly.
6. Pour the chilled mixture into the can of an ice cream freezer and freeze following the Basic Steps.

STRAWBERRY ICE CREAM

You can replace the strawberries with any other crushed or cut up sweetened fruit. Try peaches and substitute honey for sugar. The recipe makes about 1 gallon.

Ingredients

1 quart crushed sweetened
    strawberries — about 3
    pints fresh or 3 (10
    ounce) packages
    frozen
2 eggs
1 cup sugar
3 cups milk
3 cups whipping cream
½ teaspoon almond extract,
    (optional)
Dash salt

Equipment

See equipment under
    Basic Steps

1. Beat the eggs until foamy in large mixing bowl.
2. Gradually add the sugar and beat until thickened.
3. Stir in the milk, cream and flavoring.
4. Blend in the berries.
5. Chill thoroughly.
6. Pour into the can of an ice cream freezer and freeze following the Basic Steps.

SUPER-RICH VANILLA CUSTARD ICE CREAM

You will have just enough egg whites left over to make an angel food cake to serve with this expensive ice cream. The recipe makes about 1 gallon.

Ingredients	Equipment
1½ quarts whipping cream (6 half-pint cartons)	See equipment under Basic Steps
1 quart plus 1 cup milk	Large saucepan
12 egg yolks	
3 cups sugar	
5 tablespoons pure vanilla extract	
1 teaspoon salt	

1. Pour the cream and milk into a heavy saucepan and heat just until tiny bubbles appear around the edge. DO NOT BOIL.
2. Beat the egg yolks until thick and lemon-colored, about 5 minutes.
3. Gradually add the sugar, beating constantly, and beat until thick.
4. Very slowly pour 1 cup of the hot milk into the egg yolk mixture, beating constantly.
5. Now slowly beat the warmed egg yolk mixture into the remaining milk-cream mixture in the saucepan, stirring constantly.
6. Cook over low or medium-low heat, stirring constantly, until mixture will coat a metal spoon. This may take 5 to 10 minutes at low heat. Stir constantly and DO NOT LET IT BOIL.
7. Remove from heat and stir in the vanilla and salt.
8. Chill thoroughly.
9. Strain the mixture into the can of your ice cream freezer and freeze following the Basic Steps.

LEMON CUSTARD ICE CREAM

The flour in this recipe helps thicken and smooth the ice cream. If a tart flavor appeals to you, use 1 pint of buttermilk for half of the milk. The recipe makes about 3 quarts.

Ingredients	Equipment
2 cups sugar	See equipment under Basic Steps
¼ cup flour	Large saucepan
¼ teaspoon salt	
1 quart milk	
4 eggs, beaten	
1 cup lemon juice	
3 cups whipping cream	

1. Combine the sugar, flour and salt in a saucepan.
2. Gradually stir in the milk.
3. Cook and stir over medium heat until thickened. Then cook and stir 2 minutes longer.
4. Blend a small amount of the hot mixture into the beaten eggs.
5. Gradually stir the warmed egg mixture into the milk in the saucepan. Cook and stir 1 minute. DO NOT BOIL.
6. Pour into a large mixing bowl and blend in the lemon juice and cream.
7. Chill thoroughly.
8. Pour the chilled mixture into the can of an ice cream freezer and freeze following the Basic Steps.

HAWAIIAN SHERBET

Buttermilk gives a delightful, refreshing tang to this recipe. Unfrozen it is as good a "milk shake" as it is a sherbet. The recipe makes about 3 quarts.

Ingredients	Equipment
½ gallon buttermilk	See equipment under Basic Steps
1 can (6 ounces) pineapple-orange or pineapple juice concentrate, thawed	
2 cups sugar	
Pinch salt	

1. Combine all the ingredients and mix them until the sugar dissolves.
2. Chill thoroughly.
3. Pour into the can of an ice cream freezer and freeze following the Basic Steps.

ORANGE SHERBET

This sherbet is wonderful in winter, as well as summer. The recipe makes about 1 gallon.

Ingredients

1½ quarts (6 cups) milk
2 cups sugar
¼ teaspoon salt
2 tablespoons grated orange peel
2½ cups fresh orange juice
⅓ cup lemon juice

Equipment

See equipment under Basic Steps

1. In large bowl mix the milk, sugar and salt until the sugar dissolves.
2. Stir the peel and juices together and gradually add them to the milk, stirring constantly. The mixture will look curdled, but it turns out delicious.
3. Chill thoroughly.
4. Pour into the can of an ice cream freezer and freeze as in Basic Steps. Use ⅓ cup of rock salt for each 2 inches of ice for this recipe.

DIET VANILLA ICE CREAM

Egg yolks and gelatin help give a smooth, rich texture. There are approximately 45 calories per ½ cup serving. The recipe makes about 1 gallon.

Ingredients

11 cups reconstituted instant nonfat dry milk or skim milk
3½ envelopes unflavored gelatin
5 egg yolks
3 tablespoons pure vanilla extract
1 teaspoon salt
Artificial sweetener to equal 3 cups sugar

Equipment

See equipment under Basic Steps
Large saucepan
Metal spoon

1. Measure 5 cups of the milk into the saucepan.
2. Sprinkle the gelatin over the milk in the saucepan.
3. Beat the egg yolks well, then blend them into the milk in the saucepan.
4. Cook and stir over medium-low heat about 20 minutes or until the mixture will coat a metal spoon and gelatin has dissolved. DO NOT BOIL.
5. Stir in all the remaining ingredients including the 6 remaining cups of milk and chill thoroughly.
6. Strain the mixture into the can of your ice cream freezer and freeze following the Basic Steps.

DIET CHOCOLATE ICE CREAM

Prepare Diet Vanilla Ice Cream and add 1 to 2 tablespoons chocolate extract along with the vanilla. Use more chocolate extract for stronger flavor, if desired. Follow the Basic Steps for freezing.

Snack Foods, Pickled Foods, & Condiments

Everybody loves to snack. Snacking is not only an American phenomenon; people all over the world nibble their way through the day. Japanese have their sushi-bars for their favorite raw fish snacks; Koreans can stop for spicy grilled shrimp and beef any time of day; Indians nibble on spiced dried lentils; Germans pause for sausages and cold cuts; the British made an institution of the mid-afternoon snack; probably the hardiest prehistoric tribes of hunters and gatherers survived because they could find more to nibble throughout the day than less fortunate tribes. Americans, however, seem especially addicted to fattening snacks that lack nourishment.

In this chapter you will find snack foods that are both delicious and good for you. Peanut butter, almond butter or mixed nut butters may be habit forming, but they are definitely good for you. They are also excellent sources of protein and the B-vitamins. Try a bit of nut butter spread on a slice of your homemade whole wheat bread — that should tide you over until dinner. Soybeans can be roasted to make a low-calorie munch that is high in protein. Granola, the popular mix of whole grain cereals and nuts, costs pennies to make at home and, like peanut butter, may be habit forming.

Pickled foods make their appearance in this chapter, too. Pickling is another ancient means of preserving food. The first brine was probably salt water. Pickling, along with fermenting and cooking over a fire, most likely evolved as soon as prehistoric hunters and gatherers collected more snack foods than they could eat at one time; extra provisions had to be stored in something; the pot had to be invented before civilization could proceed. The Chinese love pickled condiments and sauerkraut is actually their invention. Pickled cucumbers come from the Mediterranean, pickled tomatoes are a New World addition to the old technique of pickling. The pickled foods in this chapter are the perfect accompaniments for your homemade sausages, cold cuts, cheeses and breads.

Condiments — flavored vinegars, mayonnaise, mustard and catsup, also complement your homemade foods. It would not be right to spread just any old mustard or mayonnaise on your homemade cold cuts! You will find some picnic specialties, such as pickled eggs and pickled watermelon rinds, in this section, too. With these recipes you will be ready to arrange a truly royal feast; the sumptuous banquet of food and drink you made yourself will be complete.

Recipes

PEANUT BUTTER

You have probably seen the commercial that compares peanut butters and promotes the one that tastes "like fresh-roasted peanuts." You can make peanut butter that actually does taste like that, all by yourself, at home — for fun and even some savings. Once you try fresh peanut butter you will never buy brand name spreads again. Shop carefully for the peanuts. If you buy salted nuts in the can you will not save money. If you buy raw peanuts or peanuts in the shell you will be saving money. Check bulk peanuts for freshness. A blender is necessary to make peanut butter. Some peanut butter lovers use the fine cutting blade of an electric food grinder, but a blender makes delicious peanut butter, too. This recipe makes 2¾ cups of peanut butter.

Ingredients	Equipment
1 pound shelled raw peanuts (with or without skins)	Cookie sheet
	Blender
¼ cup salad oil	Rubber spatula
¼ teaspoon salt or to taste	Peanut butter jar or other glass container

1. If you wish, roast the peanuts by spreading them on a cookie sheet and baking in a preheated 300°F oven about 15 minutes or until browned. Cool.
2. Put 1 cup of roasted or raw peanuts in your blender's container, add 2 tablespoons oil and blend about 1 minute, or slightly less if you want chunky peanut butter.
3. Stop the blender and push the peanuts to the blades, if necessary. Blend a few more seconds, until the butter is the desired texture.
4. Remove the peanut butter from the blender with a rubber spatula and put it in a jar.
5. Repeat the blending process with the remaining peanuts and oil, blending about 1 cup peanuts at a time.
6. Stir in the salt.
7. Cover tightly and refrigerate until ready to use. Chilling firms up the peanut butter and prevents the oil from separating. Just stir the oil back into the peanut butter if it does separate.

NUT AND SEED BUTTERS

If peanut butter makes you ecstatic, wait till you try one of these butters. Spread them on bread, crackers or celery chunks, if you can wait. Addicts usually settle for a finger or a spoon. If you want to make a larger batch, double or triple the recipe but continue to blend the nuts in small quantities unless you have a nut grinder or heavy duty blender. The recipe makes ¼ cup of nuts or seed butter.

Ingredients	Equipment
½ cup nuts (raw or roasted unsalted pecans, cashews, almonds or filberts) or sunflower or sesame seeds	See Peanut Butter recipe
3 tablespoons oil	
¼ teaspoon salt	

1. Blend all ingredients in your blender until smooth, stopping the blender to push the nuts to the blades, if necessary.
2. Store in covered jars in the refrigerator. The butter will firm up after a few hours in the refrigerator.

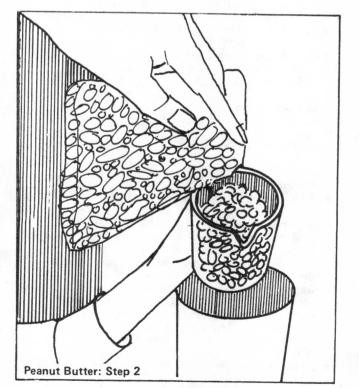

Peanut Butter: Step 2

VARIATIONS

Try any of the following combinations.

Sesame Almond: ¼ *cup each sesame seeds and almonds.*
Walnut Cashew: ¼ *cup each cashews and walnuts.*
Almond Peanut: ¼ *cup each raw peanuts and almonds.*
Pecan Sunflower: ¼ *cup each sunflower seeds and pecans.*

SOYBEAN SNACK

Cook, then roast the soybeans, season with salt and offer them for snacks. No empty calories here — soy-beans provide protein, iron and the B vitamins with fewer calories than peanuts. The recipe makes about 3 cups of Soybean Snacks.

Ingredients	Equipment
1 cup dried soybeans	Measuring cup
3 cups water	Quart container
Oil (optional)	Heavy saucepan with
Salt	lid
	Shallow pan or cookie
	sheet
	Tightly covered
	container for storage

1. Wash the beans, pick them over and discard any that are not perfect. Drain.
2. Put the beans and 3 cups water in a 1 quart container or bowl and refrigerate or freeze overnight. This softens the beans; they are harder than peas or pinto beans because of their high protein content.
3. Thaw, if frozen. Pour the beans and water into a saucepan, cover and simmer 1 hour.
4. Drain the beans well.
5. Spread them on a lightly greased pan or cookie sheet and roast in a preheated 350°F oven about 45 minutes to an hour or until well browned, stirring once or twice. Watch carefully for the last 15 minutes or so because the beans may scorch.
6. Remove them from the oven and sprinkle with oil (optional) and salt to taste.
7. Cool, then store in a tightly covered container.

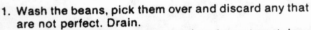

GRANOLA

Every major cereal manufacturer now packages its own brand of granola — often almost nothing but oats processed with large amounts of brown sugar. Homemade granola is better than the packaged varieties and you can vary it to suit yourself. It is much cheaper, too. Add almost any ingredients you like: chopped dried apricots, dates, raisins, dried apples or pears, cinnamon, filberts, pecans, walnuts, peanuts, sunflower seeds. Eat granola out of hand as a snack, pour on milk and eat as cereal, sprinkle it over yogurt or ice cream, stir it into almost any cookie batter, keep a covered coffee canful in the car for long

Granola: Step 5

trips. This recipe makes about 2 quarts. Store it in tightly covered cans or jars.

Ingredients	Equipment
2½ cups rolled oats	Measuring cups (metal)
1½ cups whole wheat cereal (granular, shreds or flakes — your choice)	Large mixing bowl
	Saucepan
1½ cups flaked coconut	Cookie sheets
1 cup wheat germ	Spatula
1 cup sliced or chopped almonds or other nuts	Cans or jars with tight-fitting lids
1 cup chopped toasted soybeans (see Soybean Snack recipe)	
½ cup sesame seeds	
½ cup oil	
½ cup honey	
2 teaspoons vanilla	

1. Preheat the oven to 350°F.
2. In a large mixing bowl combine the oats, wheat, coconut, wheat germ, almonds, soybeans, and sesame seeds.
3. In a saucepan heat the oil, honey and vanilla together just until blended.
4. Pour over the grain mixture in the bowl and toss to blend.
5. Spread the granola on cookie sheets and toast in the preheated oven for about 20 minutes. Turn the granola often, moving the mixture at the edges to center with a spatula for even browning. Watch carefully during the last few minutes as browning can go quickly.
6. Remove from the oven; cool, then store in tightly covered jars or cans.

Pickled Foods

Basic Equipment

1. **Mixing bowl, pots and pans.** Use stainless steel, aluminum, enamel or glass containers for preparing, mixing or heating the brine. The pickling solution turns murky when it touches other metals.
2. **Cheesecloth.** The spices you use for pickling are tied in a cheesecloth bag.
3. **Standard sized glass canning jars with two-piece, self-sealing lids.** Read and follow the sealing directions that come with these lids. Do not try to adapt old jars for canning; they will not seal properly. Pint and quart jars are used in the recipes that follow.
4. **Ladle or slotted spoon.**
5. **Wide-mouth funnel.** A funnel that fits in the tops of the jars makes filling them easier.
6. **Knife or spatula.** Air bubbles must be removed from the pickles; running a knife around the inside of the jar releases the bubbles.
7. **Water-bath canner.** Pickles must be processed in a boiling water-bath to help retard spoilage and retain flavor. Water-bath canners are available in house and hardware stores. These are large, deep pots with tight-fitting covers. They have racks that fit inside, usually with handles for easy lifting. You can easily

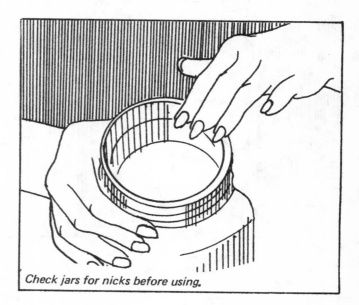
Check jars for nicks before using.

put together a water-bath canner by finding a rack, such as a round wire cake rack, that will fit inside a large deep pot. The pot must have a snug-fitting cover and must be deep enough to leave several inches of space above the tops of the jars sitting on the rack.

8. **Large kettle or pot.** You will need a large pot for additional boiling water.

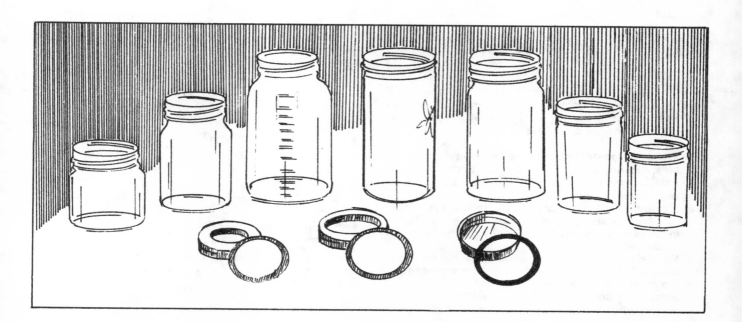

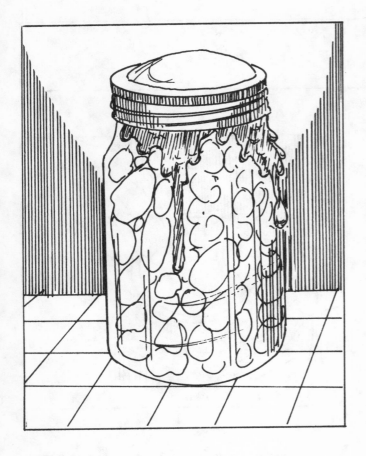

Basic Steps

1. Wash the jars and lids and all other equipment in hot suds, rinse well and dry. Keep the jars hot in a pan of hot water or in the dishwasher on "dry" cycle.
2. Fill the water-bath canner with 4 to 5 inches of hot water. Put the rack in place, put the canner on the range and begin to heat. Begin to heat more water in a tea kettle or large pot.
3. Prepare the pickles and brine or syrup as the recipe directs.
4. Put a wide mouth funnel in a jar and spoon or ladle in the pickles, packing firmly but not jamming them.
5. Pour the boiling syrup within ½ inch of top of jar.
6. Run a table knife or spatula down side of jar to release any air bubbles. If there were large air bubbles you may have to pour in just a little more syrup to bring it up to within ½ inch of top of jar.
7. Wipe the top rim and the threads of the jar with a clean damp cloth.

9. **Tongs.** You will need long-handled tongs to lift the jars out of the boiling water.
10. **Timer.** All canned foods must be processed for precisely the full time specified in the recipes.
11. **Hot pads.**
12. **Racks or folded dishcloths.** Once the pickles have been processed they need to cool on racks or dishcloths.

Basic Ingredients

Pickling preserves food with brine (water and salt) vinegar and sugar. Each of these ingredients retards spoilage of the fruits or vegetables. Most pickle recipes use a combination of these preservatives.

1. **Fruits or vegetables.** Pick perfect fruits or vegetables; pickling can not improve what you start with, only preserve it. Thoroughly wash the fruits or vegetables.
2. **Pickling salt** or **pure granulated salt.** Iodized table salt can darken pickles; uniodized table salt may make cloudy pickles because of its anti-caking ingredients.
3. **Vinegar.** Vinegar should be 4-6% acidity. Read the label and buy only white distilled or cider vinegar.
4. **Granulated white sugar.**
5. **Spices.** Fresh whole spices give the best flavor. Ground spices may darken the pickles.

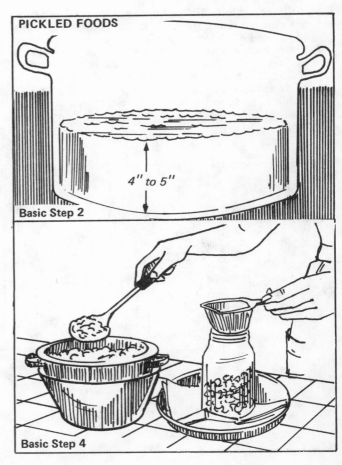

PICKLED FOODS

4" to 5"

Basic Step 2

Basic Step 4

PICKLED FOODS

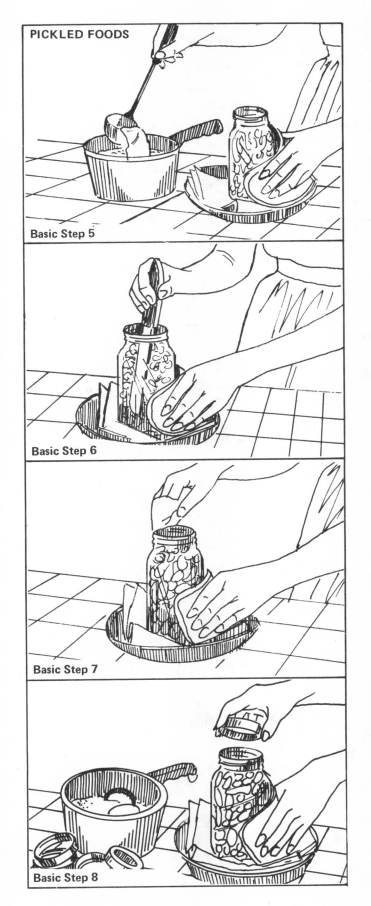

Basic Step 5

Basic Step 6

Basic Step 7

Basic Step 8

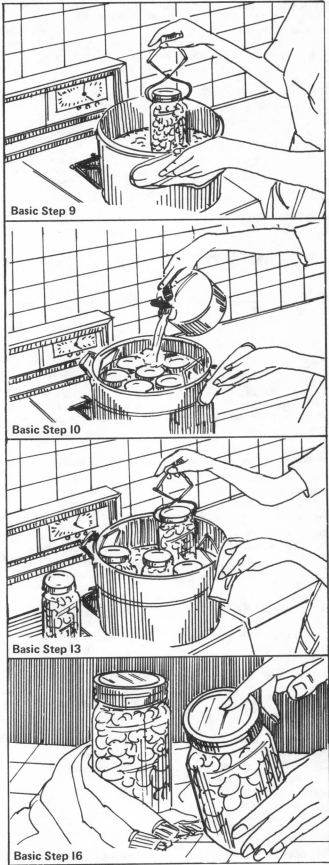

Basic Step 9

Basic Step 10

Basic Step 13

Basic Step 16

8. Put on the lids and bands and adjust, following manufacturer's directions.
9. The water in the water-bath canner as well as the water in the kettle should be boiling by now. Carefully lower the sealed jars into the boiling water and stand them on the rack. The jars must not touch each other.
10. Pour enough more boiling water down side of the canner to cover the jars by 1 inch.
11. Cover the canner and quickly heat until it boils.
12. When the water boils again, set your timer and process for the time given in the recipe.
13. When the time is up, turn off the heat, remove cover and, with long-handled tongs, carefully lift out the jars and set them on folded dishcloths or rack. Leave enough space between the jars for the air to cool them. Do not cover jars, but be sure they are out of any drafts.
14. Let the jars cool, undisturbed, at least overnight.
15. When they are cool, test the seal as the manufacturer directs and remove the screw bands.
16. Carefully look over the jars. If any show bubbles or leakage, use those jars at once, or repack and reprocess.
17. Wipe the jars with a clean damp cloth and store in cool, dark dry place.

Recipes

STORAGE

Except for recipes that indicate refrigerator storage, pickles belong in a cool, dark, dry place until you are ready to eat them. Once opened, they should be kept in the refrigerator.

FRESH-PACK DILLS

These are quick-dills. They marinate in brine just over-night, not for weeks. Select perfect, just-ripe pickling cucumbers, about 3 to 5 inches long. You should be able to pack 7 to 10 whole cukes in each quart jar. Pickles make another great gift from your kitchen. The recipe makes 7 quarts.

Ingredients	Equipment
17 to 18 pounds pickling cucumbers	See Basic Equipment
2 gallons water	Vegetable brush
1½ cups pure granulated salt	Large enamel or glass pan, bowl or casserole
1½ quarts vinegar	Measuring cups and spoons
¾ cup pure granulated salt	7 standard quart-size glass canning jars with 2-piece self-sealing lids
¼ cup sugar	
2¼ quarts water	
2 tablespoons whole mixed pickling spice	
⅓ cup whole mustard seed	
12 to 14 cloves garlic	
2 dozen heads fresh or dried dill or ½ cup dried dill seed	

1. Wash the cucumbers well, scrubbing thoroughly with a brush. Leave just a tiny bit of stem end but be sure to cut off the blossom completely. Drain the cucumbers.
2. Combine 2 gallons water and 1½ cups salt to form the brine. Pour the brine over the pickles in a large enamel or glass container and let it stand overnight.
3. Drain.
4. Measure the vinegar, ¾ cup salt, sugar and 2¼ quarts water into a large kettle or pot. Tie the whole mixed pickling spice in a cheesecloth bag. Add it to the kettle and heat to boiling.

Fresh-pack Dills: Step 7

84

5. Pack the cucumbers in clean, hot quart jars.
6. Put about 2 teaspoons of mustard seed, 1 or 2 garlic cloves and 3 heads of fresh dill or 1 tablespoon of dried dill seed in each quart jar.
7. Remove the spice bag from the kettle; then pour the boiling liquid into the cucumber-filled jars to within ½ inch of the top.
8. Follow the Basic Steps 6 through 12. Process in a boiling water-bath for 20 minutes. Continue Basic Steps 13 through 17.

8. Combine the sugar, vinegar, and spices in a large pot or kettle. Heat to boiling.
9. Add the cucumber and onion slices and cook over high heat for 5 minutes.
10. Pack into clean hot pint jars to within ½ inch of top.
11. Follow Basic Steps 6 through 12. Process in a boiling water bath for 5 minutes. Continue Basic Steps 13 through 17.

◆◆◆◆◆◆◆◆◆◆◆◆◆◆◆◆◆◆◆◆◆◆◆◆

CRISP PICKLE SLICES

These fragrant pickles are packed with onion slices. The recipe makes 7 pints.

Ingredients	Equipment
6 pounds medium size pickling cucumbers	See Basic Equipment
1 pound small white onions	Vegetable brush
2 large garlic cloves	Knife
⅓ cup salt	Large enamel or glass container
4½ cups sugar	2 trays ice cubes
3 cups white vinegar	Measuring cups and spoons
2 tablespoons mustard seed	7 standard pint-size glass canning jars with two-piece self-sealing lids
1½ teaspoons turmeric	
1½ teaspoons celery seed	

1. Wash the cucumbers well, scrubbing thoroughly with a brush. Drain.
2. Cut off both ends and discard. Slice the unpeeled cucumbers ⅛- to ¼-inch thick. (You should have about 4-quarts of slices.)
3. Peel and slice onion and peel the garlic cloves.
4. Combine the cucumber slices, onion slices and garlic in large enamel or glass container.
5. Sprinkle with salt; mix thoroughly.
6. Cover with ice cubes and let it stand for 3 hours.
7. Drain thoroughly and remove the garlic cloves.

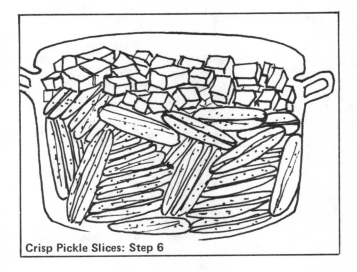

Crisp Pickle Slices: Step 6

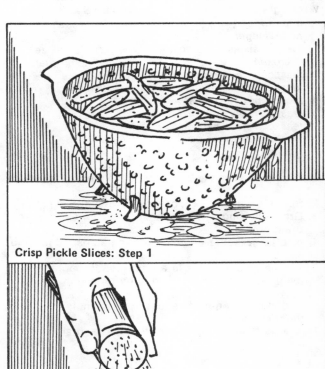

Crisp Pickle Slices: Step 1

Step 5

PEPPERY GREEN TOMATO PICKLES

Here is a perfect way to use extra green tomatoes or any green tomatoes left in the garden when the first frost comes. If you do not like them hot and spicy, reduce the amount of pepper. This recipe makes 4 pints.

Ingredients	Equipment
6 pounds green tomatoes	See Basic Equipment
¼ cup granulated salt	Wooden Spoon
3 cups sugar	Measuring cups and
2½ cups vinegar	spoons
2 (3-inch) sticks cinnamon, broken	4 standard pint-size glass canning jars with 2-piece self-sealing lids
1 teaspoon whole cloves	
1 teaspoon whole allspice	
1½ teaspoons celery seed	
1¼ teaspoons dry mustard	
1 teaspoon black pepper	
1 teaspoon cayenne pepper	

1. Wash and stem the tomatoes. Slice them into a large kettle.
2. Sprinkle with the salt, cover and let stand overnight.
3. Drain thoroughly, then rinse with cold water and drain again.
4. In a large kettle combine the tomatoes, sugar and vinegar.
5. Tie the whole spices in a cheesecloth bag and add them to the kettle along with the remaining seasonings.
6. Add more vinegar, if necessary, to completely cover the tomatoes.
7. Heat to boiling; then lower the heat and simmer for

about 30 minutes, stirring occasionally with a wooden spoon to prevent sticking.

8. Remove the spice bag and pack the tomatoes into 4 clean, hot pint jars as directed in Basic Steps 4 through 12. Process in a boiling water-bath for 5 minutes. Continue Basic Steps 13 through 17.

◆◆◆◆◆◆◆◆◆◆◆◆◆◆◆◆◆◆◆◆◆◆◆◆◆◆◆◆◆◆◆

DILLY BEANS

Dilly beans are a favorite at luncheons. Even kids enjoy these crisp green beans. The recipe makes 3 pints.

Ingredients	Equipment
2 pounds fresh green beans	See Basic Equipment
3 cups white vinegar	3 standard pint-size glass canning jars with 2-piece self-sealing lids
3 cups water	
¼ cup pure granulated salt	
4 cloves garlic, split	Saucepan
1½ teaspoons dill seed or 3 sprays fresh dill weed	Measuring cups and spoons
1 teaspoon cayenne pepper	

1. Wash the beans well. Remove the ends and trim so they will fit, standing upright, in the pint jars.
2. Pack them into the clean hot jars.
3. Measure all remaining ingredients into a saucepan and heat to boiling.
4. Pour the boiling liquid into jars, filling to within ½ inch of top.
5. Proceed as in Basic Steps 6 through 12. Process in a boiling water-bath for 10 minutes. Continue Basic Steps 13 through 17.

◆◆◆◆◆◆◆◆◆◆◆◆◆◆◆◆◆◆◆◆◆◆◆◆◆◆◆◆◆◆◆

PICKLED CAULIFLOWER

Crisp and spicy, Pickled Cauliflower is perfect for relish trays or gift-giving. The recipe makes 2 to 3 pints, depending on the size of the cauliflower.

Ingredients	Equipment
1 medium head cauliflower	See Basic Equipment
2 to 3 hot red peppers	Measuring cups and spoons
2½ cups vinegar	2 or 3 pint-size glass jars with two-piece, self-sealing lids
2½ cups water	
¼ cup pure granulated salt	
1 teaspoon garlic powder	Saucepan

1. Wash the cauliflower and separate it into flowerets.
2. Pack the flowerets into clean hot pint jars.
3. Slice or chop the peppers and divide among the jars of cauliflower.
4. Measure all the remaining ingredients into a saucepan and heat to boiling.
5. Cover and simmer for 10 minutes.
6. Pour the liquid over the cauliflower in the jars to within ½ inch of the top.
7. Follow Basic Steps 7 through 12. Process in a boiling water-bath for 10 minutes. Continue Basic Steps 13 through 17.

4. Cover and simmer for 15 minutes.
5. Pack into clean hot pint jars as in Basic Steps 4 through 12. Process in boiling water-bath 10 minutes continue Basic Steps 13 through 17.

◆◆◆◆◆◆◆◆◆◆◆◆◆◆◆◆◆◆◆◆◆◆◆◆◆◆◆◆◆◆◆◆

CRISPY PICKLED ONIONS

Crispy Pickled Onions are great for snacking or for making your own Gibsons. Makes 4 pints.

Ingredients	Equipment
3 quarts small whole white onions	See Basic Equipment Measuring cups and spoons
3 cups vinegar	
3 cups water	4 standard pint glass canning jars with two-piece, self-sealing lids
¼ cup sugar	
1 teaspoon salt	
	Saucepan

1. Peel the onions and wash well.
2. Pack them loosely into 4 clean, hot pint jars.
3. Measure the vinegar and remaining ingredients into a saucepan and heat to boiling.
4. Cover and simmer for 20 minutes.
5. Pour the liquid over the onions in the jars to within ½ inch of the top.
6. Proceed as in Basic Steps 6 through 12. Process in a boiling water-bath 10 minutes. Continue Basic Steps 13 through 17.

◆◆◆◆◆◆◆◆◆◆◆◆◆◆◆◆◆◆◆◆◆◆◆◆◆◆◆◆◆◆◆◆

WATERMELON RIND PICKLES

You will need the rind from half a large watermelon. Cut out the fruit, wrap and refrigerate it for later use. Or, save watermelon rind from meals or picnics; keep the rind in a plastic bag in the refrigerator until you have enough to pickle. Cooking time depends on the tenderness of the melon rind. Early summer melons will be more tender and cook more quickly than later melons. This recipe makes 2 pint jars or 4 half-pint jars.

Ingredients	Equipment
2 quarts cubed watermelon rind	See Basic Equipment Measuring cups and spoons
1 quart water	
3 tablespoons salt	Colander or strainer
1 quart water	2 standard pint-size (or 4 half-pint size) glass canning jars with 2-piece self-sealing lids
1 pint white vinegar	
5 cups sugar	
5 (3-inch) sticks cinnamon, broken	
5 teaspoons whole cloves	
5 teaspoons whole allspice	

1. Cut the green rind and all the pink edges from half a watermelon. Cut the rind in 1-inch cubes or fancy shapes and then measure enough for 2 quarts.

PICKLED MUSHROOMS

Slice any large mushrooms, but leave small mushrooms whole. Pickled Mushrooms are delicious with homemade smoked shrimp or oysters. The recipe makes about 3 pints, depending on size of the mushrooms.

Ingredients	Equipment
1 pound fresh mushrooms	See Basic Equipment
1 large onion, thinly sliced	Large saucepan
1 clove garlic, minced	Measuring cups and spoons
2 cups white vinegar	
2 cups water	3 pint-size glass jars with two-piece self-sealing lids
½ cup olive oil	
1 bay leaf	
1 teaspoon powdered thyme	
½ teaspoon pepper	

1. Wash the mushrooms well. Cut off the tough end of the stem. Slice, if large.
2. Put the onions, mushrooms, and garlic in a large saucepan.
3. Measure the remaining ingredients. Add them to the saucepan and heat to boiling.

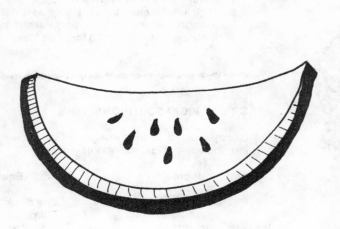
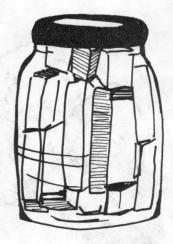

2. Wash the rind and put it in a large bowl.
3. Combine 1 quart water and the salt; pour over the rind in the bowl and let it stand overnight.
4. Drain the rind, rinse with cold water, then put the rind in a large kettle.
5. Add enough water to cover. Simmer for 30 minutes.
6. Drain well.
7. Heat 1 quart of water to boiling.
8. While it is heating, tie the spices in a small cheesecloth bag; then add it to the boiling water with the vinegar and sugar. Stir until the sugar dissolves; then boil for 5 minutes longer.
9. Pour the syrup over the watermelon rind and let it stand overnight.
10. Heat the rind and syrup to boiling and simmer about 10 minutes or until the rind becomes translucent. Remove the spice bag.
11. Pack into 2 hot, clean pint jars (or 4 half-pint jars) as in Basic Steps 4 through 12. Process in a boiling water-bath for 5 minutes. Continue Basic Steps 13 through 17.

NOTE: you may skip Basic Steps 8 and 9. Instead, simmer the rind in syrup until tender — anywhere from 1½ to 4 hours. Pack in jars following the other Basic Steps.

◆◆◆◆◆◆◆◆◆◆◆◆◆◆◆◆◆◆◆◆◆◆◆◆◆

PICKLED EGGS

Pickled Eggs are hard-cooked eggs that are refrigerated in vinegar, salt and spices. They are delicious in salads, at barbecues and on picnics. No boiling water-bath process is necessary since the eggs are kept in the refrigerator. You can vary the spices to suit your own taste. Mix and match flavors as you wish — the only limit is what you have on your spice shelf. The recipe is for one dozen eggs.

Ingredients	Equipment
1 dozen medium eggs	Large saucepan
3 cups cider vinegar	Measuring cups and
1 tablespoon sugar	spoons
1 teaspoon salt	1 standard quart-size jar
1 teaspoon pepper	with 2-piece, self-
1 teaspoon mixed pickling	sealing lid
spice	

1. Put the eggs in saucepan; cover with cold water. Heat slowly to boiling.
2. Reduce heat, cover and simmer for 15 minutes.
3. Cool the eggs under cold running water. Roll the eggs gently between your palms to crack the shell. Peel them.
4. Pack the peeled eggs into the quart jar.
5. Combine all remaining ingredients in a saucepan and heat to boiling. Reduce the heat and simmer for 5 minutes.
6. Pour the liquid over the eggs in the jar.
7. Seal the jar and refrigerate.
8. Let the eggs "season" in the refrigerator at least a week before serving. Lift the eggs out of the jar to serve. Pickled eggs will keep several months in their pickling solution in the refrigerator.

NOTE: You can add beet juice for bright purple eggs, dill seed, mustard seed, liquid smoke, garlic, onion, brown sugar or almost any other seasonings to the pickling mixture.

SAUERKRAUT

You may think sauerkraut is German because of the name, but this tart and tangy fermented cabbage is really Chinese in origin. Workers building the Great Wall of China ate fermented cabbage and rice. Try it hot with some cooked apple slices, caraway seed and perhaps just a whiff of white wine, or cold with chopped celery, onion and green pepper as a slaw. Our recipe is for a small batch that you can manage in even a tiny kitchen; it makes 2 quarts.

Ingredients	Equipment
5 pounds firm-headed cabbage 5 tablespoons salt	*Sharp knife and/or kraut or other shredder* *Large mixing bowl* *1- to 2-gallon crock* *Clean cloth or plastic bag* *Plate or other round flat object that will fit snugly inside the crock* *Wooden spoon* *Weight to hold plate down (jar of water, clean block of wood, rock or brick)*

1. Remove the outer leaves and any bad parts of the cabbage. Cut it in quarters and remove the core.
2. Shred the cabbage with a sharp knife or shredder. The shreds should be no thicker than a dime.
3. Toss the cabbage with the salt in a large mixing bowl. Mix thoroughly.
4. Pack the cabbage firmly into the crock.
5. Let it stand several minutes, then press down firmly with a wooden spoon or your hands until juice comes to the top.
6. Cover the cabbage in the crock with a clean cloth. (See NOTE)
7. Put the plate in place over the cloth, then weight the plate to keep the cabbage under the liquid and to keep the cloth wet.
8. Set the crock where the temperature will stay between 65°F and 68°F and let it ferment about 4 weeks, checking crock daily. Skim off any mold or scum that forms. Replace scummy cloth with a clean cloth when necessary.
9. After fermentation you can store the kraut by any of the following methods: crock, refrigeration, freezing or canning.

Crock

Leave the kraut in its crock and simply move it to a cooler place, less than 60°F but above 32°F. Be sure that the top of the kraut is covered with a plastic bag or weighted plate so no air can get in. Should the top layer spoil, just throw it out and be more careful about covering kraut in the future.

Canning

Heat the finished kraut and juice in a large kettle. Simmer but do not boil. Pack the kraut into clean hot quart jars,

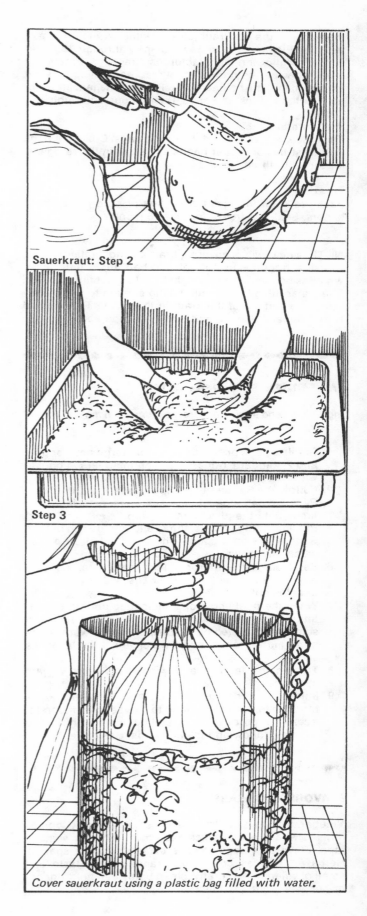

Sauerkraut: Step 2

Step 3

Cover sauerkraut using a plastic bag filled with water.

then pour in the hot kraut juice to within ½ inch of top of jar. (See Pickled Foods, Basic Steps 7 through 12.) Seal with lids, following manufacturer's directions. Process in a boiling water-bath for 20 minutes. Start timing as soon as jars go into the boiling water. Remove the jars and cool as directed in Pickled Foods, Basic Steps 3 through 17.

Refrigeration
Pack the kraut in heavy-duty plastic bags. Close the bags with twist-ties or rubber bands and store in the refrigerator for up to three months.

Freezing
Pack the kraut in glass freezer jars or rigid plastic containers. Seal and freeze for up to 6 months.

NOTE: a new way of covering kraut during fermentation is to use a large heavy-duty plastic bag about half full of water as both cover and weight to hold kraut under liquid. The water-filled bag should be big enough to completely cover the surface of the kraut in the crock. This method would replace Steps 6 and 7 of the recipe above.

JAR-FERMENTED SAUERKRAUT

Ingredients and equipment are the same as in the Sauerkraut recipe.

1. Sterilize knife or shredder, spoon, large bowl or pan, and 2 standard 1-quart glass canning jars in boiling water.
2. Follow the Sauerkraut recipe, Steps 1, 2 and 3.
3. Pack the cabbage into the quart jars, pressing down firmly until the juice comes to top.
4. Put lids on the jars just firmly enough to keep out air.
5. Set the jars on a cookie sheet or in shallow pan to catch any leaks.
6. Set them aside at room temperature for about 2 weeks or until bubbling stops. Discard any juice that bubbles out.
7. When the bubbling stops, indicating end of fermentation, check to be sure both jars are full of juice. If some has bubbled out, replace it with a warm weak brine made from 1 quart water and 2 tablespoons salt.
8. Tighten the jar lids and wipe the outside of jars clean.
9. Mildly-flavored kraut will take about 2 weeks. For a tarter taste, let it cure for up to 10 weeks. Refrigerate, freeze or process in a boiling waterbath for 15 minutes, following Pickled Foods, Basic Steps.

FLAVORED VINEGARS

Vinegar, the basis of almost every salad dressing, can be infused with a whole spice-cabinet of different seasonings. Flavored vinegar makes salad dressings sparkle. Herbs and spices completely transform the taste and smell of vinegar. Any pretty, clean bottle can hold vinegar or become a gift container.

Ingredients	Equipment
Regular, cider or white wine vinegar	Glass bottle, jar or vinegar cruet
Any of the following herbs: Sprigs of fresh parsley, dill, sage, thyme, marjoram, fennel, anise, tarragon, mint, sage, chervil, savory or any other herb that grows in your garden.	

1. Pour the vinegar into a bottle and add an herb of your choice.
2. Cork or cover the bottle and let it stand in a cool place for two or three weeks to steep.
3. Remove the herbs or strain the vinegar, if you wish. Some herbs look decorative when left floating in the bottle.

For a fiercely hot vinegar, fill a small bottle with fresh cayenne pepper, or any small hot pepper, and pour in vinegar. Let it steep for a few days. When you have used all the hot vinegar on spinach, greens and other vegetables, just add more vinegar to the remaining peppers. The peppers are hot enough to season several refills of vinegar.

You can use dried herbs if fresh ones are not available. Use 1 teaspoon of dried herb for each pint of vinegar. Let it steep for a week, then taste and alter the amount of herb to please your palate.

CATSUP

This recipe makes a little less than 1 quart of catsup, depending on the size tomatoes you use. You will not need to bottle and process this amount, just pour it into a refrigerator container and keep it chilled.

Ingredients	Equipment
¼ cup white or cider vinegar	Measuring cups and spoons
1 (3-inch) stick cinnamon, broken in small pieces	Custard cup
½ teaspoon whole cloves	Saucepan
½ teaspoon celery seed	Wooden spoon
6 large ripe tomatoes	Sieve or food mill
½ cup water	Blender
¼ cup minced onion	Small strainer
3 tablespoons sugar	Knife
1 teaspoon salt	Refrigerator container
Dash cayenne pepper	

1. Measure the vinegar, cinnamon, cloves and celery seed into a saucepan and boil 1 minute. Remove them from the heat, pour into a custard cup or other container and set aside.
2. Cut the stems from the tomatoes and quarter them into a saucepan. Add the water and onion and heat to boiling. Stir with a wooden spoon to mash the tomatoes.
3. Lower the heat and simmer, stirring occasionally to prevent sticking, about 20 minutes.

Catsup: Step 6

4. Press through a sieve or food mill. If you do not mind chunky catsup with a few seeds, blend the catsup in a blender.
5. Return the puree to the saucepan, stir in the sugar, salt and pepper and simmer, stirring occasionally to prevent sticking, about 30 to 45 minutes or until reduced to about ½ its original volume.
6. Strain the vinegar-spice mixture into the catsup and simmer another 10 to 30 minutes, depending on how thick you would like your catsup.
7. Remove from the heat and cool.
8. Store in the refrigerator in a clean container with a tight-fitting lid.

◆◆◆◆◆◆◆◆◆◆◆◆◆◆◆◆◆◆◆◆◆

CREAMY MUSTARD SAUCE

Select a small covered container to become your special mustard pot. After you taste this sauce you will always want some on hand in the refrigerator. The recipe makes about ¾ cup.

Ingredients	Equipment
¼ cup mustard seed	Measuring cups and
½ cup vinegar	spoons
¼ cup water	Blender
2 tablespoons flour	Rubber spatula
2 teaspoons sugar	Small saucepan
½ teaspoon salt	Refrigerator container
¼ teaspoon celery seed	with cover
⅛ teaspoon ground nutmeg	
⅛ teaspoon turmeric	

1. Grind the mustard seed in a blender at medium speed about 5 seconds.
2. Add the vinegar and water and blend at high speed until smooth.
3. Pour into a small saucepan; stir in the remaining ingredients and cook and stir over medium-low heat just until mixture comes to a boil and thickens.
4. Pour the mustard into a container, cover and refrigerate.

MAYONNAISE

Before the days of the electric blender only Cordon Bleu cooks would tackle making mayonnaise at home. Adding oil drop by drop to beaten egg yolks to form an emulsion was once too tricky for average cooks. But the blender changed all that. The only skills making mayonnaise now requires are patience and a steady hand. You must add the oil very slowly. Mistakes are easily repaired. If your mayonnaise curdles, pour it out of the blender into a custard cup, whip another egg or egg yolk in the blender. Then, while the blender is running, gradually add the curdled mixture through the opening in the top of the blender's cover. The recipe makes one cup of mayonnaise.

Ingredients	Equipment
1 egg or 2 egg yolks	Measuring cup (glass)
1 tablespoon red wine	Measuring spoons
vinegar, white wine	Blender
vinegar, herb-flavored	Rubber spatula
vinegar or lemon juice	Refrigerator container
½ to 1 teaspoon dry	with tight fitting lid
mustard	
½ teaspoon salt	
½ cup salad oil	
½ cup olive oil	

1. Put the egg or egg yolks in a blender and blend at high speed for 10 seconds or until frothy.
2. Add the vinegar, mustard and salt and blend at medium speed for a little more than a minute, very slowly adding oil in a fine, even stream while the blender is running.
3. Use a rubber spatula to remove all the mayonnaise from the blender's container. Put the mayonnaise in a refrigerator container and refrigerate until ready to use. Mayonnaise will keep about 2 weeks in the refrigerator.

◆◆◆◆◆◆◆◆◆◆◆◆◆◆◆◆◆◆◆◆◆

VARIATIONS

Herb Mayonnaise

Add 2 or 3 sprigs of washed fresh herbs such as parsley, chives, dill, marjoram, tarragon, basil, thyme or oregano to the egg before blending. Or use about ½ teaspoon of a dried herb.

Bloody Mary Mayonnaise

Prepare the mayonnaise as the recipe directs, then stir in 1 tablespoon of tomato paste, ½ teaspoon each lime or lemon juice and Worchestershire sauce, ¼ teaspoon each dill and celery seed and a dash of hot pepper sauce.

Curry Mayonnaise

Prepare the mayonnaise as recipe directs, then stir in 1 tablespoon curry powder, 1 tablespoon cider vinegar, 2 teaspoons crumbled dried onion and 1 teaspoon garlic powder.

Liqueurs, Cordials, & Bounces

"Behold this cordial julep here/ That flames and dances in his crystal bounds,/ with spirits of balmy fragrant syrups mixed."

Milton's verse gives away the cherished recipe for liqueurs and cordials. The basic recipe is one of the best kept secrets of the liquor industry. Flavored spirits are priced luxury items — but they are just spirits (brandy, vodka, Scotch or grain alcohol) mixed with flavored syrup. Some of the recipes for flavorings are closely guarded secrets: Drambui, Chartreuse and Benedictine cannot be reproduced. But you can come very close to the original by using commercial extracts. They are easy to make and cost much less than the original liqueur.

Liqueurs and cordials are two words for the same kind of drink. When you feel like being formal and very chic, call the drink a liqueur; when you feel like being cozy and informal, call the drink a cordial.

Bounces, old-fashioned after-dinner drinks made by steeping fresh fruit in spirits, are delicious plain or made into dessert sauces.

Liqueurs and bounces add a gracious touch to your dinners. Your guests will bask in an atmosphere of warmth and friendship when you serve them one of these distinctively flavored elixirs. Liqueurs were the result of medieval and Renaissance distillers trying to concoct love potions, cure-alls and life-prolonging drugs. No wonder you feel warm and relaxed when you sip a liqueur after dinner! There is something hypnotic about an aromatic drink the color of stained glass windows shimmering in a small glass. You can make a whole sorcerer's cabinet of magic potions by following the simple recipes in this chapter.

To make a liqueur at home all you do is stir the alcohol and sugared flavoring together. Commercial manufacturers use a fancier means to make liqueurs and cordials: percolation. They put the flavorings into the top part of a coffee pot apparatus and the spirits in the bottom part. Then they heat the pot until the spirits and flavorings "perk." Sometimes just the alcohol vapors pass through the flavorings and then recondense inside the pot.

We have discovered a way to make instant liqueurs with sugared commercial extracts. So, enjoy a Creme de Menthe, a Drambui type liqueur, a Blackberry Brandy or Cherry Bounce. They are simple to mix, economical and they make any dinner an important event.

Basic Equipment

1. **Quart sauce pan or larger pan**
2. **Measuring spoons**
3. **Measuring cup**
4. **Large spoon for stirring**
5. **Empty fifth, 1-quart liqueur or liquor bottle.** (A fifth equals 25.4 ounces. A quart is 32 ounces.)

Basic Ingredients

1. **Spirits.** Vodka, gin, brandy, Scotch or grain alcohol — different liqueurs are based on different spirits. Cherry Heering is based on brandy; Creme de Menthe is based on grain alcohol or vodka; Drambui

is based on Scotch. Check the recipe for the appropriate spirit. The amount of spirit used depends on size of decanter or bottle you use. A fifth is 25.4 ounces and a quart is 32 ounces. With either size you will probably have a couple ounces left over because of the additional ingredients.

2. **Sugar.** Use white granulated sugar.
3. **Water.** Water is usually used for the sugar syrup mixture. Occasionally sugar is added without water. Recipes for bounces call for dry sugar poured directly on the fruit. If your tap water has a strong mineral or chlorine taste, use bottled water.
4. **Fruit Extracts.** Extensive research and experimenting have successfully duplicated the extracts of famous liqueurs. Take advantage of these commercial extracts; you cannot come as close to the original liqueurs experimenting on your own. A French line of extracts, Noirot, is reliable. New brands of extracts frequently appear; consult with a home winemaking shop for further information.

ADDITIONAL INGREDIENTS

1. **Glycerine.** Food grade glycerine adds body and smoothness to a liqueur. Some recipes call for glycerine; in other recipes it is optional.
2. **Food coloring.** When an extract lacks color, the recipe sometimes calls for food coloring. Food coloring does not add to the taste of a liqueur, only to its appearance.

BASIC STEPS

1. Make a sugar syrup either in a sweet strength or a medium strength as follows:

LIQUEURS

Basic Step 1

Basic Step 5

Basic Step 4

Basic Step 7

Sweet Syrup
2 cups white granulated sugar
1 cup water

Medium Syrup
1 cup sugar
½ cup water

The strength of syrup will depend upon the recipe. Some cordials such as Blackberry Brandy or Apricot Brandy require no sugar syrup. Put the sugar and water in a saucepan and bring it just to a boil.

2. Cool the sugar syrup a few minutes.
3. Thoroughly clean your liqueur or liquor bottle. You do not have to sterilize it.

4. Pour the required amount of syrup into the bottle.
5. Pour in the required amount of extract.
6. If glycerine or food coloring are called for, add them now.
7. Fill the bottle to the top with whatever spirits you are using. You will need to purchase a fifth or quart of spirit; there will be a couple ounces left over because of the additional ingredients. Since there is nearly a seven ounce difference between a fifth and a quart, a liqueur made with a quart of spirit will have a stronger alcoholic taste than a liqueur made with a fifth of spirit. Let your preference be your guide.
8. Put the top on the bottle and shake the bottle until all the ingredients are thoroughly mixed.
9. Let the liqueur cool before drinking.

RECIPES

Liqueurs From Extracts

All the following recipes follow the Basic Steps and use the Basic Equipment.

◆◆◆◆◆◆◆◆◆◆◆◆◆◆◆◆◆◆◆◆◆◆◆◆◆◆◆◆◆◆

GREEN ANISETTE

This liqueur is licorice flavored and bright green.

Ingredients	Equipment
2 cups sugar syrup — sweet	See Basic Equipment
1 bottle Noirot Green Anisette Extract	
1 fifth or 1 quart of vodka or grain alcohol	

Follow the Basic Steps

◆◆◆◆◆◆◆◆◆◆◆◆◆◆◆◆◆◆◆◆◆◆◆◆◆◆◆◆◆◆

WHITE ANISETTE

Water-clear, White Anisette is lightly licorice flavored.

Ingredients	Equipment
2 cups sugar syrup — sweet	See Basic Equipment
1 bottle Noirot White Anisette Extract	
1 fifth or 1 quart of vodka or grain alcohol	

Follow Basic Steps 3-9

APRICOT BRANDY

Apricot Brandy is one of the most popular flavored brandies. You use no sugar in this recipe.

Ingredients	Equipment
1 bottle Noirot Apricot Brandy Extract	See Basic Equipment
1 fifth or 1 quart of brandy	

Follow Basic Steps 3-9

◆◆◆◆◆◆◆◆◆◆◆◆◆◆◆◆◆◆◆◆◆◆◆◆◆◆◆◆◆◆

BLACKBERRY BRANDY

When cold weather rolls around, try this old-time favorite "warmer-upper" — Blackberry Brandy. The recipe uses no sugar.

Ingredients	Equipment
1 bottle Noirot Blackberry Brandy Extract	See Basic Equipment
1 fifth or 1 quart of brandy	

Follow the Basic Steps

BENEDICTINE TYPE LIQUEUR

Here is one of the oldest liqueurs; it has a carefully guarded secret formula. You cannot duplicate it exactly, but you will come fairly close with this recipe.

Ingredients	Equipment
1 bottle Noirot Reverendine Extract	See Basic Equipment
8 ounces sugar syrup — medium	
1 fifth or 1 quart of brandy	

Follow the Basic Steps

B & B TYPE LIQUEUR

A drier version of Benedictine Type, B & B Type Liqueur uses no sugar.

Ingredients	Equipment
1 bottle Noirot Reverendine Extract	See Basic Equipment
½ bottle Noirot French Yellow Brandy Extract	
1 fifth or 1 quart of brandy	

Follow Basic Steps

CHERRY BRANDY

Here is another favorite fruit-flavored brandy.

Ingredients	Equipment
1 bottle Noirot Cherry Brandy Extract	See Basic Equipment
1 cup sugar syrup — medium	
1 fifth or 1 quart of brandy	

Follow the Basic Steps

COINTREAU TYPE

You will relish this fine Triple Sec type liqueur. It is flavored with dried green orange peels from Curacao. This liqueur is what gives Spanish sangria its zing.

Ingredients	Equipment
1 bottle Noirot Orange Triple Dry Extract	See Basic Equipment
1 cup sugar syrup — medium	
1 fifth or 1 quart of vodka or grain alcohol	

Follow the Basic Steps

GREEN CHARTREUSE TYPE

Chartreuse is a famous liqueur made by a French religious group from their carefully guarded secret formula.

Ingredients	Equipment
1 bottle Noirot Green Convent Extract	See Basic Equipment
1 cup sugar syrup — medium	
1 fifth or 1 quart of vodka or grain alcohol	

Follow the Basic Steps

CREME DE BANANA

If you like bananas, you will love this banana flavored drink. A pretty yellow, Creme de Banana can form the base of many exotic drinks.

Ingredients	Equipment
1 bottle Noirot Banana Extract	See Basic Equipment
2 cups sugar syrup — sweet	
1 fifth or 1 quart of grain alcohol	

Follow the Basic Steps

CREME DE CASSIS TYPE

This liqueur is flavored with black currants.

Ingredients	Equipment
1 bottle Noirot Black Currant Extract	See Basic Equipment
2 cups sugar syrup — sweet	
1 fifth or 1 quart of vodka or grain alcohol	

Follow the Basic Steps

CREME DE COCOA

Cocoa dominates the taste of this delightful liqueur.

Ingredients	Equipment
1 bottle Noirot Cocoa Extract	See Basic Equipment
2 cups sugar syrup — sweet	
1 fifth or 1 quart of vodka or grain alcohol	

Follow the Basic Steps

CREME DE MENTHE

Many people love a Creme de Menthe frappe — it is so refreshing. You can also use this liqueur in another popular "creme" drink — the Grasshopper.

Ingredients	Equipment
1 bottle Noirot Green Mint	See Basic Equipment
2 cups sugar syrup — sweet	
1 fifth or 1 quart of vodka or grain alcohol	

Follow the Basic Steps

CREME DE NOYAU

This liqueur has a bitter almond taste — from the kernels of fruit pits, not almonds.

Ingredients	Equipment
1 bottle Noirot Sweet Almond Extract	See Basic Equipment
2 cups sugar syrup — sweet	
1 fifth or 1 quart of vodka or grain alcohol	

Follow the Basic Steps

GOLDWASSER or DANTZIGER TYPE

From Germany, Goldwasser is flavored with orange peels that make tiny flecks of floating "gold."

Ingredients	Equipment
1 bottle Noirot Dantzig Extract	See Basic Equipment
2 cups sugar syrup — sweet	
1 fifth or 1 quart of vodka or grain alcohol	

Follow the Basic Steps

KUMMEL TYPE LIQUEUR

"Kummel" is German for caraway seeds. Caraway seeds supply the main flavor for this liqueur.

Ingredients	Equipment
1 bottle Noirot Kummel Extract	See Basic Equipment
2 cups sugar syrup — sweet	
1 fifth or 1 quart of vodka or grain alcohol	

Follow the Basic Steps

TIA MARIA TYPE

A Jamaican liqueur — coffee flavored and perfect over ice on hot afternoons.

Ingredients	Equipment
1 bottle Noirot Cafe Sport	See Basic Equipment
1 cup sugar syrup — medium	
1 fifth or 1 quart of rum	

Follow the Basic Steps

VANDERMINT TYPE LIQUEUR

If you like the flavor of chocolate and mint combined, Vandermint Type Liqueur is for you. You can use it in desserts, too.

Ingredients	Equipment
1 bottle Noirot Chocolate Mint Extract	See Basic Equipment
10 ounces sugar syrup — sweet	
1 fifth or 1 quart of vodka	

Follow the Basic Steps

KAHLUA TYPE LIQUEUR

Mexico's contribution to sophisticated after dinner drinks, Kahlua Type Liqueur is coffee flavored. You can make a sinfully rich mocha sauce with this liqueur.

Ingredients	Equipment
1 bottle Noirot Moka Extract	See Basic Equipment
2 ounces glycerine	
12 ounces sugar syrup — sweet	
¼ teaspoon Noirot Vanilla Extract	
1 fifth or 1 quart of vodka	

Follow the Basic Steps

CHERRY HEERING TYPE

Here is an outstanding reddish brown cherry liqueur. The true Cherry Heering is made in Denmark by the Peter Heering firm. It is a traditional holiday favorite. Try it poured over ice cream.

Ingredients	Equipment
1 bottle Noirot Cherry Brandy Extract	See Basic Equipment
½ teaspoon Noirot Vanilla Extract	
10 ounces sugar syrup — sweet	
1 ounce glycerine	
1 fifth or 1 quart of brandy	

Follow the Basic Steps

SWISS CHOCOLATE CHERRY

This tastes like a liquid version of a chocolate covered cherry. Delicious!

Ingredients	Equipment
½ bottle Noirot Cocoa Extract	See Basic Equipment
½ bottle Noirot Cherry Brandy Extract	
2 ounces glycerine	
1 fifth or 1 quart of vodka	

Follow the Basic Steps

VARIATION I

Here is another way to concoct quick liqueurs or cordials.

Steps for Variation I

1. Put all ingredients into the bottle except the dry sugar and the spirit.
2. Add one cup of the spirit.
3. Pour in the dry sugar.
4. Shake the bottle back and forth a bit to wet the sugar.
5. Fill the bottle to the top with the spirits.
6. Continue to shake the bottle for 15 minutes or more, until the cordial is very clear.
7. Cool before serving.

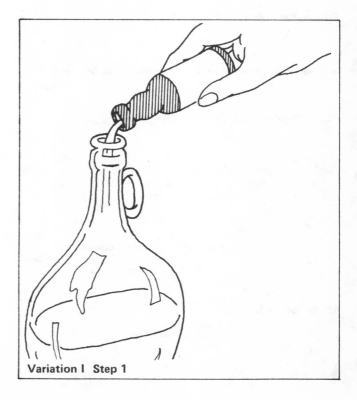

Variation I Step 1

GALLIANO TYPE

This drink tastes like the famous Italian licorice-flavored liqueur. It is bright yellow.

Ingredients	Equipment
1 bottle Noirot Yellow Genepy Extract	*See Basic Equipment*
2 ounces glycerine	
3 drops yellow food coloring	
1½ cups dry granulated sugar	
1 fifth or 1 quart of vodka	

Follow the steps for Variation I

◆◆◆◆◆◆◆◆◆◆◆◆◆◆◆◆◆◆◆◆◆◆◆◆◆◆◆◆◆◆

DRAMBUI TYPE

The origin of this liqueur is Scottish and made from a secret formula. But, you can make a drink astonishingly similar to the authentic liqueur.

Ingredients	Equipment
1 bottle Noirot Lorbuis Extract	*See Basic Equipment*
Dry white granulated sugar to taste, starting with ¼ cup	
1 fifth or 1 quart of Scotch	

Follow the steps for Variation I

◆◆◆◆◆◆◆◆◆◆◆◆◆◆◆◆◆◆◆◆◆◆◆◆◆◆◆◆◆◆

VARIATION II — INSTANT LIQUEURS

This is an even quicker method of making liqueurs. You can make a single glass or a fifth of the following liqueurs — or experiment with other extracts. Be sure you are using an extract containing sugar.

Ingredients	Equipment
Extract containing sugar	Fifth or quart liquor bottle, or single glass
Spirits	Measuring cup

Steps for Variation II.

1. Wash out a liqueur or liquor bottle or even just a glass.
2. Mix equal parts of the extract with equal parts of the spirit.

DRAMBUI TYPE

Mix equal parts Creative Cordials Scotch Heather Extract and Scotch.

◆◆◆◆◆◆◆◆◆◆◆◆◆◆◆◆◆◆◆◆◆◆◆◆◆◆◆◆◆◆

GALLIANO TYPE

Mix equal parts Creative Cordials Italian Gold Extract and vodka.

◆◆◆◆◆◆◆◆◆◆◆◆◆◆◆◆◆◆◆◆◆◆◆◆◆◆◆◆◆◆

KAHLUA TYPE

Mix equal parts Creative Café Mexico Extract and vodka.

BOUNCES

Old-fashioned, sweet and refreshing. Bounces are made by steeping fresh fruit in spirits. They are delicious plain or made into spirited dessert sauces.

Basic Ingredients

Ripe fruit (as perfect as
   possible — no bruises
   or mold)
White granulated sugar
Spirit: 1 quart vodka, gin,
   grain alcohol, brandy
   or Scotch

Basic Equipment

Wide-mouthed ½ gallon
   jar with tight fitting lid
Measuring cup
Strainer (optional)
Funnel (optional)
Fancy decanter or
   liqueur bottle.

BASIC STEPS FOR BOUNCES

1. Wash and stem the fruit.
2. Put the fruit into a clean, wide-mouthed jar, breaking the skins of the fruit as you do so.
3. Add the sugar by pouring it directly over the fruit.
4. Pour the spirit into the jar. Do not stir.
5. Tightly cap the jar.
6. Set the filled jar aside in a cool dark place for about two months. Shake the jar a couple times a month to redistribute the sugar and juices.
7. Strain the liqueur off of the fruit into a bowl. Discard the fruit.
8. Funnel or pour the liqueur into a bottle or fancy decanter.

RASPBERRY BOUNCE

Imagine the distinctive essence of raspberries preserved in a liqueur!
One-half gallon   *Age 2 months*

Ingredients

1 quart red or black
   raspberries
2 cups white granulated
   sugar
1 fifth or quart vodka, gin,
   grain alcohol, brandy
   or Scotch

Equipment

See Basic Equipment
for Bounces

Follow the Basic Steps for Bounces

CHERRY BOUNCE

Cherry Bounce is bright red. Make it in late summer and proudly serve it at Thanksgiving.
One-half gallon   *Age 2 months*

Ingredients

1 quart red sour cherries
2 cups white granulated
   sugar
1 fifth or quart vodka, gin,
   grain alcohol, brandy
   or Scotch

Equipment

See Basic Equipment
for Bounces

Follow the Basic Steps for Bounces

DAMSON PLUM BOUNCE

A good way to use your extra plums, Damson Plum Bounce will warm you on cold winter evenings.
One half-gallon   *Age 2 months*

Ingredients

1 quart Damson plums
2 cups white granulated
   sugar
1 fifth or 1 quart vodka, gin
   or grain alcohol

Equipment

See Basic Equipment
for Bounces

Follow the Basic Steps for Bounces

WINE

Everyone has a definite idea of what wine is. But, a German might explain that wine is a delicate yellow liquid that smells like early spring flowers. A Frenchman probably would wax eloquent about his beloved full-bodied, ruby red wine. An American might tell you that wine is a luxury item saved for special occasions.

If you would like to enjoy a Rhine wine, a Burgundy — even Champagne — but think you cannot afford them, consider making wine at home. For the cost of a few simple pieces of equipment, such as a polyethylene wastebasket, some modern ingredients to insure success, like sulphite sterilizers, and with the basic steps given in this chapter you can make a wide variety of wines, red, white and sparkling.

Wine from grapes was the main beverage of classical antiquity. Greeks and Romans fermented a thick sweet wine and diluted it with water for their meals. They sipped it through straws or from ornate goblets while reclining on couches; sitting upright at meals was barbarian. The northern barbarians did not adopt Roman dining manners, but they did learn to cultivate the grape. In England, King Alfred vigilantly protected vineyards from marauding Danes. And, thanks to the industrious monks in countless well-ordered monasteries throughout England and Europe, the art of winemaking, along with much of classical culture, survived to flower again during the Renaissance.

Enjoying a fine wine with your meal sometimes makes the difference between merely eating and truly dining. Flickering candlelight and shimmering jewel-red wine — that is the proper setting for poetry, song and love.

BASIC EQUIPMENT

Winemaking is like cooking. With a few basic pieces of equipment, the proper ingredients and a bit of careful attention, you can become a vintner in your own home with a great degree of success.

If you wish you may go on to more elaborate equipment; however, the following basic items will be sufficient.

1. **Beginner's book.** Before you make any wine you will need a complete up-to-date winemaking book to guide you. Choose an American publication written within the last ten years — check the copyright to make sure the book is not a reprint of an old publication. You need to know the latest American methods, equipment and procedures. This chapter will give the basic equipment, ingredients and steps as well as many superb recipes.

2. **Primary fermentor.** The primary fermentor is the first vessel used in making wine. It holds the "must" — a mixture of fruit juice, additives, sugar and water. A wastebasket or similar container is an excellent primary fermentor. Be sure it is made of polyethylene and is odorless and pale colored. Dark colored polyethylene containers will discolor the wine. The primary fermentor should be one-third larger than the amount of must: use a three-gallon primary fermentor to make one or two gallons of wine.

3. **Plastic sheet.** A plastic sheet covers the primary fermentor while the must is fermenting. This is necessary to keep out bugs, dirt, fruit flies and other unwanted objects. A sheet about a yard square and approximately 1½ to 2-mil thickness is best. The sheet should be tied loosely around the primary.

4. **Sulphite.** Two ounces of sodium metabisulphite or potassium metabisulphite, known more commonly as "sulphite," dissolved in a gallon of warm water makes enough sterilizing solution to use for three or four months, providing it retains its strong odor. The solution must be kept tightly capped or it will lose its strength. This solution is used to sterilize everything that comes into contact with the wine. It prevents the formation of mold and vinegar bacteria. To sterilize with sulphite, rinse each item with the solution and catch the solution in a bowl or large container. Pour the sulphite back into its original container and save it to use again. Sulphite is a chemical; it should be clearly labeled and locked high out of the reach of children.

5. **Stirrer.** You use a long-handled spoon or stick to stir the must throughout the winemaking process. Be certain the stirrer is plastic, wooden or stainless steel.

6. **Syphon.** The syphon transfers the must from one vessel to another. Various types of syphons are available. You can syphon with plain plastic tubing or buy any kind of syphon with rigid tubes attached or with priming bulbs on them. A five-foot length of vinyl tubing (food grade, FDA approved), ⅝-inch in diameter inside and ⅞-inch outside in diameter, syphons wine easily. There are also automatic plastic syphons that eliminate starting the prime with your mouth. These have a rubber or plastic priming bulb attached to the unit. With one squeeze of the bulb the syphoning begins. If you syphon with a plain vinyl tubing you have to suck on the end of the syphon hose to start the prime. Another self-priming syphon has a syphon hose somewhat larger than the standard size and considerably longer. On the end that goes into the primary fermentor it has a valve that is adjustable so the sediment will not be picked up. On the other end it has a self-priming bulb with a faucet-like valve. The bulb starts the prime. The valve starts the flow of the liquid when it is depressed or stops the flow when released.

Whatever syphon you choose, you put one end into the vessel containing the must then prime the other end into the empty secondary fermentor. The priming starts the flow of wine from the first container to the second.

7. **Secondary fermentor.** A secondary fermentor is used after the must has fermented in the primary fermentor for a few days. You should use a glass gallon jug for one-gallon batches or a glass five-gallon jug (car-

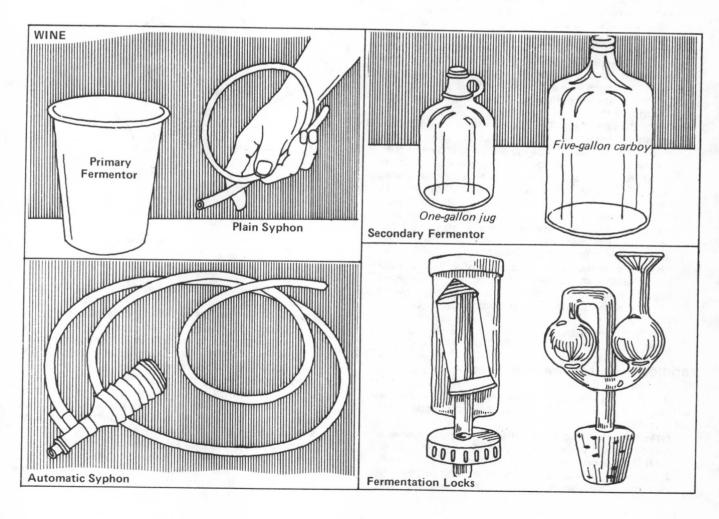

WINE

Primary Fermentor

Plain Syphon

Secondary Fermentor

One-gallon jug

Five-gallon carboy

Automatic Syphon

Fermentation Locks

boy) for five-gallon batches rather than rigid or collapsible containers. The size depends upon the quantity of wine being made. The secondary fermentor should be the same capacity as the amount of must and has to have a closed neck. The wine will remain in secondary fermentation for a period of four to five months on the average, but there will be periodic rackings (syphonings) from one secondary to another.

8. **Fermentation lock.** The fermentation lock is also known as an air lock, water trap, or water lock, air trap. A fermenttation lock fits into a rubber or cork stopper or into a plastic screw cap and attaches to the secondary fermentor. The lock allows the carbon dioxide produced to escape from the secondary fermentor and keeps out bugs and dirt. The lock should be half-filled with the sulphite sterilizing solution. There are many types of fermentation locks — glass and plastic in various shapes and sizes. Most locks are made of plastic. One basic shape — that of a small cylinder with a cap on the end — comes in assorted sizes and is called the Handy, Vinty, Hobby, Listo or Econolock. The design of the cap varies somewhat with each of these locks. Another type of plastic lock, the Vintage, looks like a pretzel with a stem on one end and a cap on the other. Or you can use a "U"-shaped glass lock that has round bulbs on the curves of the "U." Stoppers for these locks come in many styles. You can use a white rubber stopper shaped like tapered corks with a hole in the center. A number 6 or 6½ fits both one-gallon and five-gallon jugs. Or you can use a plastic screw cap with a hole in the center; this will fit most one-gallon and some half-gallon jugs. A red rubber cap with a hole in the center fits over the necks of one-gallon jugs. Larger red rubber caps fit five-gallon jugs. Rubber caps protect the entire top of the jug; most fermentation locks will fit into them.

9. **Hydrometer and jar.** The hydrometer, a scientific instrument essential for successful winemaking, measures the strength of the sugar in the wine. The hydrometer is a hollow glass bulb or cylinder weighted at the base. It extends to a long, slender, hollow, glass tube. You will see a scale printed on paper inside the tube. The hydrometer measures the natural sugar in the must, plus any sugar added to the must. The hydrometer keeps a check on the progress of fermentation and provides a control on the potential alcohol the winemaker can produce in his wine by showing the specific gravity. By using the hydrometer from the very beginning of the winemaking process, you can determine the alcohol content of your wine at the end of fermentation. The hydrometer jar is a tall, thin, plastic or glass container that floats the hydrometer in a sample taken from the must.

ADDITIONAL WINEMAKING EQUIPMENT

These additional pieces of equipment are not essential but they do make the job easier and the end product more professional.

1. **Grape crusher and apple crusher.** Using a crusher is more efficient than stomping barefooted on grapes. Best for large quantities of grapes, the crusher breaks the grapes' skins with its toothed rollers and lets the juice run out. It does not compress the

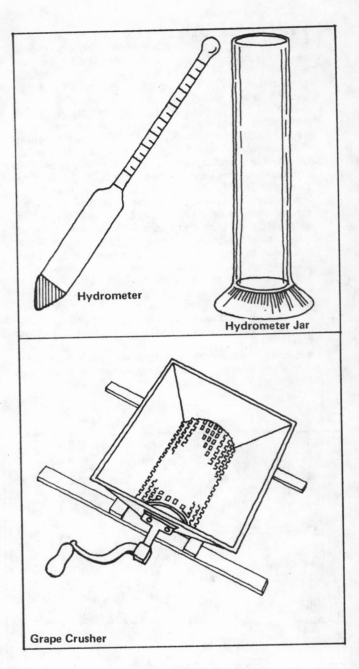

Hydrometer

Hydrometer Jar

Grape Crusher

grapes — that is the job of a grape press. The standard size for a grape crusher is 18x20 or 18x22 inches. Mini-crushers are also available.

Apples and pears require an apple crusher that is much stronger and heavier than the grape crusher. The apple crusher is helpful if you are faced with a large quantity of apples to process.

2. **Grape press.** The grape press takes over where the crusher leaves off — it compresses the grapes and extracts the juice after they have been crushed. The best grape press is a wooden container usually shaped like a basket with wooden slats to hold the grapes. You fill the basket almost to the top with grapes. The attached metal plunger has a round disc on the end that is coated to prevent the wine from reacting with the metal. When you screw down the

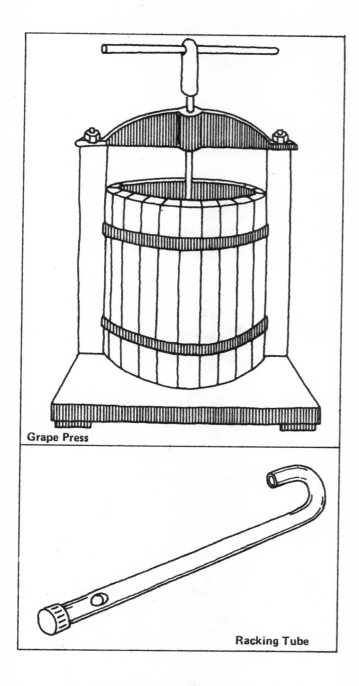

Grape Press

Racking Tube

floating particles on the first racking from the primary fermentor; they would not be needed for juice or concentrate fermentation. A strainer which will fit into a funnel is best. Funnels have many uses. They make returning the sulphite to the sulphite jug easier. They are useful for adding sugar syrup and other liquids, such as glycerine, to the wine.

5. **Vinometer.** A vinometer is a small glass instrument that measures the alcoholic content of a finished dry wine. It is useless for a sweet wine since the sugar content of the wine interferes with the reading.

6. **Thermometer.** A good thermometer is a most useful piece of additional equipment. You can make wine without it, however. An immersion-type thermometer, either floating or non-floating, is the best thermometer for winemaking. You immerse the thermometer in the must when you add the yeast or when you take a hydrometer sample. You can also use it to control your fermentation conditions by checking the room temperature.

7. **Mortar and pestle.** Use the mortar and pestle to crush additive tablets. The bulb on the end of the pestle pulverizes ingredients as you rotate it against the bowl of the mortar.

8. **Fermentation bag.** A nylon fermentation bag of a medium-close weave is a marvelous luxury for the home winemaker. Most fermentation bags hold about 20 pounds of crushed fruit depending upon the firmness of the fruit. Use the bag as a straining bag if you wish. You can entirely eliminate straining the fruit pulp from the must. All you do is place the crushed fruit, the fruit from a can of wine base, or dried ingredients inside of the bag, then tie the bag and place it in the primary fermentor to ferment along with the liquid and additives. When the recipe directs, merely take the bag out of the primary and lightly squeeze it. Then wash it out and rinse it for the next batch of wine.

9. **Racking tube.** The racking tube is a rigid plastic tube carved on one end like a hook. It can be attached to the flexible syphon hose and hooked over the edge of the primary or secondary fermentor to make syphoning easier. You can minimize the problem of picking up sediment from the bottom of the fermentor by making a hole about one inch from the end of the racking tube. The actual end has a cap on it. The wine syphons through the hole leaving most of the sediment behind.

10. **Baster.** A plastic cooking baster helps you transfer samples of must to the hydrometer jar. Or you can use it to start the prime on a syphon tube instead of using your mouth.

11. **Acid testing kit.** For those who enjoy the science of winemaking, an acid testing kit uses the titration method and contains a special strength sodium hydroxide and phenolphthalein. Follow the instructions included in the kit when first mixing your must and test before adding any additional acid. This is more important when you are using fresh fruit since the natural acid in the fruit can vary from year to year and from crop to crop.

12. **Wine thief.** A wine thief is a long glass tube that looks like an over-sized glass straw. Use it when you sample your wine; it provides a sterile way of sampling and will not disturb the wine.

13. **Wine bottles.** Wine bottles are not necessary for making wine, but they are the traditional way of stor-

plunger, the disc squashes the grape pulp and the grape juice flows down to a container below. The most commonly used grape press holds about 60 pounds of crushed fruit and sits about 20 inches high.

3. **Oak kegs.** The traditional oak kegs require continual attention to keep them free from mold, bacteria and vinegar. Unless you are very experienced and willing to devote a great amount of time to your kegs, you would do better to use glass jugs — you court failure when you use a wooden keg. However, large batches of wine made in barrels over twenty gallons in capacity stand a better chance of success than smaller batches.

4. **Strainers and funnels.** A strainer and funnel of plastic or stainless steel help you catch various

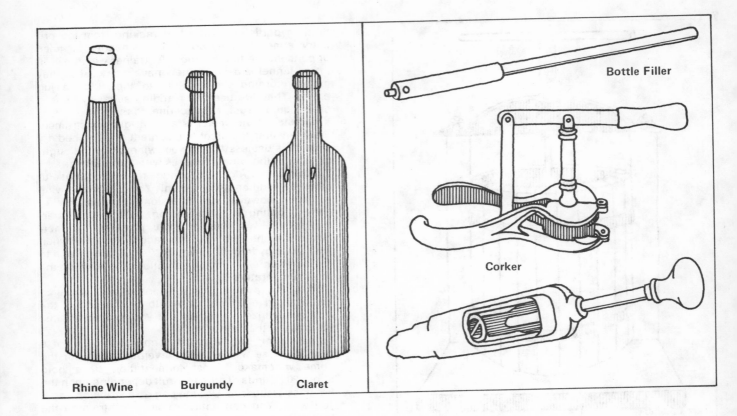

Rhine Wine   Burgundy   Claret

Bottle Filler

Corker

ing and serving wine. If you wish you can store your wine in large glass jugs in a cool, dark, dry place — but that is not very romantic. The choice of bottles is up to you. The most common selections are:

1. The green Burgundy bottle — graceful, sloped shaped — usually for Burgundy and other red wines.
2. The green Claret bottle — high shouldered — usually for Claret or Bordeaux type wines.
3. The green or amber Hock bottle — tall, slender and tapered — green for Moselle type wines and amber for Rhine type wines.
4. The amber or green Port bottle — wide and broad shouldered, sometimes squatty — for Port or dessert type wines.
5. The clear Burgundy, Claret or Hock bottle — for Rosé wines and even some red or white wines.

Available sizes run anywhere from a "split" which is a quarter bottle holding about six and one-half ounces to a Rehoboam which is about 156 ounces. The common sizes usually used by the home winemaker are:

Split, 6.5 ounces (Quarter Bottle)
Half Bottle, 13 ounces
Fifth, 25 to 26 ounces

14. **Bottle filler.** When you bottle wine, a bottle filler prevents spills and stains. It can be of plastic, metal or aluminum. The filler is a long metal tube with one end that attaches to the syphon. It has a valve for regulating the flow of wine at the other end. You use a bottle filler by attaching it to the end of the syphon. Start the prime by sucking on the end of the filler. Put the filler down into the wine bottle and push against the bottom of the bottle — this depresses the valve. Fill to the top of the bottle. When you pull out the

filler, the wine will be at the proper level for corking. Some fillers have a valve sensitive enough to release the wine without being pressed down.

15. **Corker.** A corker is not necessary for bottling in gallon jugs — you can use screw caps or a number 14 tapered cork which is put in by hand. However, a corker must be used with untapered wine corks to insure a snug fit. The cork itself has to be larger than the mouth of the bottle; the corker's job is to compress the cork and plunge it into the wine bottle. Corkers are made of wood, metal or plastic. The metal ones are easiest to handle and last the longest.

16. **Corks.** For bottling in wine bottles choose straight wine corks, T-corks, plastic wine stoppers or screw caps. Corks are the best way to bottle the wine — the wine will breathe more properly while aging in a corked bottle.

Number nine, premium first and chamfered corks fit the averaged size wine bottles. Lesser grades and

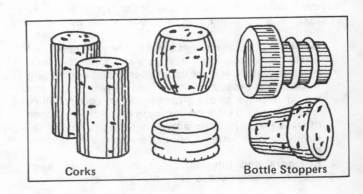

Corks   Bottle Stoppers

non-chamfered corks are also available. Number 7 corks fit Portuguese bottles, and number 8 corks fit some off-sized bottles.

17. **Wine bottle labels.** Wine bottle labels are usually sold in packages of one dozen and come pre-gummed or not pre-gummed. They are totally unnecessary, but they look classy. Many winemakers label each bottle with a piece of masking tape, but for gift-giving or serving, fancy labels are impressive.

18. **Decorative wine bottle capsules and bottle webbing.** You can dress up your bottled wine with a professional touch by putting a plastic, foil or lead capsule over the neck of the bottle. These capsules come in a variety of colors — red, gold, white, pink, blue or silver. Usually they are packed by the dozen. Straw bottle webbing, much like the kind used on commercial bottles, is available, too. The webbing goes over the wine bottle like a glove. Most webbing comes packaged in lots of ten.

19. **Wine log sheets.** Accurate record keeping insures repeated successes and prevents repeated failures. It is so easy to forget what you did many months back. A handy, efficient way to keep records is with log sheets and a loose-leaf log book. You can buy or make log sheets. Include such categories as: yeast used, specific gravity after sugar was added, date yeast was added, dates of rackings, other ingredients used and crucial steps in the procedure.

Basic Ingredients

1. **Fruits, vegetables, flowers and concentrates.** Wine can be made from any fruit, vegetable or flower. In fact, wine can be made from nearly anything — even water! That does not mean that every "anything" will make a good wine. The best wines are made from fruit, and the best fruit wine is, of course, grape.

Some people like to experiment with vegetables for novelty wines. Flower wines, like vegetable wines, are interesting and fun to make, but the wine is never superior or even excellent.

Wine from fruit is by far the most popular and satisfying kind to make. Some winemakers — the real old timers — swear there is nothing like wine made from fresh fruit. True, fresh fruit makes delicious wine, but so does a fruit juice concentrate. Fruit juice concentrates are not artificial; they are made from fresh fruit that has been sorted, cleaned, crushed, pressed, strained and concentrated into small, extra-strength quantities. The work has all been done for the winemaker. You merely reconstitute the product back into its natural state — pure juice. There is no fruit pulp involved. One small can of a vinifera concentrate equals approximately sixteen pounds of vinifera grapes.

Canned, frozen and dried fruits can also be used to make wine. Frozen and canned fruits tend to make a light bodied wine — pleasant but not a wine an expert would rate "superior." Dried fruits work well and are not difficult to use. They eliminate the crushing, pitting and de-stemming. The wines are unexpectedly good.

2. **Water.** Water is used in most home winemaking. If you were to use fruit juice with no water, you would have a very, very strong fruity wine that would really be more like a liqueur. In the case of vinifera grapes (true winemaking grapes), however, you do not have to use water. There is no advantage to using distilled or boiled water in your wine unless your water has a bad taste.

3. **Sugar.** You use plain white granulated sugar for winemaking. Sugar is converted into alcohol by the yeast. Naturally, the less sugar present in the must, the less alcohol. Of course, the yeast will only tolerate so much sugar, so there is a limit to the amount you can add.

4. **Yeast.** There is no such thing as a no-yeast wine recipe. Without yeast, fermentation is absolutely impossible. Those who claim they make no-yeast wines are actually using the wild yeast that is present on the skins of the fruit or that floats about in the air. Wild yeast is laden with mold and bacteria and can not tolerate as much alcohol as a good wine yeast.

Wine yeast is available in dry or liquid form, in an all-purpose type, plus numerous special strains, Bordeaux, Chablis, Rhine and many, many more. Do not try to make wine with baker's yeast. Baker's yeast is only for baking. It is too fast acting for winemaking. Wine should ferment slowly; wine yeast sets the proper rate of fermentation. Compare the following:

Baker's Yeast	Wine Yeast
1. *Produces a soft, hard to clear sediment that flares up easily.*	1. *Produces a firm, sticky, sediment that does not flare up. This makes clarification easier.*
2. *Speeds fermentation too much and produces a poor quality wine.*	2. *Produces a proper rate of fermentation.*
3. *Leaves a "yeasty" flavor even after aging.*	3. *Does not leave a "yeasty" flavor.*
4. *Does not have the alcohol tolerance of wine yeast.*	4. *Has proper alcohol tolerance.*

5. **Additives.** Home produced wine has vastly improved in quality over the years, thanks to the use of additives. You can produce a high-quality balanced wine by helping nature with the following additives.

Acid

Acid blend, which comes in tablet or powder form, is a mixture of citric, malic and tartaric acid. The natural acid in the fruit is usually deficient in one way or another. The proper portion of acid in wine is of prime importance. Acid blend insures the correct proportion and improves the fermentation. It gives the wine the proper tartness and inhibits the growth of harmful bacteria.

Campden tablets

Campden tablets (either potassium metabisulphite or sodium metabisulphite) sterilize the must and kill off any wild yeast. This enables the good wine yeast to operate properly. Campden tablets also eliminate bacteria that cause haze and turn your wine to vinegar.

Nutrient

Nutrient usually contains diammonium phosphate (or urea), potassium phosphate and sometimes magnesium sulphate. It is an essential aid to the wine yeast. Yeast feeds on sugar, oxygen, and certain chemicals. Usually not enough of these necessary chemicals are present in a must to nourish the yeast properly; therefore, nutrient must be used. Certain recipes may call for a super-nutrient — often referred to as energizer — that contains thiamine. Energizer is frequently recommended for wines made from a fruit or vegetable that is very deficient in the fermentable chemicals. When you make a recipe that calls for more than the normal amount of sugar you will want to use an energizier. Sometimes, if the fermentation becomes slow, or gets stuck before all the sugar has fermented, an energizer is added to the must to help the process.

Tannin

Tannin is found in the skins, seeds and stems of fruit — especially grapes. The red vinifera grape contains more tannin than any other. Some other fruits contain sufficient natural tannin for winemaking, but most fruits and vegetables need an additional amount to give the wine the bite or astringency it needs. Tannin also aids in clarification. You can buy it in powder or tablet form.

Pectic enzyme

Pectic enzyme is a fining or clearing agent. Most fruits contain pectin — it thickens jam and jelly by holding the solids in suspension. The pectic enzyme inhibits the congealing action of the pectin and helps to clear the wine. Available in powder or tablet form, it should be used in all musts.

Anti-oxidant tablets

Anti-oxidant, ascorbic acid (Vitamin C), is necessary for certain wines, especially white wines. It is usually added before bottling and helps prevent oxidation of the wine that would spoil the flavor and color. You can buy anti-oxidant in powder or tablet form.

Stabilizers

Stabilizer tablets of potassium sorbate are used if you sweeten the wine before bottling. The tablets prevent a renewal of fermentation; they are not effective for stabilizing an active fermentation. Stabilizers should be used only if you sweeten your wine before bottling.

Sparkolloid

Sparkolloid is another fining or clearing agent. When added to the wine, it carries the suspended solids to the bottom of the fermentor. The cleared wine then may be racked off (syphoned) from the sediment. Use sparkolloid only when your wine will not clear on its own by the time it is stable, and only after pectic enzyme has been tried. There are other fining agents such as egg whites, bentonite and isinglass. Bentonite and isinglass are difficult to use. Egg whites are totally unsatisfactory.

Glycerine

Glycerine is not a necessary additive. It is used if more body is desired in a finished wine, to hide some slight "off flavors," or to sweeten the wine. Since it does sweeten, never use glycerine if you want a dry wine.

HYDROMETER INSTRUCTIONS

Most hydrometers have three scales:
1. Specific gravity . . . . 990 to 1.170
2. Balling . . . . 0% to 39% sugar by weight
3. Potential alcohol . 0% to 22% alcohol by volume

1. **Specific Gravity.** This scale will register the amount of sugar in a liquid. Your hydrometer shows a specific gravity (density of soluble solids) of 1.000 when floating in pure water. Temperature changes will cause some variation, but this can be corrected (see Temperature Corrections). The specific gravity increases as the amount of sugar added increases.
2. **Balling.** The balling scale also registers the amount of sugar in a liquid. But, it measures the percentage of sugar by weight. An instrument having a balling scale, but no specific gravity scale, is often called a saccharometer. All winemaking recipes in this chapter refer to the specific gravity (hydrometer) scale.
3. **Potential Alcohol.** The potential alcohol scale registers the percentage of alcohol that will be produced if all of the sugar present in the must converts to alcohol. If fermentation stops before all the sugar is converted, the potential alcohol will not become actual alcohol. To determine the potential alcohol of a must, a hydrometer reading must be taken before fermentation begins.

How to Use your Hydrometer

After you have added the sugar to your must, take a sample of the must and put it into the hydrometer jar. Reach in the jar and spin the hydrometer between your fingers to dislodge any air bubbles. When the hydrometer stops spinning, it will float at a figure on the stem. Take care that the hydrometer is not leaning against the side of the jar but is floating free. Holding the jar at eye level, read the scale where the surface of the liquid cuts across the stem, below the ring of bubbles. You will then know how much sugar is in your must and what your potential alcohol content is.

If you do not have enough sugar in the must for the type of wine you wish to make, you can add more sugar. Five ounces of sugar added to one gallon of must will raise the gravity 10 points on the hydrometer. If you have too much sugar for the type of wine you want, add more water.

Starting Gravity

1. *Dry wine.* 1.085 to 1.100.
2. *Sweet table wine.* It is better to make a dry wine and sweeten after the fermentation is complete.
3. *Strong dessert wine.* 1.120 starting gravity; add sugar in stages to increase the percentage of alcohol.

Temperature Corrections. Most hydrometers are calibrated to be read at 60°F. If your must is not 60°F make the following corrections:

Temperature of Must	Correction
70°F	Add 1
77°F	Add 2
84°F	Add 3
95°F	Add 5
105°F	Add 7

For example, if the temperature of the must is 105°F and the reading on the hydrometer is 1.190, add 7. Then the correct hydrometer reading would be 1.197.

BASIC STEPS

One 3 gallon primary fermentor — polyethylene wastebasket or comparable container
Plastic sheet (approximately 36 inches square)
String or loose elastic tie for plastic sheet — long enough to fit around primary fermentor
Small funnel (optional)
Measuring cup
Measuring spoons
Large spoon for stirring

Hydrometer and hydrometer jar (optional)
Thermometer (optional)
Syphon
Fermentation lock
Sulphite sterilizing solution
2 glass jugs (1 gallon each)
5 wine bottles
5 corks or T-corks, plastic wine stoppers or 28mm screw caps, depending on type of wine bottle used.
Secondary fermentor

1. All equipment used to prepare the must has to be washed and rinsed in hot water two or three times. Then it has to be sterilized by rinsing it with the sulphite solution. Do not re-rinse with water after sulphiting.

2. Begin preparing the must by adding the fruit or concentrate to the primary fermentor.
3. Add the water.
4. Crush all tablets and add them to the primary.
5. Add the remainder of the ingredients except for the yeast and stir.
6. If using a hydrometer, take a hydrometer reading and adjust the sugar (see Hydrometer Instructions).
7. Cover with a plastic sheet and tie the sheet lightly with a string or loose elastic tie.
8. After 24 hours and when the must has cooled to at least 70°F, add the yeast. Follow whatever instructions are printed on the brand of yeast you are using.
9. Cover by tying the plastic sheet around the primary fermentor again.
10. Do not stir until fermentation begins (foam and bubbles). Then, stir daily.
11. Ferment until the specific gravity reaches 1.040. Or, if not using a hydrometer, ferment for three or four days.
12. Sterilize any equipment that is going to come into contact with your wine (syphon, glass jug, etc.) and rack (syphon) the wine into the glass jug leaving any sediment behind.

Basic Step 1   Basic Step 2   Basic Step 4

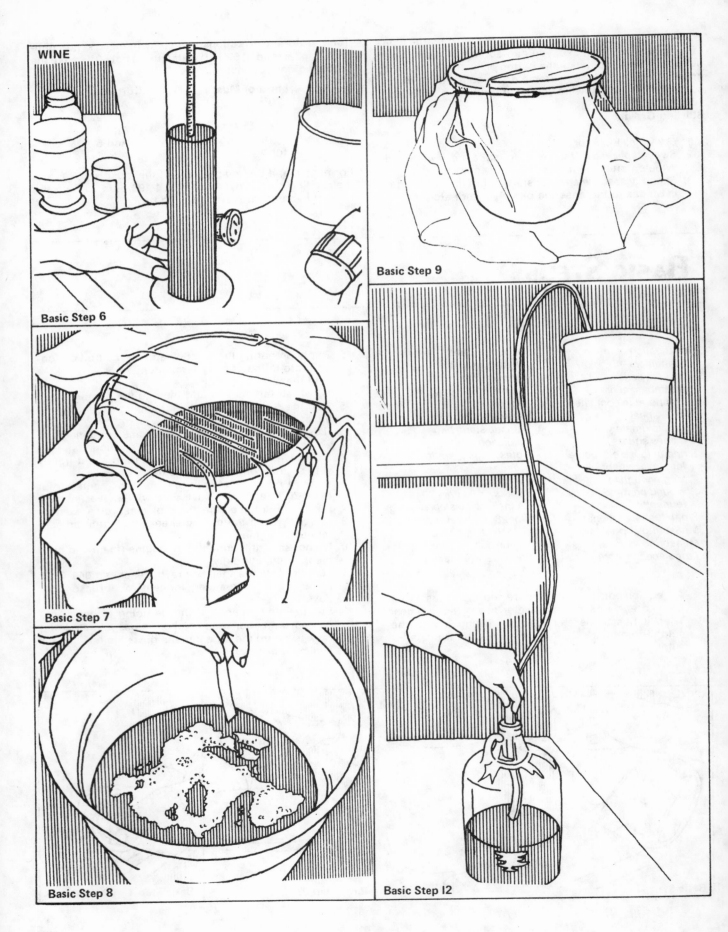

WINE

Basic Step 6

Basic Step 9

Basic Step 7

Basic Step 8

Basic Step 12

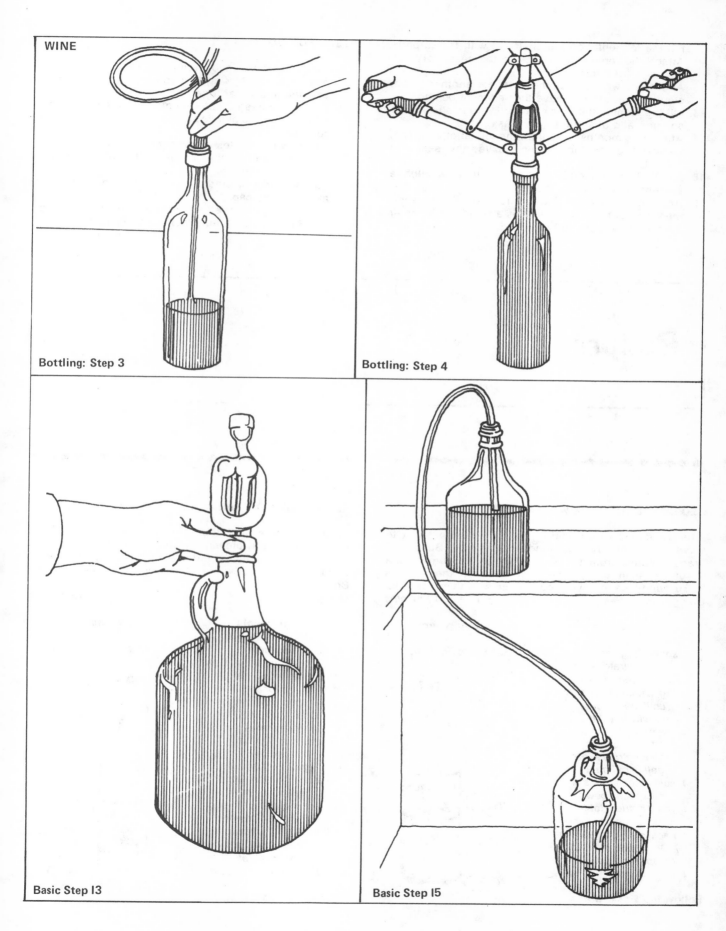

WINE

Bottling: Step 3

Bottling: Step 4

Basic Step 13

Basic Step 15

13. Fill the fermentation lock half full with the sulphite.
14. Attach the fermentation lock to the secondary fermentor (glass jug).
15. After three weeks, rack the wine into another clean, sterilized glass jug. Leave the sediment behind.
16. Fill the fermentation lock half full with fresh sulphite solution and attach it to the glass jug.
17. After three months, rack the wine into another clean, sterilized glass jug. Again, leave any sediment behind.
18. Fill the fermentation lock half full with fresh sulphite solution and attach to the jug.
19. After another month, if wine throws little or no sediment and/or the wine maintains a steady hydrometer reading, it is ready to be bottled.

STEPS FOR BOTTLING

1. Wash the bottles and sterilize with half-strength sulphite solution. Mix equal parts of prepared sulphite solution and water together.
2. Soak the corks in half-strength sulphite for an hour or two. Or, rinse plastic stoppers or screw caps in the solution.
3. Fill the wine bottles by syphoning from the secondary fermentor into the bottles. Fill to about 1½ to 2 inches from the top.
4. Put the corks or plastic stoppers into the bottles or attach screw caps.
5. When using corks, allow the bottles to stand upright for 48 hours after filling, then lay them on their sides.

Recipes

RED BURGUNDY TYPE WINE

A heavy-bodied, ruby Red Burgundy is the perfect wine to serve with beef. True Burgundy comes from Burgundy, France. Wines from the Cote D'Or of Burgundy were coveted even in Roman times. You can savor the richness of Burgundy made in your own home with this recipe.
One gallon   *Age at least 12 months*

Ingredients

1 *small Burgundy concentrate — vinifera*
½ *to ¾ pound white granulated sugar or until the specific gravity is 1.095*
Warm water — add enough to the concentrate to make 1 gallon of liquid
4 *acid blend tablets or 3 teaspoons powder*
1 *yeast nutrient tablet or 1 teaspoon powder*
1 *pectic enzyme tablet or ½ teaspoon powder*
1 *campden tablet*
1 *Burgundy wine yeast*

Follow the Basic Steps

Equipment

See Basic Equipment

RED BORDEAUX TYPE WINE

Bordeaux, named after the Bordeaux vineyards in France, is full-bodied and pleasantly dry. It is lighter in alcohol content than Burgundy and is a superb table wine. Bordeaux can be red or white. This recipe is for a scarlet red Bordeaux.
One gallon   *Age at least 12 months*

Ingredients

1 *small Bordeaux concentrate — vinifera*
½ *pound white granulated sugar or until the specific gravity is 1.075 to 1.080*
Warm water — add enough to the concentrate to make 1 gallon of liquid
3 *acid blend tablets or 2½ teaspoons powder*
1 *yeast nutrient tablet or 1 teaspoon powder*
1 *pectic enzyme tablet or ½ teaspoon powder*
1 *campden tablet*
1 *Bordeaux wine yeast*

Follow the Basic Steps

Equipment

See Basic Equipment

BEAUJOLAIS TYPE WINE

Serve bright red Beaujolais with your special gourmet meat dishes, or bring it out for light luncheons. It is a versatile type of Burgundy wine with a distinctive fruity taste.
One gallon   *Age 12 months*

Ingredients

1 small Beaujolais concentrate — vinifera
½ to ¾ pound white granulated sugar or until the specific gravity is 1.090
  Warm water — add enough to the concentrate to make 1 gallon of liquid
3 acid blend tablets or 2¼ teaspoons powder
1 yeast nutrient tablet or 1 teaspoon powder
1 pectic enzyme tablet or ½ teaspoon powder
1 campden tablet
1 Beaujolais wine yeast

Equipment

See Basic Equipment

Follow the Basic Steps

ROSÉ WINE

Everybody enjoys a good rosé wine. Now you can serve your own light-bodied rosé. The color varies from pale pink to orange-pink to deep rose. Try it with cheese and crackers for an elegant snack.
One gallon   *Age 12 months*

Ingredients

1 small rosé concentrate
½ to ¾ pound white granulated sugar or until the specific gravity is 1.095
  Warm water — add enough to the concentrate to make 1 gallon of liquid
2 acid blend tablets or 1½ teaspoons powder
1 yeast nutrient tablet or 1 teaspoon powder
1 pectic enzyme tablet or ½ teaspoon powder
1 campden tablet
1 all-purpose wine yeast

Equipment

See Basic Equipment

Follow the Basic Steps

CHIANTI TYPE

Chianti, a dry, vividly red Italian table wine, tastes harsher than most red wines. Dried elderberries and oak chips create the typical harsh Chianti flavor. Enjoy Chianti with spaghetti or other pasta dishes — *buon gusto!*
One gallon   *Age at least 12 months*

Ingredients

1 small red blend concentrate — vinifera
¾ pound white granulated sugar or until the specific gravity is 1.095
  Warm water — add enough to the concentrate to make 1 gallon of liquid
4 acid blend tablets or 3 teaspoons powder
2 ounces dried elderberries
¼ ounce oak chips
1 pectic enzyme tablet or ½ teaspoon powder
1 campden tablet
1 Chianti wine yeast

Equipment

See Basic Equipment
Fermentation bag

1. Follow Basic Steps 1 and 2.
2. Put the dried elderberries in the fermentation bag and place the bag in the primary fermentor.
3. Continue Basic Steps 3 through 11.
4. Remove the fermentation bag and squeeze it lightly. (Discard the elderberry pulp and wash the fermentation bag for future use.)
5. Continue Basic Steps 12 through 14.
6. Take a hydrometer reading daily and when specific gravity reaches 1.010, rack the wine into another clean, sterilized glass jug.
7. Add the oak chips.
8. Fill the fermentation lock half full with sulphite solution and attach it to the glass jug.
9. After three weeks to one month, taste the wine. It should have the taste of Chianti. If not, leave the chips in one more week.
10. Rack the wine into another clean, sterilized glass jug, straining out oak chips.
11. Continue Basic Steps 16 through 19.

RHINE TYPE WINE

One of the most popular white wines, Rhine wine comes from the Rhine vineyards of Germany. This wine is light-bodied and dry to semi-dry. Rhine Type Wine is sure to become one of your prized wine recipes.
One gallon   *Age at least 12 months*

Ingredients

1 small Rhine wine
    concentrate — vinifera
½ pound white granulated
    sugar or until the
    specific gravity is
    1.080
Warm water — add
    enough to the
    concentrate to make 1
    gallon of liquid
5 acid blend tablets or 3¾
    teaspoons powder
1 yeast nutrient tablet or 1
    teaspoon powder
1 pectic enzyme tablet or
    ½ teaspoon powder
1 campden tablet
1 Rhine wine yeast

Equipment

See Basic Equipment

Follow the Basic Steps

CHABLIS TYPE WINE

Chablis is a white Burgundy. True Chablis comes from a special area of Burgundy, France. You will be proud to serve this crisply dry, flinty tasting wine with your favorite fish entrees.
One gallon   *Age at least 12 months*

Ingredients

1 small Chablis
    concentrate — vinifera
½ to ¾ pound white
    granulated sugar or
    until the specific
    gravity is 1.095
Warm water — add
    enough to the
    concentrate to make 1
    gallon of liquid
2 acid blend tablets or 1½
    teaspoons powder
1 yeast nutrient tablet or 1
    teaspoon powder
1 pectic enzyme tablet or
    ½ teaspoon powder
1 campden tablet
1 package Chablis wine
    yeast

Equipment

See Basic Equipment

Follow the Basic Steps

VARIATION I

Fresh Fruit Wines

When you make wine from fresh fruit — grapes, strawberries, blackberries, or other fruit — you use a fermentation bag to hold the crushed fruit pulp. Variation I follows the Basic Steps and tells you when to add your fermentation bag to the primary fermentor and when to remove the bag.

Steps for Variation I

1. Follow Basic Step 1. Then, stem, clean and crush the fruit. If you are using soft fruit, all you have to do is break the skins so the juices will flow.
2. Put the crushed fruit into the fermentation bag and tie the bag with a string.
3. Put the fermentation bag in the primary fermentor.
4. Continue Basic Steps 2 through 11.
5. After Basic Step 11, remove the fermentation bag from the primary fermentor and gently squeeze the juices into the primary fermentor.
6. Discard the fruit pulp in the bag.
7. Wash and rinse the fermentation bag for future use.
8. Continue Basic Steps 12 through 19.

RED OR WHITE GRAPE WINE
From Labrusca (Native American) Variety Grapes

Many Americans think all grape wines are made from our native American labrusca grapes — Concord, Niagara, Catawba, Delaware. In reality, the European and California grape wines are made from the vinifera variety grapes, such as Pinot Noir, Cabernet Sauvignon, Chenin Blanc. The types of vinifera are numerous. Labrusca variety grapes do not make the best wine, although many would argue the point. Your homemade labrusca grape wine will have a "foxy" fresh taste.
One gallon   *Age 8 to 12 months*

Ingredients

5 to 6 pounds grapes
2½ to 3 pounds white
    granulated sugar or
    until the specific
    gravity is 1.100
1 gallon warm water
1 yeast nutrient tablet or 1
    teaspoon powder
1 pectic enzyme tablet or
    ½ teaspoon powder
1 campden tablet
1 all-purpose wine yeast

Equipment

See Basic Equipment
Fermentation bag with
    string tie

Follow the steps for Variation I

ELDERBERRY WINE

Elderberry wine evokes nostalgic pictures of a slower-paced, more gracious time. Elderberry wine is deep, deep red with a nice body — and so delicious. Age improves it. Do not rush to enjoy it too soon. Sip it slowly and relax.

One gallon   *Age at least 12 months.*

Ingredients

2½ pounds fresh
      elderberries
¾   to 1 pound white
      granulated sugar or
      until specific gravity is
      1.095
1   gallon boiling water
3   acid blend tablets or 2¼
      teaspoons powder
1   yeast nutrient tablet or 1
      teaspoon powder
1   pectic enzyme tablet or
      ½ teaspoon powder
2   campden tablets
1   all-purpose wine yeast

Equipment

See Basic Equipment
Fermentation bag with
string tie

Follow steps for Variation I

STRAWBERRY WINE

Strawberry wine, a romantic, fresh-tasting rosé is perfect for light suppers or luncheons. Serve it poured over a tall goblet of fresh strawberries for an elegant dessert.

One gallon   *Age 6 months*

Ingredients

3½ pounds strawberries
2   pounds white granulated
      sugar or until the
      specific gravity is
      1.090
1   gallon warm water
1   acid blend powder tablet
      or ¾ teaspoon powder
1   yeast nutrient tablet or 1
      teaspoon powder
1   pectic enzyme tablet or
      ½ teaspoon powder
1   campden tablet
1   all-purpose wine yeast

Equipment

See Basic Equipment
Fermentation bag with
string tie

Follow the steps for Variation I

BLUEBERRY WINE

Blueberries are a bit difficult to ferment; so, do not be discouraged if the fermentation is sluggish. The wine will be a pretty, light red and marvelously fruity.

One gallon   *Age 3 to 6 months*

Ingredients

3   pounds blueberries
1   pound raisins
2   pounds white granulated
      sugar or until the
      specific gravity is
      1.095
1   gallon warm water
2   acid blend tablets or 1½
      teaspoons powder
1   energizer tablet
1   pectic enzyme tablet or
      ½ teaspoon powder
1   campden tablet
1   all-purpose wine yeast

Equipment

See Basic Equipment
Fermentation bag with
string tie

Follow the steps for Variation I

BLACKBERRY WINE

Blackberries make a brilliant, ruby red wine — a mellow fruit wine you will be proud to serve your guests.

One gallon   *Age 12 months*

Ingredients

4   pounds blackberries
2½ pounds white granulated
      sugar or until specific
      gravity is 1.095
1   gallon warm water
1   acid blend tablet or ¾
      teaspoon powder
1   yeast nutrient tablet or 1
      teaspoon powder
1   pectic enzyme tablet or
      ½ teaspoon powder
1   campden tablet
1   all-purpose wine yeast

Equipment

See Basic Equipment
Fermentation bag with
string tie

Follow the steps for Variation I

PEACH WINE

Call to mind the taste of succulent summer peaches, then imagine that wonderful flavor captured in a sauterne type wine. Now, go ahead and make this golden-hued peach wine. If you want to capture even more sunny peach flavor, use a couple more pounds of the fruit in your recipe.

One gallon   *Age 3 to 6 months*

Ingredients

2½ pounds peaches
  2 pounds white granulated
      sugar or until the
      specific gravity is
      1.090
  1 gallon warm water
  2 acid blend tablets or 1½
      teaspoons powder
  1 yeast nutrient tablet or 1
      teaspoon powder
  1 tannin tablet or ¼
      teaspoon powder
  1 pectic enzyme tablet or
      ½ teaspoon powder
  1 campden tablet
  1 all-purpose wine yeast
  1 teaspoon anti-oxidant
      powder for bottling

Equipment

See Basic Equipment
Fermentation bag with
  string tie

Follow the steps for Variation I with the following changes:

1. When cleaning the fruit, pit the peaches.
2. When bottling add 1 teaspoon of the anti-oxidant powder. This will preserve the color and the flavor.

CHERRY WINE

Try a glass of Cherry Wine — crisp, cold and refreshingly tart! Make this fruit wine, an old-time favorite of winemakers, and bask in compliments when friends admire the sprightly taste and color. Cherry Wine is a pretty rosé wine; it may vary in color from a light pink to a deep reddish pink.

One gallon   *Age 3 to 6 months*

Ingredients

  2 pounds sour cherries or 3
      pounds sweet cherries
2½ pounds white granulated
      sugar or until the
      specific gravity is
      1.095
  1 gallon warm water
  3 acid blend tablets or 2¼
      teaspoons powder
  1 yeast nutrient tablet or 1
      teaspoon powder
  1 pectic enzyme tablet or
      ½ teaspoon powder
  1 campden tablet
  1 all-purpose wine yeast

Equipment

See Basic Equipment
Fermentation bag with
  string tie

Follow the steps for Variation I

PLUM WINE

Plum wine is a very delicate rosé wine. Spring-time fresh and piquant tasting, plum wine is one of the most cherished fruit wines.

One gallon   *Age 3 to 6 months*

Ingredients

2½ pounds plums, pitted
2½ pounds white granulated
      sugar or until the
      specific gravity is
      1.095
  1 gallon warm water
  2 acid blend tablets or 1½
      teaspoons powder
  1 yeast nutrient tablet or 1
      teaspoon powder
  1 pectic enzyme tablet or
      ½ teaspoon powder
  1 campden tablet
  1 all-purpose wine yeast

Equipment

See Basic Equipment
Fermentation bag with
  string tie

Follow the steps for Variation I

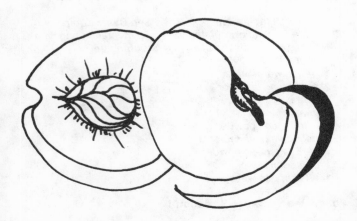

APPLE WINE

A good Apple Wine often resembles a German light wine. It is delicate in flavor and subtle in aroma. The variety of apples used will affect the taste. Use fresh tart apples for the best result.
One gallon   *Age 3 to 6 months*

Ingredients	Equipment
6 pounds apples	See Basic Equipment
2½ pounds white granulated sugar or until the specific gravity is 1.095	Fermentation bag with string tie
1 gallon warm water	
3 acid blend tablets or 2¼ teaspoons powder	
1 yeast nutrient tablet or 1 teaspoon powder	
1 tannin tablet or ¼ teaspoon powder	
1 pectic enzyme tablet or ½ teaspoon powder	
1 campden tablet	
1 all-purpose wine yeast	

Follow the steps for Variation I except for the following:

1. If possible, crush and press the apples. Use only the juice. If not possible, chop the fruit and proceed with the Basic Steps.

CRANBERRY WINE

Cranberry Wine has a very distinctive taste. If you like cranberries, you will love this wine. Make a dry cranberry wine using this recipe, or sweeten it just before bottling. The wine usually turns a cheery orange-red. A clear Cranberry Wine has a tendency to become cloudy after six months — this will not affect the taste, only the looks.
One gallon   *Age 12 months*

Ingredients	Equipment
2 pounds cranberries	See Basic Equipment
1 pound raisins	Blender
3 pounds white granulated sugar or until specific gravity is 1.095	Fermentation bag with string tie
1 gallon warm water	
1 yeast nutrient tablet or 1 teaspoon powder	
1 pectic enzyme tablet or ½ teaspoon powder	
1 campden tablet	
1 all-purpose wine yeast	

Follow the steps for Variation I except for the following:

1. When crushing the fruit, crush the cranberries and chop the raisins at the same time by putting part of each into a blender and adding part of the water.
2. Turn the blender to "Chop" for a few seconds. Be careful not to make a puree!
3. Empty it into the fermentation bag.
4. Put more cranberries, raisins and water in the blender and chop. Continue until all raisins and cranberries have been processed.

RHUBARB WINE

Rhubarb Wine can vary in color from clear to light pink to a golden color. It is a favorite of many winemakers. Because of its oxalic acid, ferment only the rhubarb juice, not the pulp. Never use hot water with rhubarb.
One gallon   *Age 6 months*

Ingredients	Equipment
2½ pounds rhubarb	See Basic Equipment
2½ pounds white granulated sugar or until specific gravity is 1.095	Strainer or fermentation bag
1 gallon cool water	
1 acid blend tablet or ¾ teaspoon powder	
1 energizer	
1 tannin tablet or ¼ teaspoon powder	
1 pectic enzyme tablet or ½ teaspoon powder	
1 campden tablet	
1 all-purpose wine yeast	

1. Cut up the rhubarb.
2. Put the rhubarb into the primary fermentor.
3. Pour the sugar over the rhubarb to extract the juice.
4. Cover with a plastic sheet and let stand 48 hours.
5. Strain the fruit through a strainer or fermentation bag, catching the juice in the primary fermentor.
6. Squeeze the bag as hard as possible or press hard against strainer to press the fruit dry.
7. Discard the fruit pulp.
8. Add the cool water.
9. Follow Basic Steps 4 through 10.

VARIATION II

FLOWER WINES

Not many flowers make passable wines, but dandelions and roses produce remarkably delicate beverages. The steps for Variation II tell you when to add the flowers to your must and when to remove them. Flower wines usually call for raisins to provide sugar and flavor.

Steps for Variation II

1. Follow Basic Step 1. Then, wash the flowers thoroughly.
2. If using any raisins, chop them.
3. Put the raisins and flowers into the fermentation bag and tie the bag with a string.
4. Put fermentation bag into the primary fermentor.
5. Continue Basic Steps 3 through 11.
6. Remove the fermentation bag and squeeze.
7. Discard the flowers and raisins.
8. Wash and rinse the fermentation bag for future use.
9. Continue Basic Steps 12 through 19.

DANDELION WINE

An old-time, country favorite, Dandelion Wine is pale yellow and light-bodied. Dandelions bloom in the early spring; you only use the petals to make wine. The tender, early greens can go into salads.
One gallon   *Age 3 to 6 months*

Ingredients	Equipment
7 cups dandelion petals (petals only)	*See Basic Equipment*
1 pound golden raisins, chopped	*Fermentation bag with string tie*
2½ pounds white granulated sugar or until the specific gravity is 1.095	*Small paring knife*
1 gallon hot water	
5 acid blend tablets or 3¾ teaspoons powder	
1 energizer	
1 tannin tablet or ¼ teaspoon powder	
1 pectic enzyme tablet or ½ teaspoon powder	
1 campden tablet	
1 all-purpose wine yeast	

Follow the steps for Variation II except for the following:

1. Before bottling add 1 teaspoon of anti-oxidant powder to preserve the color and taste.

ROSE PETAL WINE

Rose Petal Wine? Try it! This is an intriguing, dainty wine. If you are adventurous and like country wines, Rose Petal Wine will be a unique addition to your wine recipe collection. It will be very light bodied. If you are entertaining a wine snob, bring out your Beaujolais or Burgundy and save Rose Petal Wine for more open-minded friends.
One gallon   *Age 3 to 6 months*

Ingredients	Equipment
2 quarts fresh, dark red rose petals	*See Basic Equipment*
2½ pounds white granulated sugar or until specific gravity is 1.095	*Fermentation bag with string tie*
1 gallon cool to warm water	*Small paring knife*
6 acid blend tablets or 4½ teaspoons powder	
1 energizer tablet	
1 tannin tablet or ¼ teaspoon powder	
1 campden tablet	
1 all-purpose wine yeast	

Follow the steps for Variation II

VARIATION III

Wine from Frozen Fruit

You can freeze fresh fruit and later make wine from it. Freezing breaks down the tissues of the fruit so the fruit requires little or no crushing. Of course, frozen fruit is available year-round at the grocery store, should you suddenly decide to make wine. The steps required to make wine from frozen fruit are almost identical to the steps for fresh fruit wines.

Steps for Variation III

1. Follow Basic Step 1. Then, put the thawed fruit into a bowl and lightly crush it with a spoon or fork. If the

fruit is a soft fruit such as blackberries or raspberries, you can eliminate this step.

2. Put the fruit into the fermentation bag and tie the bag.
3. Put the fermentation bag into the primary fermentor.
4. Follow Basic Steps 3 through 11.
5. Remove the fermentation bag and squeeze excess juice back into the primary fermentor.
6. Discard the fruit pulp.
7. Wash and rinse the fermentation bag for future use.
8. Follow Basic Steps 12 through 19.

CHERRY WINE FROM FROZEN CHERRIES

Cherry wine looks much like a Portuguese rosé wine. This delectable wine, made from frozen cherries, may be lighter colored than a wine made from fresh cherries.
One gallon   *Age 3 to 6 months*

Ingredients	Equipment
3 pounds frozen cherries	See Basic Equipment
2½ pounds white granulated sugar or until the specific gravity is 1.095	Large mixing bowl Large spoon or fork Fermentation bag with string tie
1 gallon warm water	
2 acid blend tablets or 1½ teaspoons powder	
1 yeast nutrient tablet or 1 teaspoon powder	
1 pectic enzyme tablet or ½ teaspoon powder	
1 campden tablet	
1 all-purpose wine yeast	

Follow the steps for Variation III

BLACKBERRY WINE FROM FROZEN FRUIT

This blackberry wine will be paler than the wine made from fresh blackberries, but it is still a luscious red wine. Blackberry wine has a satisfying fruity flavor.
One gallon   *Age 12 months*

Ingredients	Equipment
3 to 4 pounds frozen blackberries	See Basic Equipment
2½ pounds white granulated sugar or until specific gravity is 1.095	Large mixing bowl Large spoon or fork Fermentation bag with string tie
1 gallon warm water	
1 acid blend tablet or ¾ teaspoon powder	
1 yeast nutrient tablet or 1 teaspoon powder	
1 pectic enzyme tablet or ½ teaspoon powder	
1 campden tablet	
1 all-purpose wine yeast	

Follow the steps for Variation III

VARIATION IV

Wine from Dried Fruit

Making wine from dried fruit is easier than making wine from fresh fruit; however, the wine may be slightly lighter in color and body. There is not as much mess with dried fruit as there is with fresh fruit. The steps are almost the same as making wine from fresh fruit with the following variations.

Steps for Variation IV

1. Follow Basic Step 1. Then, put the dried fruit into the fermentation bag and tie the bag.
2. Put the fermentation bag into the primary fermentor.
3. Follow Basic Steps 3 through 11.
4. Remove fermentation bag and lightly squeeze excess juice back into the primary fermentor.
5. Discard fruit pulp.
6. Wash and rinse the fermentation bag for future use.
7. Continue Basic Steps 12 through 19.

DRIED WILD CHERRY WINE

Wild cherries make a light rosé wine that should please all winemakers. This recipe causes less mess than working with fresh or frozen cherries. It will be lighter bodied than wine made from fresh cherries — but delicious.
One gallon   *Age 3 to 6 months*

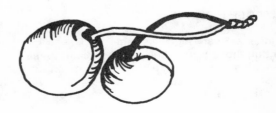

Ingredients

- 5 ounces dried wild cherries
- 2½ pounds white granulated sugar or until the specific gravity is 1.095
- 1 gallon warm water
- 3 acid blend tablets or 2¼ teaspoons powder
- 1 yeast nutrient tablet or 1 teaspoon powder
- 1 pectic enzyme tablet or ½ teaspoon powder
- 1 campden tablet
- 1 all-purpose wine yeast

Equipment

See Basic Equipment
Fermentation bag with string tie

Follow the steps for Variation IV

DRIED ELDERBERRY WINE

Elderberry wine made from dried elderberries is nearly as good as wine made from fresh elderberries — and much neater to make. If you enjoy picking and working with fresh fruit, fine, but if not, this is the answer for you. You can make elderberry wine any time of the year if you use dried elderberries.

One gallon   Age 12 months

Ingredients

- 5 ounces dried elderberries
- 1 pound raisins chopped
- 2 pounds white granulated sugar or until the specific gravity is 1.095
- 1 gallon warm water
- 3 acid blend tablets or 2¼ teaspoons powder
- 1 yeast nutrient tablet or 1 teaspoon powder
- 1 pectic enzyme tablet or ½ teaspoon powder
- 1 campden tablet
- 1 all-purpose wine yeast

Equipment

See Basic Equipment
Fermentation bag with string tie

Follow the steps for Variation IV. But put the chopped raisins into the fermentation bag with the elderberries.

DRIED ROSE HIP WINE

Rose hips are very high in vitamin C. Rose Hip Wine is delightful, though it is often rather difficult to make. The fermentation has a tendency to be sluggish and sometimes stops. Baby the fermentation, and you will have a wine in a class by itself. It may remind you of a Tokay wine.

One gallon   Age 6 months

Ingredients

- 5 ounces dried rose hips
- 8 ounces raisins, chopped
- 2 pounds white granulated sugar or until the specific gravity is 1.090
- 1 gallon hot water
- 4 acid blend tablets or 3 teaspoons powder
- 1 or 2 energizer tablets
- 1 pectic enzyme tablet or ½ teaspoon powder
- 1 campden tablet
- 1 all-purpose wine yeast or 1 Tokay wine yeast

Equipment

See Basic Equipment
Fermentation bag with string tie

Follow the steps for Variation IV. But, put the chopped raisins into the fermentation bag with the rose hips.

VARIATION V

Wine from Canned Fruit

Much of the mystery surrounding the high-priced "wine bases" found on the shelves of home winemaking shops in years past has disappeared. In reality these "bases" were nothing more than broken, canned fruit without preservatives. The winemaker today is more sophisticated than the winemaker of even five years ago — you can go to the local grocery store and simply buy a can of fruit for much less than the "wine bases" cost. Then you can make cherry wine, plum wine, peach wine — you name it! True, not all canned fruits work well, but you can make wine with any that have not had a preservative added.

Steps for Variation V

1. Follow Basic Step 1. Then, put the fermentation bag into the primary fermentor.
2. Open the canned fruit and pour the juice and fruit into the bag.
3. Tie the bag and put it in the primary fermentor.
4. Continue Basic Steps 3 through 11.
5. Remove the fermentation bag and lightly squeeze excess liquid back into the primary fermentor.
6. Discard the fruit pulp.
7. Wash and rinse the fermentation bag for future use.
8. Follow Basic Steps 12 through 19.

BLACK CHERRY WINE FROM CANNED BLACK SWEET CHERRIES

This wine will be deeper in color than sour cherry or wild cherry wine. This recipe is a rich, sumptuous addition to a basic collection of fruit wines.
One gallon   *Age 3 to 6 months*

Ingredients	Equipment
1 *(16 ounce or approximate size) can of black sweet cherries* 2½ *pounds white granulated sugar or until the specific gravity is 1.095* 1 *gallon warm water* 6 *acid blend tablets or 4½ teaspoons powder* 1 *yeast nutrient tablet or 1 teaspoon powder* 1 *pectic enzyme tablet or ½ teaspoon powder* 1 *campden tablet* 1 *all-purpose wine yeast*	*See Basic Equipment Fermentation bag with string tie*

Follow the steps for Variation V

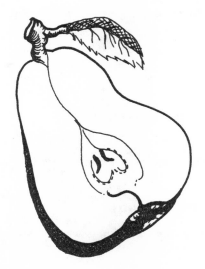

PEAR WINE FROM CANNED PEARS

Some people say pears make insipid wine, yet we found that the wine was quite pleasant — dry, very light, white and delicate.
One gallon   *Age 3 to 6 months*

Ingredients	Equipment
1 *(16 ounce or approximate size) can of pears* 2 *pounds white granulated sugar or until the specific gravity is 1.095* 1 *gallon warm water* 5 *acid blend tablets or 3¾ teaspoons powder* 1 *yeast nutrient tablet or 1 teaspoon powder* 1 *tannin tablet or ¼ teaspoon powder* 1 *pectic enzyme tablet or ½ teaspoon powder* 1 *campden tablet* 1 *all-purpose wine yeast* 1 *teaspoon anti-oxidant powder*	*See Basic Equipment Fermentation bag with string tie*

Follow the steps for Variation V, except for the following: when bottling, add one teaspoon anti-oxidant powder to preserve the color and taste.

VARIATION VI

Sparkling Wines

Sparkling wines are perfect for parties — they bubble and shimmer delightfully. For that special celebration, you should have some sparkling wine in your wine collection. Go ahead — try it! With care and caution, you can have the fun and enjoyment of making a good sparkling wine.
   You can make any wine into a sparkling wine. Just follow these directions.

Ingredients for Adding Sparkle	Equipment
2 *ounces white granulated sugar* 2 *ounces water* 1 *Champagne yeast*	*See Basic Equipment* *5 Champagne bottles* *Plastic Champagne stoppers* *5 Champagne wire hoods*

Steps for Variation VI

1. Follow Basic Steps except (and this is very important) always start out with a lower specific gravity than that given in the wine recipes — about 1.070 to

1.075. This means you add much less sugar. You must use a hydrometer.

2. After the wine has fermented to dryness and is clear and stable (about five months from the time you first make it), then you add the sparkle by following the next steps.

3. For each gallon to be sparkled, make up a sugar syrup of 2 ounces of sugar to 2 ounces of water.

4. Bring the sugar and water mixture to a boil.

5. Cool to at least 70° F.

6. Add the Champagne yeast and stir.

7. Now bottle the wine in sterilized Champagne bottles. (Use only champagne bottles.)

8. Add 4 teaspoons of the syrup mixture to each bottle.

9. Cap the bottles with plastic Champagne stoppers and wire hoods.

10. Store in a cool place for two or three months.

11. Put a bottle in the refrigerator and chill thoroughly.

12. Open the bottle. If the wine is not carbonated, try another bottle a month or two later. Have patience! Do not expect your wine to carbonate in a week or two.

13. When the wine is finally carbonated, always keep it cool. Never shake it. Wrap a towel around the bottle while carrying it to the refrigerator to chill.

COLD DUCK

True Cold Duck is a half-and-half blend of red labrusca variety grape and a white vinifera variety grape. Perfect for formal dinners or sumptuous midnight suppers, this is one of the most popular table wines.

Two gallons *Age 5 months before adding sparkle, then age 2 to 3 months more.*

Ingredients	Equipment
1 small Concord grape concentrate	See Basic Equipment
1 small white blend concentrate — vinifera	
1 pound white granulated sugar or until the specific gravity is 1.070 to 1.075	
2 gallons warm water	
10 acid blend tablets or 7½ teaspoons powder	
2 pectic enzyme tablets or 1 teaspoon powder	
2 campden tablets	
1 Champagne yeast	

Follow the Basic Steps, 1 through 19. When the wine has aged for 5 months, add the sparkle.

Ingredients for Adding Sparkle	Equipment
4 ounces white granulated sugar	10 Champagne bottles
4 ounces water	10 Plastic Champagne stoppers
2 packages Champagne yeast	10 Champagne wire hoods

Follow the steps for Variation VI

CHAMPAGNE TYPE WINE

Bubbling, crisp, dry white wine served in a tulip-shaped Champagne glass — what could be more elegant. True Champagne, of course, comes only from Champagne, France. But you can amaze your friends by making your own sparkling American Champagne.

One gallon *Age 5 months before adding the sparkle, then age 2 to 3 more months.*

Ingredients	Equipment
1 small white blend concentrate — vinifera	See Basic Equipment
¼ pound white granulated sugar or until the specific gravity is 1.070 to 1.075	
Warm water to 1 gallon	
4 acid blend tablets or 3 teaspoons powder	
1 yeast nutrient tablet or 1 teaspoon powder	
1 pectic enzyme tablet or ½ teaspoon powder	
1 campden tablet	
1 Champagne yeast	

Follow the Basic Steps, 1 through 19. When the wine has aged 5 months add the sparkle.

Ingredients for Adding Sparkle	Equipment
2 ounces white granulated sugar	5 Champagne bottles
2 ounces water	5 Plastic Champagne stoppers
1 Champagne yeast	5 Champagne wire hoods

Follow the steps for Variation VI

SPARKLING BURGUNDY

A handsome, dry, red bubbly wine, sparkling Burgundy used to be synonymous with high-class parties, formal dances and romance. Make your own delicious Sparkling Burgundy and plan a special intimate dinner for two to go with it.

One gallon

Age 5 months before adding the sparkle, then age 2 to 3 months more.

Ingredients	Equipment
1 small Burgundy concentrate — vinifera	See Basic Equipment
¼ pound white granulated sugar or until the specific gravity is 1.070 to 1.075	
Warm water to 1 gallon	
4 acid blend tablets or 3 teaspoons powder	
1 yeast nutrient tablet or 1 teaspoon powder	
1 pectic enzyme tablet or ½ teaspoon powder	
1 campden tablet	
1 Champagne yeast	

Follow the Basic Steps, 1 through 19. After the wine has aged 5 months, add the sparkle.

Ingredients for Adding Sparkle	Equipment
2 ounces white granulated sugar	5 Champagne bottles
2 ounces water	5 Plastic Champagne stoppers
1 Champagne yeast	5 Champagne wire hoods

Follow the Steps for Variation VI

◆◆◆◆◆◆◆◆◆◆◆◆◆◆◆◆◆◆◆◆◆◆◆◆◆◆

COMMON PROBLEMS

1. **Bad Flavors.** If a wine stands in its own sediment too long it may develop a bad or "off" flavor because the live yeast cells begin to feed on the sediment.

   Remedy
   The wine should be systematically racked.

   • Bad flavors also may come from fermenting in temperatures that are too warm.

   Remedy
   Your "fermentation room" should be kept at 75°F or lower. Do not allow the temperature to reach 80°F or above.

2. **Stuck Fermentation.** Sometimes a must stops fermenting before all the sugar has been converted to alcohol.

   Remedy
   The temperature may be too low for a particular yeast. Some yeasts do not tolerate temperatures below 60°F. Increase the temperature of the room

to 70°F or 75°F to allow the must to warm; check after a day or two to see if the fermentation has resumed.

   • Sometimes during the summer the fermentation becomes too warm (above 85°F), and the yeast weakens.

   Remedy
   Use a yeast starter (yeast dissolved in a little must) and ferment again. When the yeast starter is going well, add a pint of must to the starter. Once this is going well, add a quart of must. Then, after that mixture is vigorously fermenting, add a gallon of must. Gradually increase the amount of must until the entire must is fermenting properly.

3. **Exploding Bottles of Still Wine.** Bottling before fermentation is finished, and before fermentation is stable, may cause an explosion.

   Remedy
   Return all the wine to the secondary fermentors under fermentation locks until fermentation is complete and until the specific gravity is below 1.000 and steady for one month. Then bottle again.

   • Sweetening wine before bottling and not adding a stabilizer may cause bottles to explode.

   Remedy
   Same as above. Potassium sorbate or other stabilizers will not stop an active fermentation; they merely prevent renewed fermentation when sugar is added to a wine before bottling.

4. **Yeasty Taste.** A wine may taste yeasty if the wrong yeast has been used. It also may have a yeasty flavor if it has not been sufficiently racked and fined, or if you drink it before it has aged properly.

   Remedy
   None. Aging will help somewhat, but if the wrong yeast has been used, nothing can be done.

5. **Bottle Smell.** You sometimes smell sulphur when opening a bottle of wine.

   Remedy
   Allow the wine to stand uncorked for a few hours or decant the wine and wait a short time.

6. **Musty Odor.** If a musty smell is noticed when a bottle of wine is opened, it may be due to mold on or in the cork. All corks should be examined. The fungus could spread.

   Remedy
   Take out all corks. Wipe the inside of bottle necks with your sulphite solution. Insert new sulphite-soaked corks in the bottles.

7. **Flowers of Wine.** Small, whitish islets gradually spread over the surface of the wine and form a film. The wine develops a bad flavor and smell.

   Remedy
   Once the film has covered the surface there is no

remedy. If detected early enough, when only a few islets have formed and when a hint of sour, vinegary smell is noticed, the wine can be saved. First strain it through a closely woven cloth to remove the whitish particles. Next, add two campden tablets for each gallon to sulphite the wine; then bottle at once. Caution must be taken to thoroughly disinfect the bad wine's container.

8. **Oxidation.** When wine has been overly exposed to air it will oxidize. Sometimes low-acid wine made from overripe fruit will oxidize. Oxidized wine will be brownish in color and bitter in taste.

Remedy

None. This could have been prevented by fermenting at proper temperatures — 60°F to 75°F and keeping air from the wine when the primary fermentation is over.

9. **Vinegar Smell and Taste.** Wine can develop a smell and taste of vinegar and turn to vinegar (not the edible type you use for salad) when it is attacked by acetobacter (vinegar bacteria). This problem is usually caused because fermentation locks were not used or not used soon enough. Also, if secondary fermentors were not topped up, wine sometimes turns to vinegar.

Remedy

None. Any containers that have held vinegar-wine must be thoroughly sterilized with sulphite before being used again.

WINEMAKING
Glossary

Aging. Changes that take place in wine after fermentation is finished. Aging makes wine more pleasant to drink.

Aerobic Fermentation. Primary fermentation, "with air."

Anerobic Fermentation. Secondary fermentation, "without air."

Astringent. The bite or pucker taste given to wine by the tannin.

Autolyses. The live yeast's consumption of yeast sediment that gives wine a bad flavor.

Balling Scale. Hydrometer scale which gives the sugar content in percent by weight.

Body. The fullness of the wine, referring to the alcohol and glycerine content. This has nothing to do with sugar content; dry or sweet wines can be either full-bodied or thin-bodied.

Bouquet. The sum total of the wine's aromas that result from a combination of alcohol, acids and aldehydes.

Brix Scale. Balling scale.

Cap. A floating layer of fruit pulp that forms on the top of the primary fermentor during primary fermentation.

Carbon Dioxide. Gas given off by fermenting yeast.

Dry Wine. Wine which is not sweet. It contains less than 1 percent residual sugar (unfermented sugar).

False Wine. A second-run wine made by adding sugar, water and other additives to the pulp left from the first run.

Finings. Substances that clear the haze in a cloudy wine by carrying the suspended solids to the bottom of the secondary fermentor. Pectic enzyme and sparkolloid are finings.

First Run. The first wine made from the pure, undiluted juice of a fruit.

Fortification. The adding of distilled spirits to increase the alcoholic content of wine.

Labrusca Grapes. Grapes such as Concord, Niagara, Delaware—native North American grapes having a "foxy" flavor.

Lees. The yeast sediment in the bottom of a fermentor.

Must. Ingredients consisting of crushed fruit, juices, additives, etc, before fermentation.

Rack. Syphon.

Rosé. A pink or very light red wine.

Spirits. Beverages produced by distillation that have a high alcoholic content. Brandy, vodka, gin, for instance.

Starter. A living yeast culture used to start fermentation in a large volume of must.

Sulphiting. Using sulphite in musts and wines as a sterilizing agent.

Sweet Wine. Wine sweet in flavor that contains 1 percent or more residual (unfermented) sugar.

Table Wine. Dry wine—red, white or rosé, usually consumed with the main part of a meal. Table wines have from 9 percent to 14 percent alcohol.

Topping Up. Filling a secondary fermentor to the neck using wine, sugar-syrup or distilled water to minimize oxidation.

Vinifera Grape. The wine grape, European in origin, now grown in Europe and California.

White Wine. Not red, not rosé—but various colors from light yellow to deep golden to brownish.

BEER

"The joy bringer." That is what the ancient Egyptians called their beer. And that is what beer still is for thousands of Americans. At baseball games, after work, after play — nothing refreshes you on a hot day like a cold beer foaming in a chilled mug.

Beer has been bringing joy since at least 6000 BC; archeologists have found references to beer in ancient Mesopotamia. Beer was the Egyptian's favorite drink. Beer and bread were standard fare for Egyptian slaves, peasants, priests and kings. Beermaking spread throughout the Roman empire and developed into a booming industry during the Middle Ages, especially in Northern Europe where it was too cold to grow grapes for wine. Pictures of medieval revelry often show enormous joints of meat being washed down by beer or — as the British call their favorite heavy beer — ale.

European and British brewers formed guilds and provided the necessary drink for daily meals, as well as the obligatory refreshment at festivals and parties. (Water, at that time, was dangerously polluted.) In fact, ale used to be synonymous with "festival." If a medieval Englishman said he was going to a "bride-ale" he meant he was going to a wedding celebration. That is the source of our word "bridal" — from "bride-ale."

If you could take a sip of those early beers while listening to minstrels in motley singing bawdy ballads, you would find yourself drinking a heavy, highly alcoholic brew. Soon you would be adding shocking verses of your own to the minstrel's song. If we drank those old ales at baseball games, few of us would see the fourth inning. Fortunately for baseball, beers are lighter now and have a lower alcoholic content. Shakespeare's Falstaff would think us sissies for guzzling watery American lagers.

Brewing was one of the first industries in the American colonies. The Pilgrims brought beer with them on the Mayflower; they sighted Plymouth Rock just before their beer supply ran out. The first brewery was built in 1683 by William Penn; most large estates, such as George Washington's and Thomas Jefferson's, had their own breweries and experimented with different beer recipes. Americans drank the heavier British beer until the 1840s when German settlers introduced the lighter lager beers that are so popular today.

IS BEERMAKING LEGAL?

The laws on the legality of beermaking are skimpy. Winemaking is legal, but there is no clear rule on beermaking. The Internal Revenue Service considers home brewing illegal and they cite Section 5222 (a) (2) (B) of the Internal Revenue Code. The code restricts beermaking to an authorized brewery, but it refers specifically only to beer for sale to the public.

The home brewer argues that a home is not a brewery and his beer is not for sale to the public; it is for home consumption.

The IRS has not, to our knowledge, taken anyone to court for home brewing. The cost of policing would probably exceed the revenue from taxing home brews. You must be the best judge of what you do in your own home. Should you decide to brew beer at home, here are the basic equipment, ingredients and steps.

BASIC EQUIPMENT

1. **Beginning book.** A good beginning book is a handy tool. There are, of course, some really bad books for sale. Purchase a recently written book devoted to making beer. It will give you complete details, information beyond the basic steps given in this chapter, and allow you to delve deeper into the science of beermaking.
2. **Boiling kettle.** If you use compressed hops in your beer, you will need to boil them in water and in the malt. Some recipes recommend boiling all of the water with the hops. If this is done, then use a very large pot or kettle that will hold about seven gallons. Stainless steel, enamel (no chips or cracks) or pyrex glass should be used. Never use aluminum or iron. When a recipe calls for boiling only one or two gallons of water, a smaller pot is sufficient.
3. **Primary fermentor.** The first container used in fermenting beer is your primary fermentor. A polyethylene wastebasket makes a good primary fermentor. Be sure it is odorless and pale colored. Dark colored containers may fade into the beer. The primary fermentor holds the "wort" — a mixture of hops, water, malt, additives and corn sugar. The container has to be thoroughly washed with soap and hot water, rinsed with sulphite solution then re-rinsed with hot water just before filling.
4. **Plastic sheet.** While the wort is fermenting, you cover the primary fermentor with a plastic sheet. The first fermentation is not sealed. You use the plastic sheet to keep out foreign matter. Select a sheet about a yard square, 1½ to 2 mills thick, and tie it loosely around the primary with a string or loose elastic band. Some winemaking stores sell a large muslin cap, like a large shower cap, that makes a good cover for the beer's primary fermentor.
5. **Sterilizing solution.** There are conflicting views about what to use as a sterilizing agent in beermaking. For years nothing was used except hot soapy water or boiling water for cleaning the equipment. Then some authorities recommended sulphite sterilizing as in winemaking, because sulphite eliminates any residual soap. So, in recent years home beermakers have rinsed their equipment with a sulphite solution, just as a winemaker sterilized his equipment.

   A few years ago the same authorities who had recommended sulphite sterilizing solutions suddenly reversed their viewpoint and maintained that sodium metabisulphite and potassium metabisulphite nearly always react with the beer and produce hydrogen sulphite — a gas that smells like rotten eggs. They insist that sulphite is fine for the fermentation locks but not for sterilizing beer equipment. They claim that the home beermaker should thoroughly wash and rinse out his equipment with something else just prior to using the equipment — soap and hot water, for instance.

As a rule sulphite will not cause a rotten egg odor. To be safe, though, we suggest that you thoroughly wash out your equipment with very hot water, then use the sulphite and re-rinse with water. The sulphite used for winemaking is the same sulphite used for beermaking. If you use soap, then re-rinse several times with hot water. Use the equipment immediately.

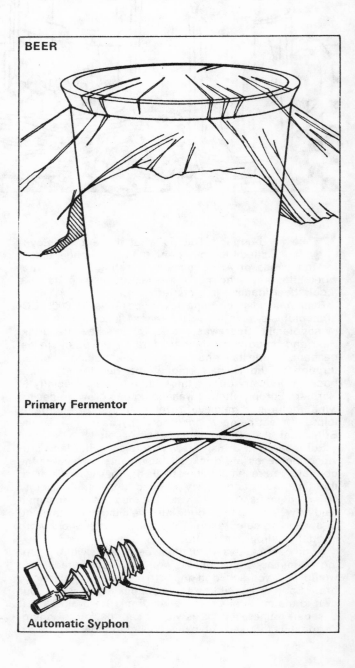

BEER

Primary Fermentor

Automatic Syphon

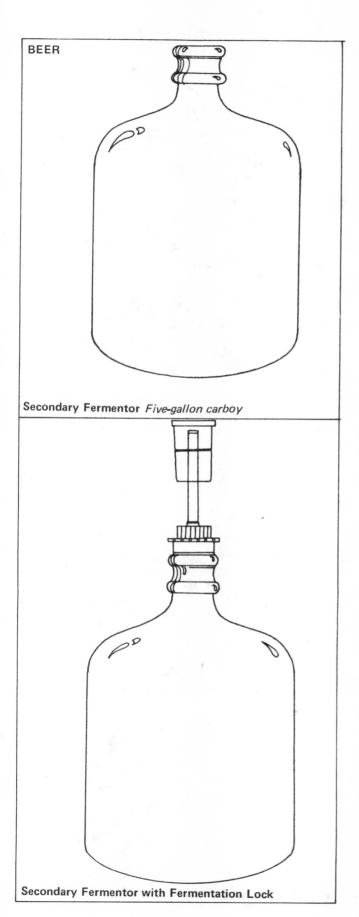

BEER

Secondary Fermentor *Five-gallon carboy*

Secondary Fermentor with Fermentation Lock

If you are delayed, wash and rinse again. Two ounces of metabisulphite or potassium metabisulphite dissolved in a gallon of warm water makes enough sterilizing solution to use for three or four months. The solution should retain its strong odor. Keep it capped tightly or it will lose its strength. If the solution does not smell strongly, do not use it. Sulphite prevents mold and bacteria growth. When you rinse with sulphite, catch the solution in a bowl or large container and pour it back into its original container. Keep sulphite clearly labeled and locked high out of the reach of children.

6. **Stirrer.** A plastic, wooden or stainless steel long-handled stirrer is best to use while making beer.

7. **Syphon.** The syphon transfers the wort from one container to another. There are many kinds of syphons available. A five foot length of food-grade vinyl tubing, ⅝-inch in diameter inside and ⅞-inch outside in diameter makes an excellent syphon. Check the chapter on wines, under Basic Equipment for details on automatic syphons. If you use a plain vinyl tube for a syphon you have to put one end in the wort and suck on the other end to start the prime flowing.

8. **Secondary fermentor.** When the wort has fermented a few days in the primary fermentor it is ready to be syphoned into a second container for airtight fer-

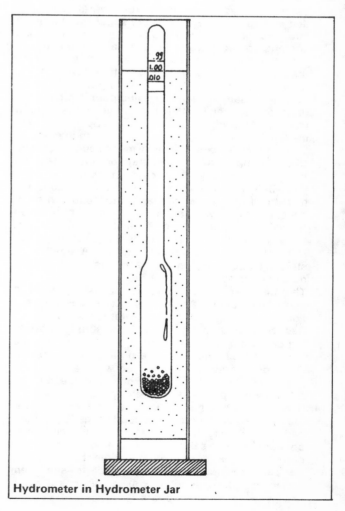

Hydrometer in Hydrometer Jar

mentation. Usually beer is made in five-gallon or larger batches; therefore, a five-gallon or large glass jug (carboy) is recommended as a secondary fermentor. If the amount of beer being made exceeds five gallons, then use one-gallon glass jugs for the excess. If you are making ten gallons, two five-gallon glass jugs would be used.

9. **Fermentation lock and stopper.** Sometimes called air lock, water trap or water lock, the fermentation lock fits into a rubber or cork stopper or into a plastic screw cap placed on the secondary fermentor. The lock allows the carbon dioxide produced by fermentation to escape and keeps out dirt and bugs. While there are many kinds of locks the most common ones are plastic. Some locks look like pretzels, some are "U"-shaped with a long stem. Stoppers also come in various styles. There are white rubber stoppers shaped like tapered corks with a hole in the center (use a number 6 or 6½ for one-gallon and five-gallon jugs). Red rubber caps, with a hole in the center, that fit over the necks of jugs are also commonly used.

10. **Hydrometer and jar.** There are special beer hydrometers available, but they are not necessary. You can use a regular triple scale hydrometer for measuring the sugar-density of the beer. The hydrometer is a hollow glass bulb or cylinder weighted at the base. It extends to a long, slender, hollow glass tube. Inside the tube there is a scale printed on paper. The hydrometer measures the natural or added sugars in the wort. It is the sugar that ferments into alcohol. Different beers have different alcoholic content, so you have to keep an accurate count of your beer's sugar level to be certain you are making the kind of beer you intended to brew. The hydrometer jar is a tall, thin, plastic or glass container. You take a sample of the wort and pour it into the hydrometer jar, then float the hydrometer in the jar for a reading of the wort's specific gravity. Specific gravity means the density of soluble particles. In the case of beer and wine, specific gravity means sugar content.

11. **Cheesecloth, fermentation bag or hops steeping bag.** If you use dry, compressed hops in your beer, you will have to boil them. Then, the boiled hops will have to be strained out of the boiling mixture through cheesecloth. Or you can use a cheesecloth or nylon fermentation bag to hold the hops like a tea bag. When you use the finished hops, they, too, will have to be strained or contained in a bag. A small hops steeping bag — nylon with a drawstring — eliminates the mess.

12. **Thermometer.** Temperature control is important in good beermaking. An immersion thermometer that floats is the best for taking careful readings.

13. **Beer bottles.** Unless you like the absurdity of drinking beer from soda pop bottles, use only returnable beer bottles. Never use wine bottles or non-carbonated drink bottles. They are too weak and will explode. A standard 12-ounce brown bottle can be drunk by one person at one sitting.

14. **Crown caps.** You have to use the same kind of caps that you see on beer or soda pop bottles. Only these caps can withstand the pressure of the beer's carbonation. Plastic safety caps can also be used; they pop off if the carbonation is too violent.

15. **Capper.** Crown caps require a capper to seal them on the lip of the beer bottle. You can buy metal, nylon or vinyl hand-model cappers.

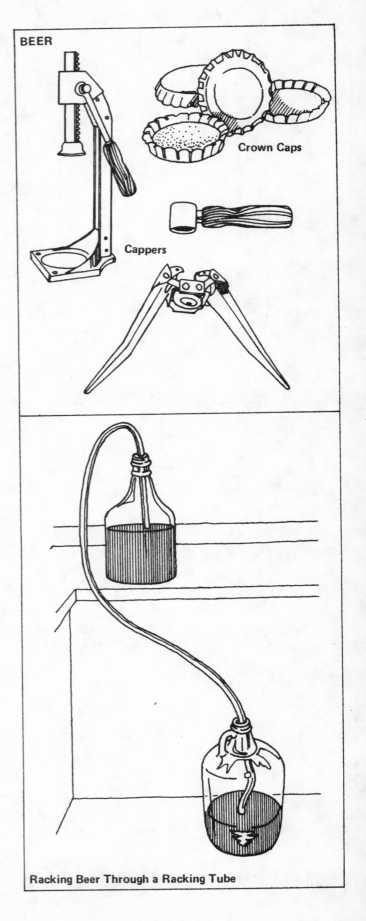

BEER

Crown Caps

Cappers

Racking Beer Through a Racking Tube

ADDITIONAL EQUIPMENT

1. **Funnels.** Funnels are useful for transferring sulphite back and forth from jug to jug in the sterilizing process or for adding sugar or sugar syrup in the bottling process.
2. **Racking tube.** Racking is another word for syphoning. You use a rigid plastic tube, curved on one end like a hook, to attach to the flexible syphon hose and hook over the edge of the primary or secondary fermentor. It makes syphoning easier. Sometimes there is considerable sediment on the bottom of the wort. If you make a hole about one inch up from the end of the racking tube (the actual end has a cap on it) then the beer can be syphoned through the hole, leaving the sediment behind.
3. **Baster.** For taking samples from the wort and transferring them to the hydrometer jar, use a plastic cooking baster. You can also use it to start the prime on a syphoning tube instead of using your mouth.
4. **Bottle filler.** Small beer bottles are easy to fill if you use a bottle filler. A plastic, metal or aluminum filler has a long tube with one end that attaches to the syphon. There is a valve for regulating the flow of beer at the other end. Attach the filler to the end of the syphon and start the prime by sucking on the end of the filler. Put the filler down in the beer bottle and push against the bottom of the bottle — this opens the valve and you can fill the bottle.
5. **Beer bottle labels.** Packaged in lots of a dozen, beer bottle labels add a little class to your home brew.
6. **Beer log sheet.** Make a record so you can repeat your favorite recipes. Include such categories as hydrometer readings, dates of racking, ingredients added, major steps in the brewing process.

Basic Ingredients

1. **Malt extract.** Canned malt extracts are available in many types and colors. Thanks to these marvelous extracts, you do not have to make your own malt. Malt extract is made from barley and gives beer its color and flavor. The malt also provides some of the sugar that ferments into alcohol. Some malt extracts have hops added, some have no hops. You can use a dry form of malt, but most people prefer the convenient extracts.
2. **Sugar.** You use corn sugar, not ordinary white cane sugar, for beermaking. Corn sugar ferments easier than cane sugar; a beer made from cane sugar tastes bad.
3. **Water.** Chlorinated water spoils the flavor of beer. Hard water may spoil lager beers, but it is fine for ales. Boil water for all beers, except the ales, to eliminate the chlorine.
4. **Hops.** The female hop plant, *humulus lupulus,* gives beer its characteristic bitter taste. Hops aid the beer's preservation and add the beer's special aroma. Without hops, beer would taste "winey."

Although hops grow wild in some parts of the world, good brewing hops are carefully cultivated. Kent, Bramblin and Fuggles are the best known hops. You can buy compressed or instant hops. Loose finishing hops that are added later in the beermaking process are also available. Be sure that you are using recently packaged hops.

5. **Additives.** These additives aid fermentation and help preserve the beer.
   Citric acid
   Aids in fermentation. Use a minimal amount so that no acid taste is present in your beer. You should add it in the primary stage.
   Energizer
   Energizer is a super-nutrient. It aids in the fermentation. Add it in the secondary stage.
   Salt
   Salt aids in the fermentation. Add it in the primary stage. Do not use very much or your beer will taste salty.
   Fining gelatin
   Add fining gelatin to the beer in the secondary stage; it will clarify the beer by carrying suspended particles to the bottom of the fermentor.
   Anti-oxidant
   Anti-oxidant is ascorbic acid. It prevents oxidation when you syphon the beer into bottles. Oxidation is a chemical reaction that happens when your beer is exposed to air; it causes deterioration and flattens the carbonation.
   Heading liquid
   Heading liquid is optional in beermaking. It is an extract, made from the bark of the Quillaia tree, that helps produce and retain a good head on the beer. Add heading liquid just before you bottle the beer.
   Campden tablets
   Campden tablets are sometimes used when mixing the wort. The tablets help prevent acetobacter, the vinegar bacteria.
6. **Yeast.** Use special beer yeast rather than Baker's Yeast. Baker's Yeast was used for beermaking at home for many years when there was nothing better available. Now you have a choice of numerous liquid or dry commercial beer yeasts. The liquids usually come in vials large enough for five to eight gallons of beer. Packages of dried beer yeast also make five to eight gallons of beer.

Additional Ingredients

Adding various grains to a beer recipe gives the beer special characteristics. Barley, for instance, adds body and makes a richer beer. Barley comes in Crystal Malted Barley, Light Malted Barley and Patent Black Malted Barley. Dried malt extract may be used instead of the canned liquid malt extract, or you can use it along with the liquid malt.

Basic Steps

1. Thoroughly wash all equipment that is going to be used to prepare the wort. Rinse it with hot water, then sterilize the equipment with sulphite solution. Thoroughly re-rinse it with clear hot water.
2. Break up the dry compressed hops and tie them in a piece of cheesecloth, fermentation bag or hop steeping bag.
3. Now put some of the water, the malt, citric acid and salt in the boiling kettle. Simmer for one to two hours.
4. After simmering the hops, discard them and wash the cloth or bag for future use.
5. Pour the hot "wort" into the primary fermentor.
6. Add the corn sugar (save 2 cups for bottling) and stir to dissolve.
7. Add the balance of the water.
8. Add the salt and citric acid.
9. Take a hydrometer reading and adjust the sugar to the recommended specific gravity for the recipe you are using. If you need to add sugar, remember that five ounces of sugar in one gallon will raise the gravity ten points on the hydrometer. If you need to lower the specific gravity, add water.
10. Cover the primary with a plastic sheet or muslin cap. If using a plastic sheet, tie it loosely with a string or elastic band.
11. After twenty-four hours, sprinkle the dry brewers'

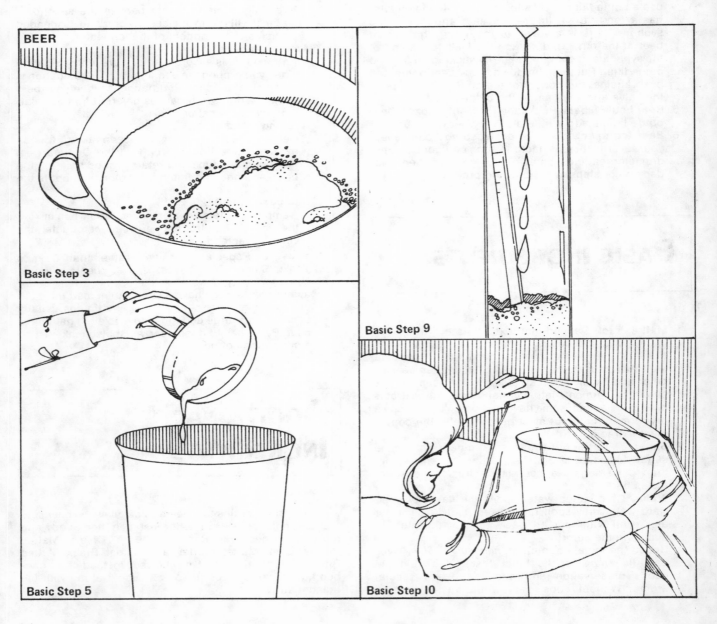

BEER

Basic Step 3

Basic Step 5

Basic Step 9

Basic Step 10

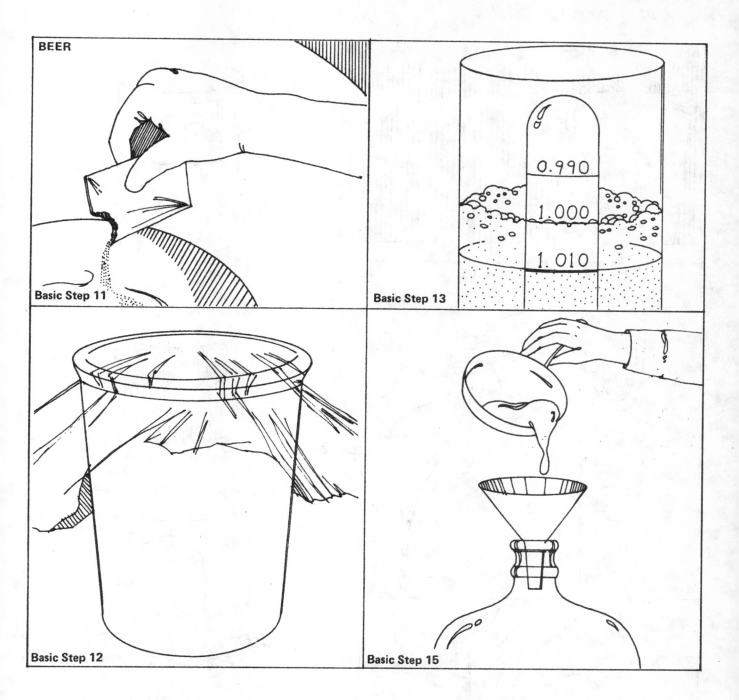

BEER

Basic Step 11

Basic Step 13

Basic Step 12

Basic Step 15

yeast on the surface of the wort.

12. Cover with the plastic sheet, tie the sheet and leave the wort alone.

13. Ferment (foam and bubbles) until the specific gravity reaches 1.010. Take a hydrometer reading every couple of days.

14. Clean and sterilize the syphon, the secondary and anything else that will come in contact with the wort. Re-rinse with water.

15. Add the fining gelatin to a cup of warm water. Pour this mixture into the bottom of the glass carboy (secondary fermentor). Please note: It may be necessary to use an additional gallon jug if the recipe makes 6 gallons of beer. Add a bit of gelatin and energizer to this jug also.

16. Syphon the wort from the primary into the secondary.

17. Add the crushed energizer or energizer powder.

18. Fill the fermentation lock half way with sulphite solution.

19. Attach the lock to the top of the carboy.

20. Two weeks later take a hydrometer reading.

21. If the hydrometer reads 1.000, it is time to bottle. The beer must be clear. If it is not clear, wait until it clears before bottling.

22. To bottle, sterilize and rinse all equipment again.

23. Crush the anti-oxidant tablets or measure out the powder and stir them into the wort.

24. Set aside two cups of the wort and warm them.

25. Syphon the remainder of the wort into the primary fermentor.

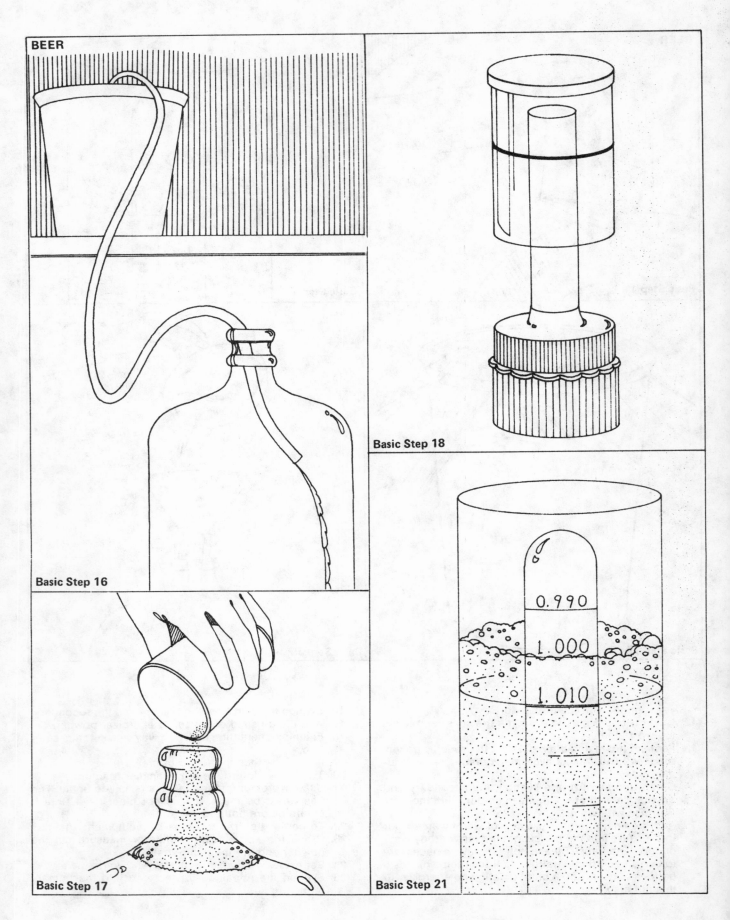

BEER

Basic Step 16

Basic Step 17

Basic Step 18

0.990

1.000

1.010

Basic Step 21

130

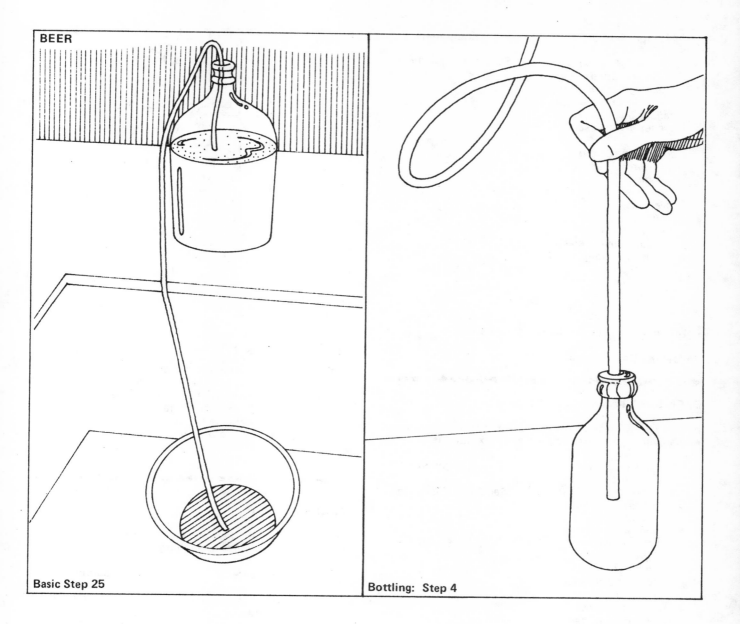

BEER

Basic Step 25

Bottling: Step 4

26. Now mix the remaining sugar into the two cups of warmed wort.
27. When the sugar-wort mixture has cooled to at least 70° F. pour it back into the wort.
28. If you are using a heading liquid, add it now and stir.

STEPS FOR BOTTLING

1. Wash your bottles in clean clear warm water.
2. Rinse each bottle out with half strength sulphite solution.
3. Re-rinse each bottle with clean, hot water.
4. Syphon the beer into the bottles, filling each bottle to within one inch of the top.
5. Cap with a crown cap.
6. Store in a cool, dry, dark place for at least two weeks.
7. After two weeks, put a bottle into the refrigerator and chill.

8. Open. If it is not carbonated, wait a longer period of time and repeat the test.
9. Age longer (perhaps 3 months) if the beer does not taste the way you think it should.

RECIPES

LIGHT BAVARIAN TYPE BEER

If you like a moderately light beer, try this one. The recipe makes 6 gallons.

Ingredients

One can (2½ pounds)
    lightly hopped malt
    extract such as Blue
    Ribbon Extra Pale Dry
6 gallons boiled water
2 ounces compressed
    hops
4 pounds corn sugar
    (reserve 2 cups for
    bottling)
1 level teaspoon citric acid
2 level teaspoons salt
4 energizer tablets
2 anti-oxidant tablets
½ teaspoon fining gelatin
1 teaspoon heading liquid
    (optional)
1 package lager beer
    yeast

Equipment

See Basic Equipment

Starting specific gravity should be 1.035 to 1.040
Terminal specific gravity should be 1.000

Follow the Basic Steps

DARK BAVARIAN TYPE BEER

A dark, hefty beer so rich and satisfying that you will relish every drop. The recipe makes six gallons.

Ingredients

One can (2½ to 3
    pounds) dark malt
    extract
6 gallons water, boiled
2 ounces compressed
    hops
4 pounds corn sugar
    (reserve 2 cups for
    bottling)
1 level teaspoon citric acid
2 level teaspoons salt
4 energizer tablets
2 anti-oxidant tablets
½ teaspoon fining gelatin
1 teaspoon heading liquid
    (optional)
1 package dark Munich
    beer yeast

Equipment

See Basic Equipment

Starting specific gravity should be 1.035 to 1.040
Terminal gravity should be 1.000

Follow the Basic Steps

VARIATION I

Beer Using Instant Hops

This variation eliminates steps 2 through 8 of the Basic Steps to produce some excellent brews.

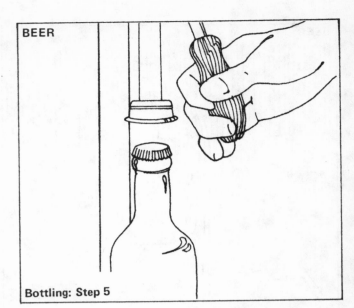

BEER

Bottling: Step 5

Steps for Variation I

1. Wash all the equipment that you use to prepare the wort. Rinse it with hot water, sterilize with sulphite solution, re-rinse with clear hot water.
2. Put the malt extract, sugar (less 2 cups), instant hops, citric acid, salt, crushed campden tablets and hot water into the primary fermentor.
3. Follow Basic Steps 9 through 28.

LAGER BEER

Here is everyone's favorite American-type beer — light, pale amber and thirst-quenching.

Ingredients

One can (2½ pounds)
    light malt extract, such
    as Blue Pale Dry
6 gallons boiled water
1 package instant hops
6 pounds corn sugar
    (reserve 2 cups for
    bottling)
1 level teaspoon citric acid
2 level teaspoons salt
4 energizer tablets
2 anti-oxidant tablets
½ teaspoon fining gelatin
1 teaspoon heading liquid
    (optional)
6 campden tablets
1 package lager beer
    yeast

Equipment

See Basic Equipment
You will not need the
    fermentation bag or
    boiling kettle

Starting specific gravity should be around 1.050
Terminal specific gravity should be 1.000

Follow the steps for Variation I

RED, WHITE AND BLUE TYPE

Many Americans prefer a very light, almost watery beer. Here is a good light beer and it is economical too! The recipe makes 9 gallons.

Ingredients	Equipment
One can (2½ pounds) light malt extract such as Blue Ribbon Pale Dry	See Basic Equipment You will not need the fermentation bag or boiling kettle.
6 gallons boiled water	
1 package instant hops	
6 pounds corn sugar (reserve 3 cups for bottling)	
1 level teaspoon of citric acid	
2 level teaspoons salt	
4 energizer tablets	
2 anti-oxidant tablets	
½ teaspoon fining gelatin	
1 teaspoon heading liquid (optional)	
6 campden tablets	
1 package lager beer yeast	

Starting specific gravity should be 1.050 to 1.060
Terminal specific gravity should be 1.000

Follow the steps for Variation I. Then, just before bottling, dilute the beer with three gallons of water.

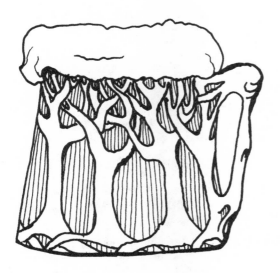

VARIATION II

Ales

Finishing hops add flavor and intensify the aroma of your beer. Ales, which are heavier than lager beers, use finishing hops. Good ale should be made from hard water. If your water is soft, add 1 ounce of gypsum to the water when boiling it.

Steps for Variation II

1. Follow Basic Steps 1 through 5.
2. Throw in the finishing hops.
3. Continue Basic Steps 6 through 15.
4. Remove finishing hops from the wort.
5. Continue Basic Steps 16 through 28. Stir the beer daily during secondary fermentation. Ferment at 50°F to 70°F.

PALE ALE

Ale has a characteristic bitter tang. Ale ferments best at 50°F to 70°F. The recipe makes 5 to 6 gallons.

Ingredients	Equipment
1 can (2½ pounds) light malt extract	See Basic Equipment
2 ounces compressed hops	
½ ounce finishing hops	
5 gallons boiled hard water	
4 pounds corn sugar (reserve 2 cups for bottling)	
¾ teaspoon salt	
1 teaspoon citric acid	
4 energizer tablets	
½ teaspoon fining gelatin	
1 teaspoon heading liquid (optional)	
2 anti-oxidant tablets	
1 package ale yeast	

Starting specific gravity is 1.035
Terminal specific gravity is 1.000

Follow the steps for Variation II

DARK ALE

Do you prefer your ale dark rather than light? Then this ale is for you. The recipe makes 5 to 6 gallons.

Ingredients	Equipment
1 can (2½ pounds) plain dark malt extract	See Basic Equipment
3 ounces compressed hops	
¾ ounce finishing hops	
3½ pounds corn sugar	
½ pound brown sugar	
5 gallons hard water	
1¾ teaspoons salt	
1 teaspoon citric acid	
4 energizer tablets	
1 teaspoon heading liquid (optional)	
2 anti-oxidant tablets	
1 package ale yeast	

Starting specific gravity is 1.035
Terminal specific gravity is 1.000

Follow the steps for Variation II

COMMON PROBLEMS

1. **Sediment in Bottom of the Beer Bottle.** Sediment will not harm you, but it looks ugly. You can minimize it when you pour the beer into your glass.

   Remedy
   Pour very slowly and at one setting. Pour the complete bottle; do not stop until you see the sediment beginning to move off the bottom and into your flowing beer.

2. **Beer Tastes Awful.** Most recipes ask you to age your recipes a short time; however, it still may not be palatable. In fact, it may be downright atrocious.

   Remedy
   Age the beer another three months.

3. **Filling Your Beer Bottles Is Difficult.** Your beer bottles fall over, break, refuse to drain properly after sulphiting. Whoops you missed a couple!

   Remedy
   Place the bottles on the case that held your used beer bottles, or use a beer or wine case — something with dividers. They make excellent supports. When you sulphite, you can put the rinsed bottles upside down and allow them to drain.

4. **The Wort Foams Up Into the Lock.** This is common. Do not be alarmed.

   Remedy
   Clean out the lock. Add fresh sulphite and continue.

5. **Your Primary Fermentor Has a Terrible Brewery Odor or Your Primary Just Plain Smells!**

   Remedy
   Baking soda is excellent for cleaning your primary.

6. **Your Beer Bottles Explode.**

   Remedy
   Give a great deal of respect to your fermented beer. It may have undetectable residual sugar. Do not shake the bottles. Carry them to the refrigerator with a glove or wrapped in a towel. Keep the bottles cool once the beer is carbonated.

Glossary BEERMAKING

Ale. A heavier beverage than most beer. Ale is "top-fermented" — the yeast rises to the top of the fermentor. Ale is stronger and bitterer than Lager Beer.

Barley. A cereal grain that is often used as the basic ingredient of beer.

Bock. A heavy, dark beer with a stronger, richer flavor than regular beer.

Carboy. A narrow necked glass jug resembling a one gallon glass jug. A carboy has no handle and is usually 5 gallons in size, but some are as large as 15 gallons. They are commonly used as a secondary fermentor.

Dortmunder. A very pale Bohemian beer.

Finishing Hops. Loose hops which are sometimes added after you boil the wort; they lend aroma to the beer.

Heading Liquid. A liquid additive that causes a thicker, longer lasting head on the beer.

Lager. A light, yellow, clear beer that ferments best at approximately 40°F. It is "bottom-fermenting" beer — the yeast settles to the bottom. "Lager" is a German word meaning "warehouse" or "store." Beer was originally called by this name because it was stored all winter. American beer is mostly the Lager beer.

Malt. Malt provides the sugar and most of the flavor and color of beer. It is made from barley.

Malt Extract. A product that results when the starch from barley or other grain is converted into sugar, which, in turn, is converted into alcohol. Malt extract is usually used by home beer makers rather than malt.

Malt Liquor. A recently invented beer that lacks the malt and hop taste of lager beer but has a higher alcoholic content. It tastes like porter or stout.

Munich. A light to dark brown beer with stronger hop flavor and stronger in alcohol than lager.

Pilsener. From the city of Pilsen, Czechoslovakia. A Bohemian beer, pale and more hop-flavored than Bavarian beer.

Porter. A variation of ale but with fewer hops and a sweeter taste.

Steam Beer. Regular beer. In the old West, where beer had to be fermented at warmer temperatures than usual, the steam process was preferred. Actually, most home brew is more of a "steam beer" than a lager.

Stout. Somewhat like a porter beer but very "malty" in taste and sweeter, yet dark and heavy.

Weiss. German beer that is usually made from wheat instead of barley. Weiss translated means "white." Weiss beer is very pale in color and quite tart tasting. It is quite foamy.

Wort. The basic mixture of ingredients for making beer, comparable to the "must" of winemaking.

SodA Pop

Making soda pop at home may seem unusual, but homemade sassafras drink and root beer were turn-of-the-century favorites. They gradually found their way to the corner drugstore's soda fountain, where flavored syrups were mixed with carbonated water. Then they went on to become the mass-produced multi-flavored carbonated drinks we consume in such enormous quantities today.

Homemade soda pop is not like any carbonated beverage you can get from the supermarket or a vending machine. It has a unique flavor — yeasty, somewhat bubbly and with just the slightest hint of alcohol. We suggest you present samples of your homemade pop for tasting without any introduction or description. Then, once everyone has had a taste, tell them what it is and how you made it. You will probably get an assortment of opinions, both before and after tasting.

You can make soda pop at home for less than it would cost to buy commercially-made pop. The first method of making pop in this chapter uses yeast to produce carbon dioxide — the bubbles. Pop made by fermentation stays bubbly for a fairly long time. This pop has a small alcohol content, about one percent. Consider it the champagne of soda pops. Adults usually like it better than children. It goes well with picnic lunches and backyard suppers. Enjoy a bottle of homemade root beer on a summer afternoon; it will cheer you up and make you think of old-fashioned soda fountains, Gibson girls and bicycles built for two. If you are planning a block party this year, why not follow a theme of the gay nineties, or turn-of-the-century America, and serve homemade pop and homemade ice cream. Have your children run an old-fashioned ice cream parlor and serve ice cream floats and sodas.

This chapter's second way of making pop uses carbonated water or club soda to produce instant soda pops. The kids all have fun sampling all the different kinds of syrups that can be made into fizzy glasses of pop. This kind of pop has no alcoholic content. It does not keep its bubble very long.

If you make soda pop with yeast you are going to be working with gas (carbon dioxide) under pressure (in a closed bottle). There are certain necessary precautions for this method. Follow our Basic Steps and Equipment suggestions exactly and you should not have problems.

Basic Equipment

1. **Measuring cups**
2. **Measuring spoons**
3. **Wooden spoon for stirring**
4. **Large plastic or enamel container.** The Root Beer recipe makes about 3 gallons; you will want a container that holds at least 4 gallons. You can use a specially-purchased plastic bucket or wastebasket, or use a large kettle or water-bath canner.
5. **Funnel and ladle or syphon.** You will need a funnel and ladle or a syphon to get the pop into the bottles. If you are adept at syphoning, use a five-foot food

grade syphon — just as for winemaking. A funnel that fits in the top of the bottles is neat and easy.

6. **Bottles.** Bottles and caps are the most important equipment in making soda pop. Save the bottles from commercial pop. Bottles must be the returnable kind, with rounded tops designed for crown caps, not screw caps. Use any size — seven-ounce, sixteen-ounce or one-quart. Do not use one-way, non-returnable or disposable bottles. They are made from weaker glass and could easily explode.

7. **Bottle caps and bottle capper.** Bottle caps and capper can be purchased at home winemaking shops. A bottle capper pushes the crown caps on bottles and crimps the edges in place. Follow the capper's directions for putting crown caps in place.

   Plastic safety caps, available in home winemaking stores, some liquor stores and supermarkets, are satisfactory and you do not need a capper to put them in place. These caps just snap on the lip of the bottle. They have a raised center with a groove running around the outer edge of the cap. They will retain the soda's carbonation and if the pressure inside builds up too much, they just pop off. You can reuse plastic caps. These caps may not fit snuggly on every size bottle, so prevent leaking by storing plastic capped bottles upright rather than on their sides. You may have an occasional bottle of pop go flat because the plastic cap did not fit tightly enough, but the safety feature more than makes up for the loss of one or two bottles of pop.

8. **Box.** Use a cardboard box, wooden box or styrofoam cooler to store the pop while it ferments.

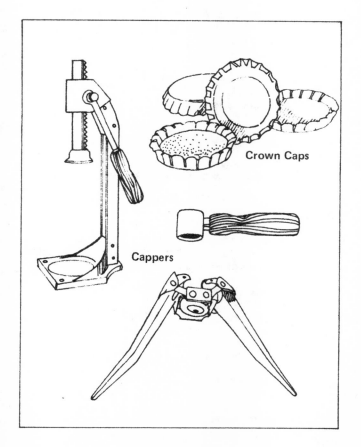

Crown Caps

Cappers

Basic Ingredients

1. **Flavoring extracts.** Use extracts that are made especially for soda pop. These may be fountain syrups, bottled extracts or flavored drink powders (Kool Aid). We prefer the bottled extracts. They come in three or four-ounce bottles, in fruit flavors, root beer, ale, cola and others. The flavored drink powders are easier to find, but do not taste as good as extracts. Never use extracts made for flavoring liqueurs. They cause excessive foaming and carbonation and you will have bottles exploding all over the ceiling.
2. **Water.** Use your tap water unless it has a strong flavor.
3. **Sugar.** Use white granulated sugar.
4. **Yeast.** Baker's yeast was once used for pop, but wine or Champagne yeasts, available in home winemaking stores, are much better. Always start with lukewarm or tepid water so the yeast can begin working. Cold water slows down yeast action and hot water may kill yeast.

Basic Steps

Ingredients	Equipment
Extract	Measuring cup
Sugar	Measuring spoons
Water	Large container for mixing
Yeast	Wooden spoon
	Funnel and ladle or syphon
	Returnable pop bottles and caps — plastic or crown
	Cardboard box, wooden box or styrofoam cooler

1. Wash all equipment, including pop bottles, in hot suds. Rinse well and dry. If the equipment is not properly cleaned you will get a bacterial growth that can make the pop slimy.
2. Shake the extract well, if using bottled extracts. Stir the extract and sugar and water together in the mixing container, stirring until sugar is dissolved.
3. Stir in the yeast until it is dissolved and well mixed.
4. Ladle or syphon the pop into clean bottles to within 1 inch of the top.
5. Cap with crown or plastic lids.
6. If you use crown lids, place the capped bottles on their sides in a cardboard or wooden box or styro-

foam cooler. Cover to keep them from drafts. If you use plastic lids, stand the bottles upright in a box or cooler.

7. Set the box of bottles aside in warm place. If the temperature is about 70°F. the pop will take one to five days to carbonate. Below 70°F. it will take longer than five days to carbonate; above 80°F. probably just 1 day to carbonate.

8. Check for carbonation. After one day take bottle and refrigerate it, standing upright, until chilled. Working over the sink, open the bottle very slowly and carefully, lifting the lid easily and gently so the carbonation cannot escape all at once. Check by looking and tasting to see if the pop is carbonated enough. If the pop is still somewhat flat, let it stand another day or more.

9. When the pop is carbonated enough, move it to a cool place or refrigerate and drink within two weeks. Always refrigerate the bottles upright and be sure to open the bottles over the sink in case they foam over.

Recipes

ROOT BEER

Homemade Root Beer is heftier — more like beer — than commercial Root Beer. It is superb with sausage and cheese sandwiches. This recipe makes about 25 (16-ounce) bottles or 12 (1-quart) bottles. You could halve the recipe for your first attempt.

Ingredients	Equipment
1 3-ounce Hires Root Beer extract	See Basic Equipment
2 pounds (4½ cups) sugar	
3 gallons tepid water	
½ teaspoon all-purpose wine or Champagne yeast	

Follow the Basic Steps

CHERRY POP

Cherry Pop, bright red and shimmering, makes a perfect birthday party beverage. If you cannot find a one-ounce size of extract, merely measure out one ounce from the larger sized extract bottle. The extract will keep. This recipe makes 10 (16-ounce) or 5 (1-quart) bottles.

Ingredients	Equipment
1 ounce cherry extract	See Basic Equipment
3 cups sugar	
5 quarts tepid water	
¼ teaspoon all-purpose wine yeast or Champagne yeast	

Follow the Basic Steps

COLA

Much more potent than store-bought colas, homemade Cola makes an unusual afternoon treat. This recipe makes 10 (16-ounce) bottles or 5 (1-quart) bottles.

Ingredients	Equipment
1 ounce Cola extract	See Basic Equipment
3 cups sugar	
5 quarts tepid water	
¼ teaspoon all-purpose wine yeast or Champagne yeast	

Follow the Basic Steps

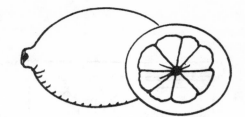

LIME SODA

You can increase this recipe for a larger batch of cooling Lime Soda. The recipe makes 10 (16-ounce) bottles or 5 (1-quart) bottles.

Ingredients	Equipment
1 ounce Lime extract	See Basic Equipment
3 cups sugar	
5 quarts tepid water	
¼ teaspoon all-purpose wine yeast or Champagne yeast	

Follow the Basic Steps

DIET SODA

Even calorie-conscious soda lovers can enjoy homemade soda. You can use any flavor of extract with this recipe. The recipe makes about 25 (16-ounce) bottles or 12 (1-quart) bottles. Make just half a recipe if you wish.

Ingredients	Equipment
3 ounces any soda extract	See Basic Equipment
6½ ounces sugar	
3 gallons tepid water	
½ teaspoon all-purpose wine yeast or Champagne yeast	

Follow the Basic Steps. But, when ready to drink, sweeten to taste with any artificial sweetener.

VARIATION I

Making Soda With Carbonated Water or Unfermented Soda

Here is a neat and simple way of making soda pop. All you do is mix the flavored syrup with carbonated water (using a soda syphon) or club soda. The soda is not quite as fizzy and does lose its carbonation quite rapidly, but you can enjoy an instant, refreshing drink. First you make the Fountain Syrup, then you mix your soda. The recipe makes one quart of Fountain Soda, enough for at least 16 glasses of soda.

Ingredients	Equipment
3 cups white granulated sugar	1 quart bottle
1 quart warm water	Saucepan
1 ounce any soda extract	Jar with lid
Carbonated water or club soda to fill a large glass	Tall glass
Ice	

1. Put the sugar into a quart bottle.
3. Fill the bottle to the neck with the warm water and mix.
3. Pour the mixture into a pan and bring it to a simmer.
4. Add the extract, stir and cool. This makes a delicious fountain syrup which you can use immediately or store in a covered jar for later use.
5. Put 1 or 2 ounces of Fountain Syrup in a tall glass.
6. Carbonate the water if you have a soda syphon or use commercial club soda.
7. Fill the glass nearly to the top with carbonated water or club soda and stir.
8. Add ice and drink immediately.

COMMON PROBLEMS

1. **Soda pop mixture did not carbonate.**

   Remedies
   - Check the temperature of your storage area. If it is below 70° F, move the soda pop to a warmer place and wait.
   - If it is over 70° F, try moving the soda pop to an even warmer place and wait longer.
   - If the above two remedies do not work, you may have added the yeast when the temperature of the water was too warm, or perhaps you did not stir well enough. Wait about 10 days more, and if there is no carbonation, then unbottle and add the yeast again. Re-bottle and wait again. Or discard the soda mixture and be more careful next time. Another trick for carbonation is to add two crushed energizer tablets to the sugar-water-extract mixture. (See chapter on wines for energizer tablets.)

2. **Soda pop bottles explode while you are waiting for soda to carbonate.**

   Remedy
   - One bottle may carbonate sooner than another. Refrigerate a couple bottles and test them. Test sooner next time. If you fear explosions, even though the bottles are protected in a box, next time use plastic safety caps. Then the cap will blow off, but the bottle will not explode.

3. **Soda pop tastes yeasty.**

   Remedies
   - Let it stand in the refrigerator a few more days. Then taste.
   - Try a different flavor next time. Some flavors disguise the yeast better than other flavors. On the other hand, homemade soda pop simply may not be to your taste.

Money Saving Tips

Apples. Along toward spring, apples sometimes seem tasteless. For more flavorful apples, simmer slices with just a bit of water, a dash each of lemon juice and cinnamon. Lemon juice is a potent flavor-perker for most foods.

Bananas, black. If they are a bargain, or you have extra bananas, mash with some lemon juice, then seal in plastic bags or small covered containers and freeze until you are ready to bake bread or cupcakes. Remember to freeze in measured amounts.

Beef. Good ground beef comes from your own grinder. Buy chuck, round or whatever is on special and tote it home to grind. Use the meat for patties, meat loaves, cold cuts or sausage.

Bread. Save every scrap and put it to use. Cut cubes and oven-toast them for croutons or puddings. Dry bread crusts, slabs or leftover slices, in a slow oven and mash or grind (in blender or grinder) to crumbs; use the crumbs for toppings, breading or crumb crusts. Or make a mighty muffin: soak 1 cup bread crumbs, ½ cup raisins, ½ cup chopped dried apricot or apples in 1 cup milk for 15 minutes. Stir together ½ cup flour, 1½ teaspoons baking powder, ½ teaspoon salt. Beat 1 egg, 1 tablespoon oil and milk mixture. Add the egg, oil and milk mixture to the flour mixture all at once, swish with a fork until moistened and then spoon into greased muffin tins. Bake in preheated 425°F oven for 20 minutes.

Butter blend. To save money, or to save on cholesterol, stretch butter by adding corn or safflower oil. Here is how: put ¼ pound (1 stick) of softened butter in blender container. Turn the blender on to "High" and gradually add ½ cup corn or safflower oil until smooth. Use a spatula to put the butter blend in tubs or onto waxed paper to form sticks. Refrigerate until needed.

Co-ops for food buying are springing up all over the country. You put time and effort into a communal purchasing program and save money by eliminating the middleman.

Cereal, leftover, cooked. Do not throw it away, but pack into a lightly greased container, cover and chill. The next morning, slice and fry it in butter, top with honey or syrup.

Cheese. Just a little bit of cheese can make a big flavor difference in almost any recipe. Dried out bits can be grated to top casseroles. Cut chunks to toss in salads, or mix in yeast or quick bread doughs. Stir into omelets, scrambled eggs, croquettes, toss with hot buttered noodles or rice or vegetables. An elegant way to use leftover cheese is to make a fondue. Just melt the cheese in warm, not boiling, wine (kirsch is traditional). Cut chunks of French or sourdough bread to dip in the fondue. Serve the fondue with tossed or fruit salad for a quick gourmet meal.

Coffee. Leftover coffee can be used as a liquid to make

gelatin for a unique dessert. Just use coffee instead of water in a gelatin recipe. Or freeze cold coffee in ice cube trays and use the cubes to keep iced coffee chilly and undiluted. Cold coffee can be part of liquid in baked goods, custards, gelatins or whips, too.

Casseroles, along with soup, are the greatest way to use up bits and pieces of food, and save money. There are many great casserole cookbooks — look for them at the library. Why buy until you have had a chance to see which one you like best?

Clearance tables of produce sometimes offer good buys, if you check to be sure the fruit or vegetable has some parts worth saving, if you can use it right away or if you can chop, mash or package and freeze it right away to use later on. Learn to know which items are too far gone to save.

Eggs. When cheap, buy a lot and freeze them. Break several whole eggs (enough for your favorite recipe for example) into a plastic sandwich bag. Tie the top and freeze them. Or break eggs into an ice cube tray to freeze. When frozen, package the cubes in plastic bags for freezer storage. Yolks and whites can be frozen separately, too. Stir yolks with a bit of sugar or salt before freezing. Always label packages with the amounts that are inside. Freeze for up to six months.

Just a few whites left over? Make meringues by beating whites until foamy. Gradually add 2 to 3 tablespoons of sugar for each egg white, beating to stiff peaks. Flavor with a dash of vanilla. Drop by spoonful on a cookie sheet lined with waxed paper and bake the rounds in a 250°F oven for several hours or until they are very dry. Top them with sweetened fruit and whipped cream. Or drop spoonsful of meringue into simmering water and poach about 5 minutes, then use them to top puddings or fruits.

Leftover yolks are the basis of hollandaise sauce and old-fashioned cooked or boiled salad dressing. They can thicken many other sauces and dressings. Cook whole yolks in simmering water and then crumble or slice over salads or vegetables for a sunny topper.

Fish, leftover. Refrigerate right after its first appearance, always well-wrapped in plastic or foil. Then, for an encore, try one of the following. Cream the fish and serve on toast. Flake and toss with water chestnuts, green pepper slices, mushrooms and mayonnaise and serve on lettuce leaves. Mix the fish with mayonnaise and stuff tomatoes. Stir into cooked brown rice with some herbs and a little cheese sauce and bake until bubbly. Mash and mix the fish with cheese, rice, chopped vegetables for croquettes. How about stirring the fish into lemon-spiked gelatin along with bamboo shoots, sliced or shredded carrots, or chopped green pepper for an elegant molded salad?

French-type dressings are cheaper when you make them. Start with ¼ to ⅓ cup vinegar to ¾ to ⅔ cup oil and season to taste. Use flavored vinegar, herbs, ground spices, anything you wish. Let the dressing stand a while so the flavors can blend before serving.

Imperfect. Some food preparation calls for the very best, but sometimes imperfect fruits or vegetables will do just as well. Overripe bananas are an example. Or bruised

fruit, if there is enough salvageable fruit to make good jams, jellies and juices.

Jars and bottles. Save them, if you have room. When empty, wash well, rinse, dry and store, along with their lids, to use for nut butters, yogurt, cottage cheese, dry cereals, soybeans, etc.

Juice, fruit. Just a few tablespoons or few cups left? Freeze juice in ice cube trays, then, when frozen, package in plastic bags. Thaw when needed. Use to glaze or baste meats, to flavor gelatin desserts or salads, to replace part of the milk in custards, to poach apples or pears or stew dried fruits. Whip the juice in your blender with ice cubes for a slushy drink. Mix a variety of juices together for a "mystery" drink.

List. Make one before you go to the store. Base your own meal plans for the week on the weekly food advertisements. Stick to the list while shopping, unless you come across an even better buy.

Leftovers. Plan ahead. Plan on 2 or more meals from a big roast or other large dishes. Save everything. Soups and casseroles are the perfect place for leftovers.

Lettuce. Do not toss out those limp outer leaves. Line a saucepan with them, then pour in fresh or frozen peas, add just a bit of liquid, cover and cook — that is what French chefs do. Lettuce will start to have brown spots when stored next to apples, avocados, melons, pears, plums or tomatoes because they give off ethylene gas.

Milk, dry (instant nonfat). Powdered, instant milk is a good buy. Reconstitute it as the package directs, chill it thoroughly. Or, mix half reconstituted milk with whole or 2% milk. Add dry milk along with other dry ingredients in

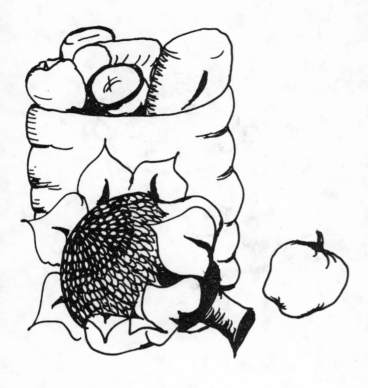

cookies, cakes, bread or other baked goods and get a nutritional bonus.

Milk, sour. Pancakes, waffles, cookies, quick breads all take sour milk in place of sweet. Just add ½ teaspoon soda to neutralize the acid. You can use sour milk that is too curdled for baking to clean your silver. Pour it over your silver in a shallow pan, let it stand overnight. Next day rub silver with a clean cloth, rinse and dry.

Meat loaf is a wonderful way to save money on the main course. Start with ground beef then add rolled oats, brown rice (cooked), leftover mashed or cubed potatoes, or anything else that will stretch the meat. Bean sprouts are a low-calorie extender. Cooked cracked wheat (bulgar wheat), chunks of cheese and chopped vegetables all go great in meat loaves. Soy granules, soy grits and powdered milk, are also excellent for stretching meat.

Natural foods. Unprocessed, raw is usually what "natural foods" means. Many natural foods stores offer savings on special items. Soybeans, sesame seeds, whole, rolled or other grains in bulk are usually a good buy. Shop wisely and you can save.

Outlet stores. You can buy not-quite-perfect items at considerable saving. Warehouse-type stores, without any fancy trappings, may be cheaper too. Day-old bread stores are quite popular now, so get there early.

Organ meats. Liver, kidney, sweetbreads, brains and heart are the most nutritious and cheapest meats available. Check the library for cookbooks specializing in recipes for these meats. They are used in many easy gourmet dishes.

Organic foods are, unfortunately, loosely defined. Some promoters have made a lot of money by using the term freely. "Organic" produce sold in "health food" stores should meet the same standards for freshness and quality as produce in supermarkets. Organic foods are grown without chemical fertilizers or pesticides. But who is to guarantee them as organic? If it is important to you, find a farmer who shares your beliefs and buy only from him.

Peanuts. Buy them in the shell to save money. Shell them yourself to make peanut butter, then use the shells for garden mulch.

Peel. Lemon, lime, orange or grapefruit peels. Buy fruit when cheap, wash thoroughly and shred or grate the rind, seal in plastic bags and freeze. Or dry the shredded peel on a cookie tray and grind it to a powder in a blender. Use the powdered fruit peels in desserts and baked goods. Squeeze the juice to freeze in foil baking cups, ice cube trays or small covered containers. If you forgot to grate peel before juicing fruit, scrape any remaining fruit from peel and cut peel in thin strips. Pour boiling water over and let stand a few minutes, then drain. Candy the peel by simmering it in a sugar syrup (one part water to two parts sugar) for 30 minutes, then let it stand several hours or overnight. Drain. Eat as is, use as a garnish or roll the candied peel in sugar, dip in melted chocolate or grated fresh ginger.

Peelings. Thoroughly scrub vegetables, such as carrots and potatoes, before you peel them, then add the peelings to soups or stocks for extra nutrition and flavor. Drain, saving soup and peelings separately. The soup you eat, the peelings go to the compost pile.

Potatoes. Leftover potatoes can make many magical encores. Shape cold mashed potatoes into patties and fry them in butter. Or form balls, roll in bread crumbs and deep fry until brown. Or press leftover mashed potatoes into a pie plate, then fill with ground beef or hash and bake for a main dish pie. Mix cold mashed potatoes with egg yolks and pipe around tops of casseroles for duchess potatoes. Make a potato souffle by beating 2 eggs yolks with 2 cups mashed potatoes, ½ to 1 cup shredded cheddar cheese. Beat 2 egg whites stiff and fold in. Pile in a souffle dish and bake at 350°F for 35 to 40 minutes.

Quantity. You are smart to buy in large quantities if the price is right, if you can use, freeze or pickle all that you buy, and if you have storage space.

Rice. Save cooked rice to add to meat loaf or ground meat for burgers. Stir cooked rice with chopped, cooked meat and tomato sauce for hash or Spanish rice. Cream rice with tuna or leftover fish, chicken or turkey. Use it in custard-type puddings or mix with chopped fruit, mandarin oranges, marshmallows and whipped cream for Heavenly Hash.

Salt. Seasoned salt is much cheaper to make than to buy. Blend iodized table salt with garlic powder, pepper, paprika, dry mustard, thyme, sesame seeds, poppy seeds and anything else you like. Put the seasoned salt in a shaker and let it stand a few days to blend the flavors. Use it on salads, vegetables, soups and casseroles.

Soup. Almost anything can go into soup: fruit, vegetables, meat, poultry, fish, bread, cheese, eggs, milk. Meat, poultry, fish and vegetable soup are actually full meals. Creamed soups make luncheons special or breakfasts worth getting up for. Cold soups, either fruit or vegetable, spark summer-weary appetites.

The French, famous for their soups, have pots that simmer perpetually. They add foods to the pot as they think of it, eat a meal a day from the pot, and on it goes — sort of an eternal meal sitting at the back of the stove. You can make long-simmering soups if you have a very low heat setting on your range, or if you have a slow cooker. If kept at 160°F you can keep a soup going for several days. Or, you can make it one day, chill, remove the fat that hardens on the surface, and heat it up for eating the next day. After that you can keep it hot for a day or two. Or you can refrigerate it for up to a week. One short cut is to ladle meal-sized amounts into plastic freezer containers, cover and freeze.

Sesame seeds are often available in bulk at cheap prices in natural foods stores. If you buy in quantity, store them in tightly covered jars or containers in a cool, dark, dry place.

Soybeans. Soybeans are a versatile, high-protein, low-fat legume. Baked, they can be served as Boston baked beans or chili. Dry-roasted they replace peanuts. Soy granules and soy grits are available as meat extenders.

Tomatoes peel easily if you plunge them into boiling water, then dip in cold water. The peels slip right off. Try this trick for peaches too.

Tea is cheaper loose than in bags. Use a strainer or tea ball to make tea from loose leaves. Tea is also a great cleaner. Let it steep a long time (30 to 40 minutes) and use to clean varnished furniture and woodwork and glass. Wipe on with a lint-free cloth, then dry.

USDA (United States Department of Agriculture) has many inexpensive or free booklets to help you learn to shop wisely and save money. Check for them at your county Extension office.

Vegetables. Save every portion of leftover cooked vegetables or of cooking liquid. Put them into clean coffee cans and cover, then stash away in the freezer and add to the cans as you clean up after each meal. When the can is full, it is soup time! Heat the vegetables and broth with a bouillon cube or two, season to taste, and maybe stir in some pasta or cooked rice. Save cooking liquid from vegetables to use in cream sauces or soups. Leftover cooked vegetables can make a great comeback after an overnight marinade in flavored vinegar or French or Italian dressing. Drain and toss with greens. Chop cold cooked vegetables to stir into souffles, hash, soups, stews, casseroles, molded salads, stuffings or sandwich fillings.

Vinegar can work wonders as a cleaning agent as well as flavor-sparker. Pour vinegar full strength into anything that is coated with hard water deposits — tea kettle, steam iron. Let them stand to loosen the deposits. Soak the shower head in vinegar. Give your automatic washer a vinegar purge by running it without clothes, just warm water and a gallon of white vinegar (it is the cheapest). Put vinegar on mosquito bites to stop the itching, sun burn to stop the pain. Mix vinegar and water to clean windows or glass. Remove smoke-filled room odors from clothes by hanging them over a tub of steaming water that has had a gallon of vinegar added. This treatment removes moth ball and fried food smells too.

Wheat, cracked. Also called bulgur, bulghur, bulghar and the like. You can often find it, in bulk, for a good savings. Serve it in place of rice, add it to meat loaves or use it as a stuffing. It has a wonderful nutty flavor.

INDEX